# Illustrator®

## CS

### A c c e l e r a t e d

YJ IT Publishing Team

Manager: **Suzie Lee**
Chief Editor: **Angelica Lim**
Developmental Editor: **Colleen Wheeler Strand**
Production Editor: **Patrick Cunningham**
Editor: **Sas Jacobs**
Proofreader: **Semtle**
Cover Designer: **Changwook Lee**
Book Designer: **Semtle**
Production Control: **Ann Lee**

---

ISBN: 89-314-3504-5

Printed and bound in the Republic of Korea.

---

**How to contact us**

E-mail: support@youngjin.com
        feedback@youngjin.com.sg
Address: Youngjin.com
1623-10, Seocho-dong, Seocho-gu, Seoul 137-878, Korea
Telephone: +65-6327-1161
Fax: +65-6327-1151

Illustrator®
CS
Accelerated

Y.

c o n t e n t s

c o n t e n t s

# Illustrator CS - Installation and the CD-ROM › › ›

## Installing the Trial Version of Illustrator CS

A trial version of Illustrator CS is included on the supplementary CD-ROM; this version only lasts for a few days following installation. If you have the full version of Illustrator CS, please follow the installation directions included with your documentation.

1 Double-click on the CD-ROM/Adobe Illustrator CS Tryout/Setup.exe file to begin the installation.

2 When the following window appears, click [Next].

3 When the following dialog box appears, close all Adobe applications and then click [OK].

4 Choose a language (e.g., US English) and then click [Next].

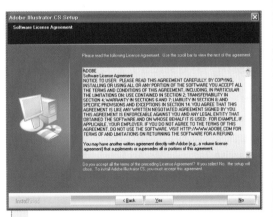

5 Before installation begins, you will be asked to agree to the license information. Click [Yes] to proceed with the installation.

6 Now it's time to choose the folder where you want the program to be installed. To change the folder, click on [Browse]. Click [Next] if you'd like to install the program in the default folder.

7 Installation will begin when you click [Next]. To change installation options, return to an earlier step of the installation process by clicking [Back].

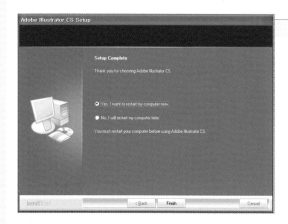

8 This is the window you will see when the program has been completely installed. Click [Finish] to end the installation process.

## Installing the Supplementary CD-ROM

1 In addition to the trial version of Illustrator CS, the supplementary CD-ROM contains all the example files used in the book. The example files are saved in the Sample folder and are arranged by chapter. You may open the files directly from the CD-ROM or copy the files to your hard drive.

Chapter | 1

# The Basics of Illustrator CS

Adobe Illustrator CS is a versatile program that can be used to create detailed illustrations both for print and the Web. Illustrator includes industry-standard drawing tools that are often used to create digital artwork such as company logos, product packaging, and cartoon characters. Because drawing in Illustrator is quite different from drawing in real life, these tools can be a little difficult for a beginner to master at first.

After introducing the basic principles of vector illustration, this chapter will help you get started by covering the Illustrator interface and its tools in detail.

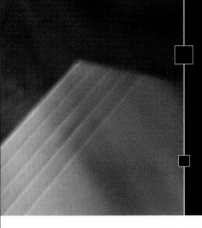

# The Illustrator Interface

This chapter provides a general overview of the main features of Illustrator CS. The Illustrator interface can seem a little daunting at first with its mix of menus, toolboxes, and palettes; this chapter will introduce you to the various screen elements through detailed explanations and simple examples.

## Vector and Bitmap Images

All computer graphics are either vector or bitmap. Vector images are created using strokes and fills that are defined using mathematical equations. Points are joined to create lines and lines are joined to create objects. Because vector images are defined using mathematical equations, vector images have small file sizes and maintain their resolution or quality even when magnified. The downside to vector images is that they cannot be made to look very realistic.

◀A Vector Image at 100% Magnification (Left) and the Same Image at 500% Magnification (Right)

Bitmap images, on the other hand, are recorded using individual pixels. The higher the image resolution, the more pixels are used to record the image; this creates sharper looking images. The opposite is true for images with lower resolutions; these often appear blurry or poorly detailed. Bitmap images are used for realistic images such as photographs and scans. When you magnify a bitmap, the image loses sharpness. If magnified sufficiently, the pixels that make up the image become discernable.

◀A Bitmap Image at 100% Magnification (Left) and the Same Image at 50% Magnification (Right)

Illustrator is a vector-based graphics program. Therefore, all text and shapes created in Illustrator are vector images. Vector images can be converted to bitmap images through a process called rasterization, but doing so will greatly reduce your ability to edit your graphics using Illustrator.

<< note

## Converting Vector Images into Bitmap Images in Illustrator CS

The [Object] - [Rasterize] command can be used to turn vector images into bitmap images. However, bitmap images cannot be converted to vector images.

❶Select the vector image, then choose [Object] - [Rasterize].

❷When the Rasterize dialog box appears, enter the appropriate settings and click [OK].

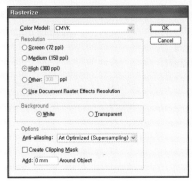

❸The vector image will be converted into a bitmap image.

When you first open Illustrator CS, you will see the welcome screen. The welcome screen contains options that make it easy for you to get started in Illustrator whether you are a new user, an upgrader, or are just looking to create a new document. Let's have a look at the options available in the welcome screen.

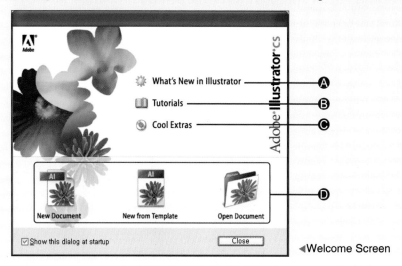

◄Welcome Screen

**A** **What's New in Illustrator**: Click this to find out about the program's new features at the Adobe Web site.

**B** **Tutorials**: You can click on this to access the Help menu.

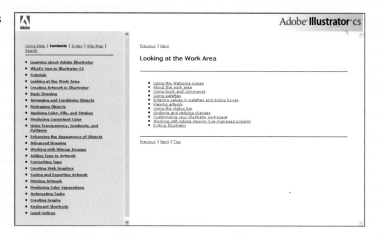

**C Cool Extras**: Clicking Cool Extras brings up a PDF document with information on templates, brushes, fonts, colors, and gradients. Sample files that demonstrate what Illustrator can do are also available.

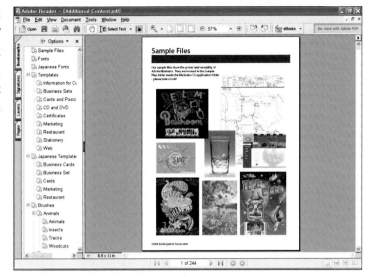

**D New Document, New from Template, or Open Document**: Clicking New Document, New from Template, or Open Document opens the respective command's dialog box. Enter the desired settings or navigate in the dialog box to create or open a new document in the document window.

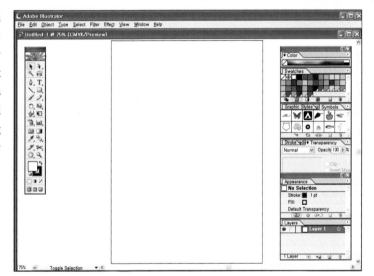

## Illustrator CS Interface

Almost all of the commands for drawing or editing artwork in Illustrator can be found in the work space—the menu bar at the top, the toolbox on the left, and the floating palettes on the right. In the center of the document window is the work area, where you'll create and edit your graphics.

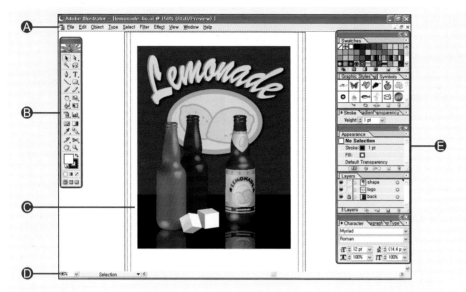

**Ⓐ Menu Bar**: Clicking on a menu item opens a drop-down menu which contains a list of commands and submenus.

**Ⓑ Toolbox**: The toolbox contains the tools that you will use to work with images.

**Ⓒ Work Area**: The work space for your drawing.

**Ⓓ Status Bar**: Displays information on the active document.

**Ⓔ Palettes**: The palettes contain preset options and various commands for modifying an image. Some of the palettes also display information on an active image or the current task.

## Menu Bar

The menu bar contains a multitude of commands for performing a wide variety of tasks in Illustrator. Some of these commands are only found in the menu bar while others can also be accessed through keyboard shortcuts, palettes, the toolbox, or status bar. Clicking on a menu item opens a drop-down menu which contains commands and submenus. In the drop-down menu, you will also find the keyboard shortcuts for accessing commonly used commands. Let's take a quick look at the type of commands found in each menu.

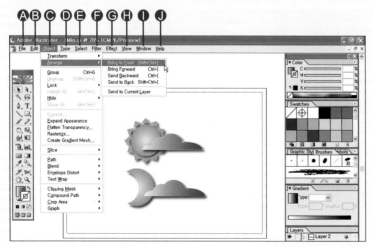

Ⓐ **File Menu**: The commands found in the File menu are basic functions that you will need in order to work in Illustrator. These commands cover areas related to creating, printing, and saving documents, importing and exporting files, adjusting document settings and exiting Illustrator.

Ⓑ **Edit Menu**: The Edit menu contains commands that help you edit an image or change the way you work in Illustrator. Commands related to image-editing include the undo and redo commands, the copy and paste commands and text-editing commands such as the Find and Replace command. You can also tailor your Illustrator environment using the Presets commands or the Color Settings, Keyboard Shortcuts or Preferences commands.

Ⓒ **Object Menu**: The Object menu contains object-related functions. A number of these functions such as the Blend command can also be accessed through the toolbox or the palettes. Some of the commonly used object commands involve changing the object's shape (Transform), position (Arrange), appearance (Expand) and how you work with objects (Group).

Ⓓ **Type Menu**: The Type menu contains commands for adjusting text properties such as font type, font size, type orientation, punctuation and style.

Ⓔ **Select Menu**: The Select menu lets you choose the fastest and easiest way to select one or more objects. It may come as a surprise to you but there are many ways to select an object. For example, you can choose one of the Same commands to select objects with the same characteristics.

Ⓕ **Filter Menu**: The Filter Menu contains commands that change an image completely to create a different style. The Artistic filters, for example, make an image appear to have been painted or created in the selected artistic style. Chapter 5 covers the topic of filters in more detail.

Ⓖ **Effect Menu**: Effects, like filters, change an image completely to create a different style. The key difference between effects and filters is that an effect can be edited after you apply it while a filter cannot be changed. See Chapter 10 for more information on effects.

**View Menu**: The View menu lets you change the view of the artboard, decide whether elements such as rulers will be shown and determine how objects are represented in the artboard.

Ⓗ **Window Menu**: In the Window menu is a list of all the palettes in Illustrator, a check mark beside a palette name indicates that the palette is opened. If there is no check mark, the palette is closed. To open or close a palette, you can check or uncheck the palette name in the Window menu. When working with more than one file in Illustrator, you can also use the Cascade or Tile commands in the Window menu to change the view of the files and switch from one file to another easily.

Ⓘ **Help**: The Help menu contains copyright information on the program and support material and resources that will help you get started in Illustrator.

## Toolbox

The toolbox, which sits at the top-left of the Illustrator window, contains many different tools for drawing and editing artwork in Illustrator. All of these tools are represented by icons corresponding to their functions, and you can activate a tool by clicking it or by typing its keyboard shortcut.

When you point at a tool in the toolbox, a tool tip showing the tool's name and its keyboard shortcut will appear. Double-clicking a tool will show the tool's options in a dialog box.

◄Placing the cursor over the Direct Selection tool reveals the name and the shortcut key for the tool.

If a tool icon shows a triangle at the bottom-right side (◢), it means that other similar tools have been grouped together with the tool. To see the hidden tools, click and hold down the mouse on the tool. Clicking on the vertical bar at the end of a group of tools will display the group in a floating window outside the toolbox. Pressing the close button (☒) will close the floating window. Holding down the [Alt] key as you click on a group of tools will toggle between the tools in the group.

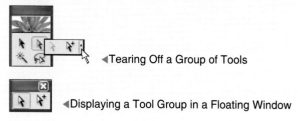

◄Tearing Off a Group of Tools

◄Displaying a Tool Group in a Floating Window

In this section, let's take a quick look at all the tools in the toolbox (these tools will be covered in greater depth later in the book). The default shortcut key(s) for each of these tools is indicated in the brackets beside the tool name. You can change the shortcut by selecting [Edit] - [Keyboard Shortcuts] from the main menu.

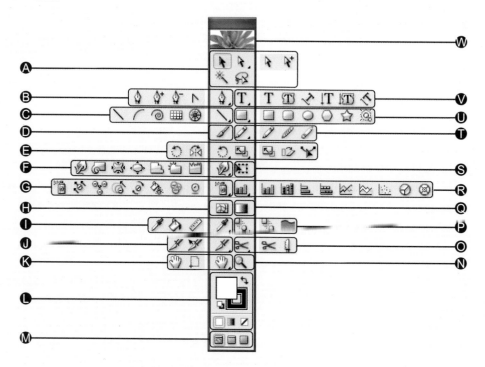

## Ⓐ Selection Tools

- *Selection Tool* [V] < >: This tool is used to select an entire object.

- *Direct Selection Tool* [A] < >: The Direct Selection tool selects object paths or anchors. You will learn about paths and anchors in Chapter 2.

- *Group Selection Tool* < >: This tool selects a single object from a set of grouped objects. Double-click once to select the entire group.

- *Magic Wand Tool* [Y] < >: The Magic Wand tool selects objects with the same color.

- *Lasso Tool* [Q] < >: Use the Lasso tool to create freeform selections.

## Ⓑ Path Tools

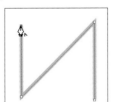 

- *Pen Tool* [P] < >: The Pen tool creates vector lines, curves, and objects. This tool is used frequently.

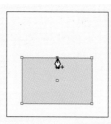 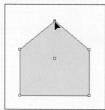

- *Add Anchor Point Tool* [+] < >: This tool adds anchor points to an object or path to change the shape of the object.

 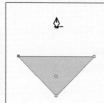

- *Delete Anchor Point Tool* [-] < >: This tool deletes anchor points from objects or paths.

 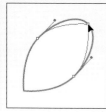

- *Convert Anchor Point Tool* [Shift]-[C] < >: The Convert Anchor Point tool is used to control direction lines or to turn linear paths into curves (and vice versa).

**◉ Line Tools**

- *Line Segment Tool* [\] < >: The Line Segment tool creates straight lines.

- *Arc Tool* < >: This tool creates arcs.

- *Spiral Tool* < >: The Spiral tool draws spirals.

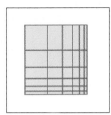

• *Rectangular Grid Tool* <⊞>: This tool creates rectangular grids.

• *Polar Grid Tool* <⊛>: The Polar Grid tool creates circular grids.

Ⓓ **Paintbrush Tool [B]** <✎>: This tool is used to add brush strokes.

Ⓔ **Transform Tools**

• *Rotate Tool* [R] <↻>: Use the Rotate tool to rotate objects.

• *Reflect Tool* [O] <⧉>: The Reflect tool creates a vertical or horizontal reflection of the object.

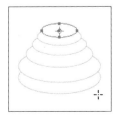

• *Scale Tool* [S] <▣>: This tool changes the size of an object.

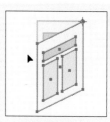

• *Shear Tool* <📐>: Use the Shear tool to adjust the slant of an object.

• *Reshape Tool* <📐>: When an anchor point is selected using the Reshape tool, the surrounding path segments are "bound" to that point; clicking-and-dragging the anchor point will reshape the selected area of the object.

**Ⓕ Warp Tools**

• *Warp Tool* [Shift]-[R] <🖌>: The Warp tool distorts the shape of an object.

• *Twirl Tool* <🌀>: This tool twirls an object.

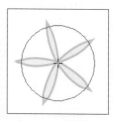

• *Pucker Tool* <🔅>: The Pucker tool pulls an object inward.

• *Bloat Tool* <🔅>: Use the Bloat tool to swell an object outward.

• *Scallop Tool* <img>: The Scallop tool creates rounded ridges along a path.

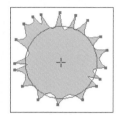

• *Crystallize Tool* <img>: The Crystallize tool creates spikes along a path.

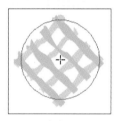

• *Wrinkle Tool* <img>: The Wrinkle tool crinkles object lines.

### Ⓖ Symbol Tools

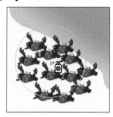

• *Symbol Sprayer Tool* [Shift]-[S] <img>: This tool sprays the selected symbol onto the work area.

• *Symbol Shifter Tool* <img>: The Symbol Shifter tool moves symbols gradually in the direction that you drag the tool.

• *Symbol Scruncher Tool* <img>: The Symbol Scruncher tool is used to pull in or spread out symbols.

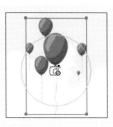

• *Symbol Sizer Tool* < >: The Symbol Sizer tool is used to increase or decrease the size of symbols.

• *Symbol Spinner Tool* < >: The Symbol Spinner tool rotates symbols.

• *Symbol Stainer Tool* < >: The Symbol Stainer tool uses the selected fill color to change the color of symbols without altering their overall brightness.

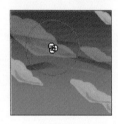

• *Symbol Screener Tool* < >: The Symbol Screener tool makes symbols transparent.

• *Symbol Styler Tool* < >: This tool alters the stylistic traits of symbols.

**Mesh Tool [U]** < >: The Mesh tool adds criss-crossed paths to an enclosed area to create a mesh of paths. Meshes can be used to create highly detailed fills that convey realistic light and shadow effects.

**❶ Color and Measurement Tools**

- *Eyedropper Tool* [I] <🖊>: Click an object with the Eyedropper tool to copy its color and stroke settings to the Color and Stroke palettes. If another object is selected when you click an object with the Eyedropper tool, its fill and stroke properties will be modified to match the clicked object.

- *Paint Bucket Tool* [K] <🪣>: Use the Paint Bucket tool to fill an object with the selected color.

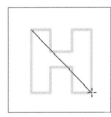

- *Measure Tool* <📏>: This tool measures the position, angle, and distance of objects.

**❷ Slice Tools**

- *Slice Tool* [Shift]-[K] <🖊>: Use the Slice tool to slice images into smaller segments for the Web.

- *Slice Selection Tool* <👆>: The Slice Selection tool selects image slices.

**❸ Move Tools**

- *Hand Tool* [H] <✋>: Use the Hand tool to drag your view of the work area. The Hand tool is very useful for quickly shifting your focus to another area of your image.

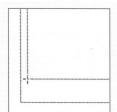

• *Page Tool* <☐>: The Page tool moves the printable area on the page.

**❶ Fill and Stroke Colors**

• *Fill Color Swatch* [X] <☐>: Shows the selected fill color, which is used for coloring an area enclosed by paths. Double-click on the swatch to open the Color Picker dialog box and select a new fill color.

• *Stroke Color Swatch* [X] <◼>: Shows the selected stroke color, which is used for coloring paths. Double-click on the swatch to open the Color Picker dialog box and select a new stroke color.

• *Swap Fill and Stroke Colors* [Shift]-[X] <↰>: Swaps the fill and stroke colors.

• *Default Fill and Stroke Colors* [D] <▣>: Sets the fill color to white and the stroke color to black.

• *Color* [<] <☐>: Changes the fill color to the last selected solid color in the Color palette.

• *Gradient* [>] <▮>: Changes the fill color to the last selected gradient in the Gradient palette.

• *None* [/] <⊘>: Removes either the fill or stroke color – whichever is selected.

**❶ Screen Modes**

• *Standard Screen Mode* [F] <▣>: Displays the image in the default window view, which includes the menu bar, title bar, and scroll bars.

• *Full Screen Mode with Menu Bar* [F] <▣>: Displays the image without a title bar or scroll bars.

• *Full Screen Mode* [F] <▣>: Displays the image without the menu bar, title bar, or scroll bars.

**❶ Zoom Tool [Z] <🔍>**: The Zoom tool is used to zoom in or out of an image.

**❶ Cropping Tools**

• *Scissors Tool* [C] <✂>: This tool cuts an object straight across between two selected points on the path.

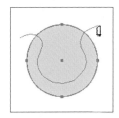

- *Knife Tool* <⬚>: Drag the Knife tool to cut an object.

### Ⓟ Auto Tools

- *Blend Tool* [W] <⬚>: Use the Blend tool to create intermediate shapes between two objects.

- *Auto Trace Tool* <⬚>: The Auto Trace tool traces a bitmap image to create paths.

### Ⓠ Gradient Tool [G] <⬚>: The Gradient tool is used to adjust the direction of a gradient.

### Ⓡ Graph Tools

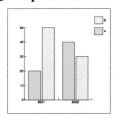

- *Column Graph Tool* [J] <⬚>: Use the Column Graph tool to create a column graph.

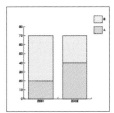

- *Stacked Column Graph Tool* <⬚>: The Stacked Column Graph tool creates a stacked column graph.

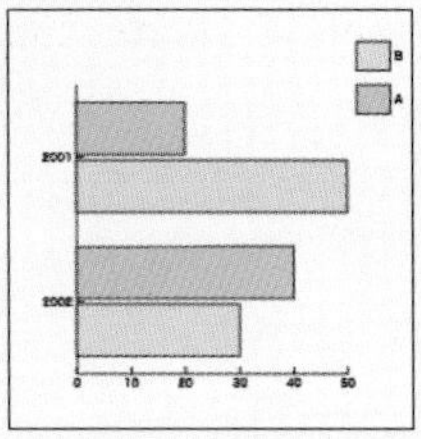

• *Bar Graph Tool* <>: The Bar Graph tool creates a horizontal bar graph.

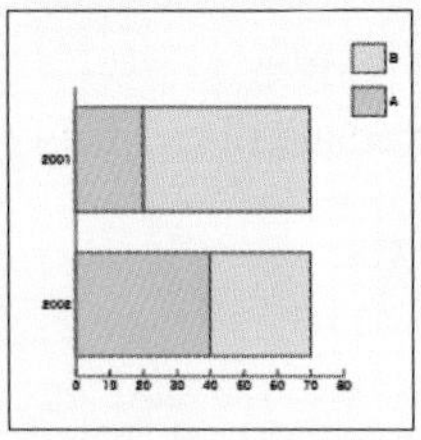

• *Stacked Bar Graph Tool* <>: Use the Stacked Bar Graph tool to create a horizontal stacked bar graph.

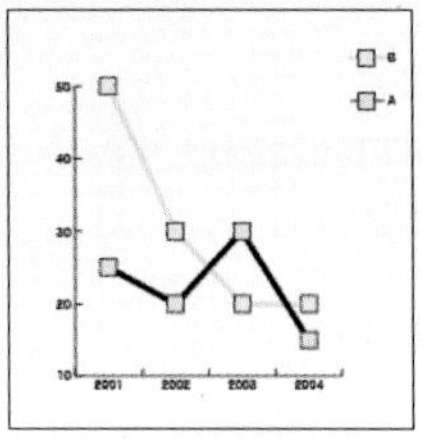

• *Line Graph Tool* <>: This tool creates a connected line graph.

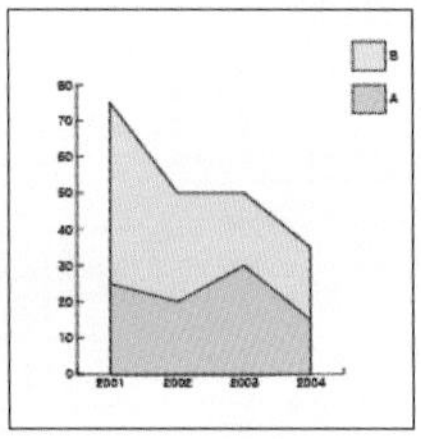

• *Area Graph Tool* <>: The Area Graph tool creates an area graph.

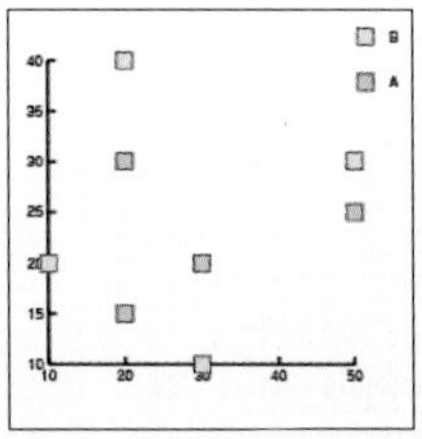

• *Scatter Graph Tool* <>: A scatter graph can be created with the Scatter Graph tool.

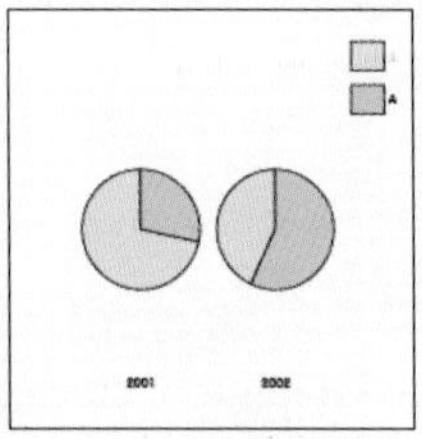

• *Pie Graph Tool* <>: The Pie Graph tool creates a pie graph.

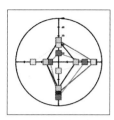

• *Radar Graph Tool* <⊛>: You can create a radar graph with the Radar Graph tool.

**❾ Free Transform Tool [E]** <✎>: Use the Free Transform tool to create a bounding box around an object. The bounding box can be used to scale, rotate, reflect, shear, or distort the object.

**❿ Freeform Line Tools**

• *Pencil Tool* [N] <✎>: Use the Pencil tool to draw freeform lines.

• *Smooth Tool* <✎>: This tool smoothes lines.

• *Erase Tool* <✎>: The Erase tool erases object anchor points or lines.

**⓫ Shape Tools**

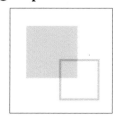

• *Rectangle Tool* [M] <▢>: The Rectangle tool creates rectangular shapes.

• *Rounded Rectangle Tool* <img>: This tool makes rectangles with rounded edges.

• *Ellipse Tool* [L] <img>: The Ellipse tool draws circles and ellipses.

• *Polygon Tool* <img>: The Polygon tool draws polygons.

• *Star Tool* <img>: This tool creates stars.

• *Flare Tool* <img>: The Flare tool adds a lens flare.

## ⓥ Type Tools

• *Type Tool* [T] <img>: The Type tool is used to enter characters. Click and drag the Type tool to create a text field, then type in the text. Alternatively, simply click on the work area to add text without a bounding box.

- *Area Type Tool* <📝>: This tool adds text inside a closed area.

- *Path Type Tool* <📝>: The Path Type tool enters text on a path.

- *Vertical Type Tool* <📝>: This tool is used to enter vertical text.

- *Vertical Area Type Tool* <📝>: This tool enters vertical text inside a closed area.

- *Vertical Path Type Tool* <📝>: The Vertical Path Type tool enters vertical text along a path.

Ⓦ **Adobe Illustrator Icon** <🖼️>: Opens up the main Illustrator page on the Adobe Web site.

# Work Area

The work area in Illustrator is divided into five sections. These sections indicate the printable and unprintable areas and the boundaries of the page.

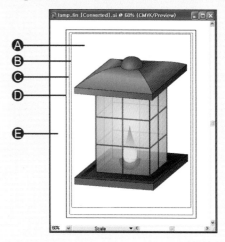

**Ⓐ Imageable Area**: The area inside the innermost dotted lines is the printable area.

**Ⓑ Nonimageable Area**: The area between the sets of two dotted lines is the unprintable margin of the page.

**Ⓒ Edge of Page**: The edge of the paper.

**Ⓓ Artboard**: This is the entire area that can contain printable artwork; it is determined by the dimensions you specify when creating your document.

**Ⓔ Scratch Area**: This is the area outside the artboard. You may work in this area, but the drawings in this area will not be printed.

<< note
## Defining Page Areas

The page size, and therefore the boundaries of the page, are determined by the printer's default settings. The document size, as well as the printing and non-printing areas of the page, can be changed by selecting [File] - [Document]. If you don't see the dotted and solid lines as shown in the figure above, see the "Showing or Hiding the Artboard and Page Tiling" note below.

<< note
## Showing or Hiding the Artboard and Page Tiling

If you do not see the solid or dotted lines demarcating the artboard window, you can turn on the lines by selecting [View] - [Show Artboard] or [View] - [Show Page Tiling]. To hide the lines, select [View] - [Hide Artboard] or [View] - [Hide Page Tiling].

If the second set of dotted lines indicating the edge of the page is not showing, it is probably because the artboard's boundary (represented by solid lines) is overlying the page boundary (represented by dotted lines). The artboard, by default, is the same size as the page, but the size of the artboard can be changed. You will be able to see the second set of dotted lines if the artboard and the page are of different sizes. To change the size of the artboard, select [File] - [Document Setup] from the menu bar.

# Status Bar

The status bar contains the Zoom pop-up menu and the Status pop-up menu. These menus pop up when you click on their respective arrow icons (▼) in the status bar. Using the Zoom pop-up menu, you can zoom in or out of an image very easily.

The Status pop-up menu lets you select the kind of information on the active document that you want displayed. When the default Current Tool option is selected, the Status menu displays the name of the currently selected tool. The tool name displayed changes when you switch to another tool. Other options in the Status pop-up menu include Date and Time, which shows you the current date and time; Number of Undos, which displays the number of undos and redos that have been applied; and the Document Color Profile, which indicates the color mode of the document. You will learn more about color modes later in this chapter.

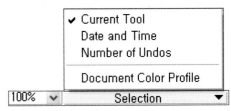

▲Status Pop-Up Menu

## << note

## Easter Eggs

In some programs, there are functions that are left deliberately undocumented so that users can be pleasantly surprised when they discover them by accident. These hidden functions, known as easter eggs, are often quirky and fun and not essential for using the software. One example of an easter egg is found in Illustrator's status bar. Holding down the [Alt] key and clicking on the arrow icon next to the Status pop-up menu reveals options that are not documented in the Adobe Help function.

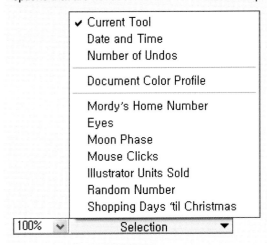

◄Easter eggs range from the quirky (Eyes) to the bizarre (Mordy's Home Number).

# Using Palettes

In Illustrator, as with many other programs, some functions are grouped into palettes and these palettes are displayed on the right-hand side of the work space. The purposes and uses of the palettes vary rather widely. Some palettes display information on an image or the current task, some contain commands for modifying an image, and others contain preset options such as styles and color swatches.

This section will briefly introduce you to all the palettes in Illustrator and show you how to manage them. Do note that this section provides only an overview, and more information on each of the palettes can be found in later chapters.

## Showing or Hiding Palettes

When you first launch Illustrator, you will see the default palettes on the right-hand side. These are the palettes that are used most often. Illustrator contains more palettes than is possible to show on screen, so you'll need to decide which are most important to your work. You can see the complete list of palettes available in Illustrator by selecting the Window menu. By checking or unchecking a palette name in the Window menu, you can hide or show a palette on the screen.

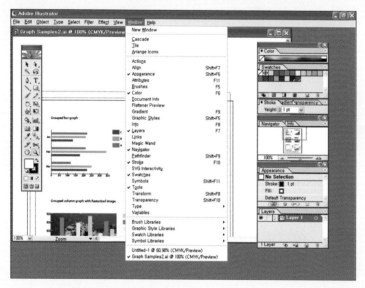

◀The list of palettes starts from [Actions] and ends at [Symbol Libraries]. A check mark indicates palettes that are currently shown in the window.

Another way to hide a palette is to click on the close button (  ) on the top-right corner of the palette. You can also minimize or maximize palettes. Click on the minimize button ( ) to show only the palette's tab and the maximize button ( ) to show the entire palette.

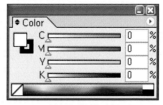

▲A Minimized Palette

◀A Maximized Palette

## Hiding the Toolbox and All Palettes

The toolbox, when combined with numerous palettes, can clutter up the work space and make it hard to review your work without distraction. A quick way to hide all this clutter is to press the [Tab] key once. Pressing the [Tab] key again will show all the palettes and the toolbox. To hide only the palettes and not the toolbox, press [Shift]-[Tab] instead. Pressing [Shift]-[Tab] again will show all the palettes.

## Showing or Hiding Palette Options

Every palette has its own pop-up menu which is opened by clicking the triangle icon ( ) at the top-right corner of the palette. On some of these menus, you can select [Hide Options] to hide some of the options on the palette. Selecting [Show Options] reveals all the palette options again.

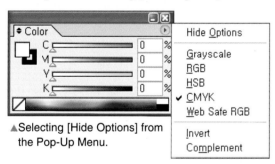

▲Selecting [Hide Options] from the Pop-Up Menu.

▲After selecting [Hide Options], all options except the color spectrum bar will be hidden.

## Moving, Grouping, or Separating Palettes

Because it is not possible to show all of the palettes at any one time, similar palettes are grouped into one window to save space. In a group containing multiple palettes, only the options for the selected palette are shown. To view a palette hidden in the group, click on the palette's tab to bring it up.

You can also move individual palettes and palette groups to other positions on the screen. To move a palette, click and drag the palette's tab to another position on the work space to create a standalone palette. Alternatively, drag it inside another palette group to pair the palette up with the group.

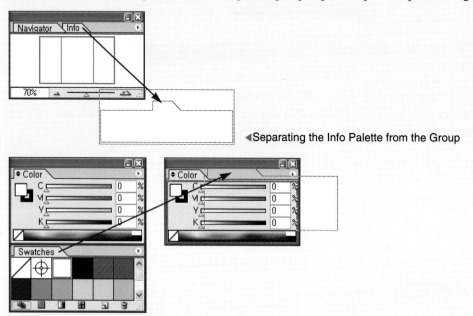

◀Separating the Info Palette from the Group

▲Pairing the Swatches Palette with the Color Palette to Form a Palette Group

You can also drag a palette to the bottom of another palette to dock it there; doing so will tether the palettes to one another. To move an entire palette group, just click and drag the palette's title bar to the new position.

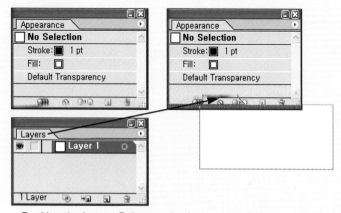

▲Docking the Layers Palette to the Appearance Palette

## Palette Descriptions

Every palette has a different role and function. In this section, let's take a closer look at each of the different palettes and see how they are used.

### Actions Palette

The Actions palette can be used to record and apply actions (e.g., automated scripts) for frequently repeated tasks. (If you're familiar with Microsoft Word, this is similar to the [Tools] - [Macro] command.) While recording commands to create actions, each step will appear beneath the name you've selected for your action. These steps can be applied separately or consecutively. You can also use the Actions palette to edit, delete, organize, and export recorded actions.

### Align Palette

This palette is used to align and distribute objects. You can align selected objects along the vertical or horizontal axis. You can also choose to align objects using their edges or anchor points as reference. The designs of the align and distribute icons in the palette are suggestive of their respective functions. Note that to use the Align palette you must select more than one object.

### Appearance Palette

This palette shows the appearance attributes of the selected object, including the fill and stroke properties, and the effects applied to the object using the Effect menu. You can use this palette to duplicate, edit, and delete attributes. A set of appearance attributes can be saved as a new style in the Styles palette.

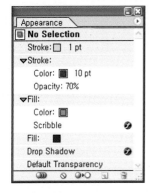

### Attributes Palette

The Attributes palette contains a mishmash of options. First, it can be used to set overprinting for the fill or stroke color of an object. The overprinting option affects the color of overlapping areas when printed; when overprinting is not selected, the color of the top object knocks out the color of the bottom object. So a yellow object will appear yellow even if it overlaps a blue object. Conversely, when overprinting is selected, the overlapping areas will turn out green.

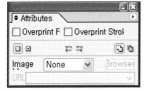

The Attributes palette can also be used to make the center point of an object visible or invisible. There are also options for selecting whether overlapping areas from the same path will be filled with color or treated as "outside" the object and left empty. Using the Attributes palette, an object can also be set to link to a Web address.

### Brushes Palette

The Brushes palette contains a wide range of brush styles that can be used with the Paintbrush tool (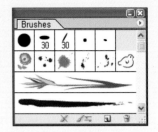) or applied to any existing path in an image. Using the Brushes palette, you can customize and add new brush styles or load Illustrator's collection of brushes from the brush library. To load a brush library, click the triangle button ( ) at the top-right side of the palette and select [Open Brush Library].

### Character Palette

The Character palette sets the character properties of text. You can open this palette by selecting [Window] - [Type] - [Character].

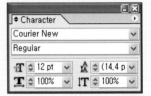

### Character Styles Palette

This palette is used to save the settings entered in the Character palette as a character style. You can click a saved style to apply it to selected text. You can open this palette by selecting [Window] - [Type] - [Character Style].

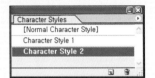

### Color Palette

The Color palette allows you to apply fill and stroke colors to a selected object. You can also use the palette's pop-up menu to specify different color modes (e.g., RGB or CMYK).

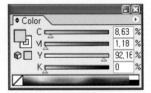

### Document Info Palette

The Document Info palette shows information on the active document. The information is grouped into different categories and these categories are shown in the pop-up menu. The categories are Document, Object, Graph Style, Brush, Spot Color Object, Patter Object, Gradient Object, Font, Linked Image, Embedded Image, and Font. You can choose [Save] to save the information as a text file.

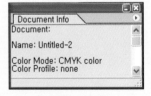

### Flattener Preview Palette

The Flattener Preview palette allows you to preview your artwork as a flattened image. Areas that will be affected by the flattening process are highlighted.

## Glyphs Palette

Glyphs are special characters or symbols that are not found in the alphabet. Every font has its own set of glyphs and you can view and insert a glyph by double-clicking on it in the Glyphs palette. The fonts–Webdings, Windings, Windings 2, and Windings 3–contain some of the more commonly used glyphs. You can open this palette by selecting [Window] - [Type] - [Glyphs].

## Gradient Palette

This Gradient palette is used to apply and edit color gradients. You can choose the gradient type, color, angle, and position.

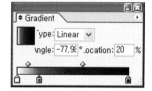

## Graphic Styles Palette

The Graphic Styles palette contains a list of styles that can be applied to objects and paths. To choose from more styles, select [Open Graphic Styles Library] from the palette's pop-up menu to access Illustrator's collection of graphic styles.

## Info Palette

The Info palette indicates the position of the cursor on the page. The position is shown in X and Y coordinates and these values change as the cursor moves. The Info palette also contains information on the current object or task, such as angle and dimension data. The palette automatically pops up when the Ruler tool ( ) is used to measure an object.

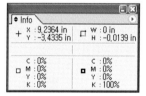

## Layers Palette

Artwork in Illustrator can be created using one layer or many overlapping layers. You can think of layers as transparent sheets on which objects are drawn. The stacked sheets combine to form a single image when viewed from above. Layers are created and manipulated using the Layers palette, which displays the content of each layer (using thumbnails) as well as the order in which the layers appear in the "stack." You will learn more about layers in Chapter 5.

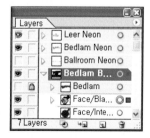

## Links Palette

This palette is used to manage bitmap images added with the [File] - [Place] command.

### Magic Wand Palette

The Magic Wand palette is used for setting the Tolerance value for the Magic Wand tool. A high Tolerance value selects a large color area, while a low value allows for less color deviation and usually results in a smaller selection.

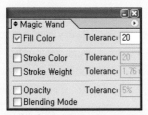

### Navigator Palette

This palette is used to zoom in and out of a document. You can also drag the red box to specify the part of the document that you want to look at.

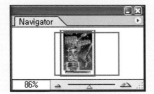

### OpenType Palette

OpenType is a font file format with two primary characteristics – OpenType fonts are compatible across Windows and Macintosh operating systems, and these fonts support a wider range of glyphs and characters than other type formats. You can tell that a font is in the OpenType format if the font name has the word "Pro" at the end. With an OpenType font selected in the Character palette, you can use the OpenType palette to modify the style of the characters. You can open this palette by selecting [Window] - [Type] - [OpenType].

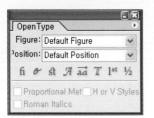

### Paragraph Palette

The Paragraph palette sets the spacing and indentation of paragraphs. You can open this palette by selecting [Window] - [Type] - [Paragraph].

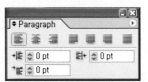

### Paragraph Styles Palette

Settings entered in the Paragraph palette can be saved as a paragraph style in the Paragraph Style palette. Clicking on a saved style applies the style to the document. You can open this palette by selecting [Window] - [Type] - [Paragraph Styles].

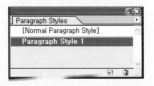

### Pathfinder Palette

The Pathfinder palette creates new paths based on overlapping objects or paths. For example, the paths for two objects can be combined to form a single object, or two objects can be divided according to the intersections of their paths. Fill colors can also be removed or changed depending on the options selected in the Pathfinder palette.

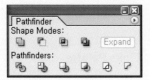

## Stroke Palette

The Stroke palette can be used to change the weight and style of an object's stroke line. Style options include choosing a design for a stroke's starting point, corners, and end points, and setting the length of the dashes and gaps for a dashed line.

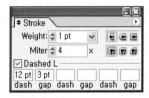

## SVG Interactivity Palette

This palette is used for adding interactivity to an image that will be placed on the Web. You can add an event to an object so that when a user performs the event, an action is triggered. For example, clicking on an object opens a link in a new window.

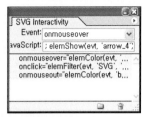

## Swatches Palette

The Swatches palette provides an easy way to select and apply commonly used colors, gradients, and patterns. Select [Open Swatch Library] from the palette's pop-up menu to load more swatches into Illustrator. Some interesting swatch libraries include the Skin Tones, Metals, and Earth Tones libraries. You can also mix your own color and save it as a color swatch.

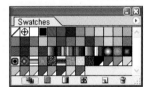

## Symbols Palette

The Symbols palette contains symbol objects that can be used in your document. Using symbols greatly reduces the size of your file and makes it easy to edit repetitive objects in your artwork. When an object is turned into a symbol, Illustrator saves only one copy of the object. Other instances of the object are linked to the symbol, and therefore do not increase the file size of your image. You can place symbols in the work area using the Symbol Sprayer tool. The other symbol tools, such as the Symbol Stainer tool, can be used to edit symbols once they're placed in the work area of your image.

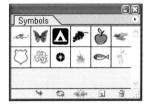

## Tabs Palette

The Tabs palette is used to display and set tabs. Text can be set to align to the left, right, or center of a tab. You can open this palette by selecting [Window] - [Type] - [Tabs].

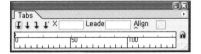

## Transform Palette

This palette is used to move, scale, rotate, and slant selected objects. It also displays the coordinates and dimensions of selected objects.

### Transparency Palette

This palette is used to change the opacity of objects and determine how objects will blend in overlapping areas.

### Variables Palette

The Variables palette is used to create and manage the variables in a template. Designers often use standard templates (without variables) if they need to create numerous images that share similar designs or layouts.

Working with a template is easy and it's rather like filling out forms. But if you need to create a large number of designs from a template, say 100 Web banner designs, the process of filling out data on a template a hundred times is still tedious. A more efficient method is to use variables to define which objects on the template are dynamic (changeable). By using variables, you can automate the process of filling out the template with a set of data.

## Basic Illustrator Commands

In this section, you will learn more about the tools, menu commands, and palettes needed to perform basic tasks in Illustrator CS. These commands represent the building blocks for working with graphics in the program.

## Changing the View

It is important to be able to move around the screen when you are working in Illustrator, and you can use many methods to change the screen view.

### Zoom Tool

You can click or drag the Zoom tool ( ) to magnify part of the image. If you hold down the [Alt] key while clicking with the Zoom tool, you will zoom out of the area. While working with other tools, you can temporarily access the Zoom tool by pressing [Ctrl]-[Spacebar] to zoom out or [Ctrl]-[Alt]-[Spacebar] to zoom in. Double-clicking on the Zoom tool ( ) sets the image magnification value to 100%.

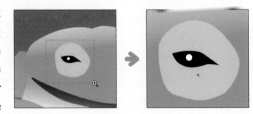

## Hand Tool

You can use the Hand tool to click and drag your view of the work area. This allows you to focus on a specific part of your image. Double-clicking the Hand tool (🖐) or pressing [Ctrl]-[0] automatically maximizes your image within the document window.

## View Menu

Another way to change the screen view is to use the View menu, which contains several commands for altering your document view – Zoom In, Zoom Out, Fit in Window, and Actual Size.

## Navigator Palette

Move the red box in the Navigator palette to move your view around the artboard. To zoom in or out from an image, click the Zoom Out (◿) or Zoom In (◺) button, or drag the triangle icon below the slider (▱). You can also specify the zoom value directly in the text box in the bottom-left corner.

## Status Bar

Type a magnification value in the Zoom pop-up menu in the status bar ( 100% ▾ ) or click on the arrow icon ( ▾ ) to select a preset zoom value.

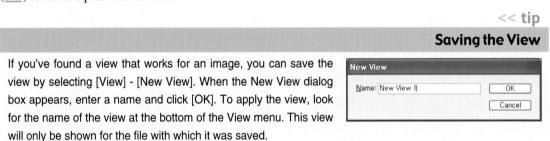

<< tip
### Saving the View

If you've found a view that works for an image, you can save the view by selecting [View] - [New View]. When the New View dialog box appears, enter a name and click [OK]. To apply the view, look for the name of the view at the bottom of the View menu. This view will only be shown for the file with which it was saved.

# Selecting Objects

Before you can move, color, or apply effects to objects, you must select them first. Objects are selected using selection tools found in the toolbox or by using menu commands.

## Selection Tools

You can use the Selection tool (▶), Direct Selection tool (▶), Group Selection tool (▶), Lasso tool (🔾), and the Magic Wand tool (🔧) to select part or all of an object. The selection tools are covered extensively in Chapter 2.

## Select Menu

The Select menu contains options for making selections.

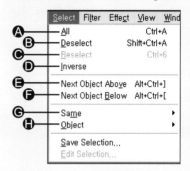

**Ⓐ All**: Selects all objects in the image.

**Ⓑ Deselect**: Deselects the current selection.

**Ⓒ Reselect**: Repeats the last selection command used.

**Ⓓ Inverse**: Deselects the current selection and selects the previously unselected areas.

▶Choosing [Select] - [Inverse] deselects the yellow star (the current selection) and selects all the other stars.

**Ⓔ Next Object Above**: Selects the object above the selected object.

**Ⓕ Next Object Below**: Selects the object below the selected object.

**Ⓖ Same**: The Same submenu contains options for selecting objects with the same attributes.

▲[Select] - [Same] Submenu

▲Choose [Select] - [Same] - [Fill Color] to select objects with the same fill color.

**Ⓗ Object**: Use the Object submenu to select similar types of objects.

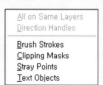

▲[Select] - [Object] Submenu

# Manipulating Objects

The Edit and Object menus contain options for manipulating objects. In this section, you will learn to copy and paste objects using the Edit menu, and to group, ungroup, and lock objects using the Object menu.

## Edit Menu

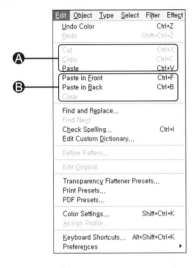

**Ⓐ Cut, Copy, and Paste**: Because you will cut, copy, or paste objects frequently when using Illustrator, it helps to remember the keyboard shortcuts for these actions. Press [Ctrl]-[X] to cut, [Ctrl]-[C] to copy, and [Ctrl]-[V] to paste.

**Ⓑ Paste in Front and Paste in Back**: The Paste in Front and Paste in Back commands let you paste an object on top of or behind other objects in your drawing.

<< note

### Paste in Front and Paste in Back

The Paste in Front and Paste in Back commands can be used to make accurate drawings and create variations of an object, as shown in the following examples:

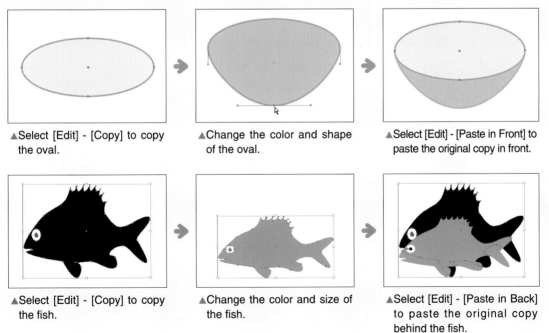

▲Select [Edit] - [Copy] to copy the oval.

▲Change the color and shape of the oval.

▲Select [Edit] - [Paste in Front] to paste the original copy in front.

▲Select [Edit] - [Copy] to copy the fish.

▲Change the color and size of the fish.

▲Select [Edit] - [Paste in Back] to paste the original copy behind the fish.

## Object Menu

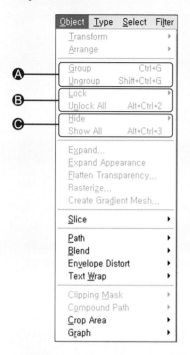

**Ⓐ Group and Ungroup**: Selecting the Group command groups any selected objects into a single unit; this is useful when you want to make changes to multiple objects at once. Selecting the Ungroup command separates selected groups into their individual parts. Double-clicking the Group Selection tool ( ) on a grouped object selects all the objects in that group.

**Ⓑ Lock and Unlock All**: This command locks objects to prevent them from being selected and edited. The Lock submenu contains three commands—Selection locks selected objects, All Artwork Above locks objects in front of a selected object (this is useful when objects overlap), and Other Layers locks the other layers (including the objects on these layers). The keyboard shortcut for the [Lock] - [Selection] command is [Ctrl]-[2]. Clicking Unlock All unlocks all the objects in your work area.

**Ⓒ Hide and Show All**: The Hide command hides an object from view. Hidden objects cannot be selected or edited. There are three commands in the Hide submenu—Selection hides selected objects, All Artwork Above hides objects in front of the selected object, and Other Layers hides the objects in the other layers. Selecting the Show All command reveals all hidden objects.

<< note

### Locking Layers in the Layers Palette

The Layers palette can be used to lock layers. In the Layers palette, clicking in the Toggles Lock box of a layer will lock the layer. The lock icon ( ) will appear when the layer is locked. Clicking on the icon will unlock the layer and the icon will disappear.

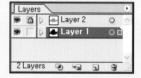

## Creating New Documents

The first few pages of this chapter dealt with using the welcome screen, including how the welcome screen can be used to create a new document. In this section, let's look at other ways of creating new documents. For example, you can open a new document or use an existing template to create a new document.

A new document in Illustrator consists of a single page that you use to draw artwork. An Illustrator document cannot have more than one page.

## Using the New Command

You can create a new document at any time by selecting [File] - [New] or by pressing the shortcut keys, [Ctrl]-[N]. When the New Document dialog box appears, enter your desired settings and click [OK].

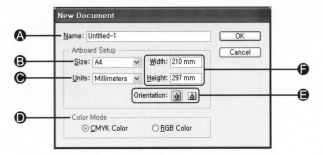

**A Name**: Enter a name for the new document.

**B Size**: Sets the size of the new document.

**C Units**: Determines the unit of measurement for width and height.

**D Color Mode**: Choose the color mode of the new document—CMYK for printing and RGB for Web images.

**E Orientation**: Choose a portrait ( ) or landscape ( ) orientation for the document.

**F Width and Height**: Specifies the document size using width and height dimensions. If dimensions are entered manually, "Custom" will appear in the Size drop-down menu.

## Using Templates

Templates are preset documents, and there is a wide variety of templates to choose from in Illustrator. There are blank templates for doing artwork in odd sizes, such as CD disc labels and business cards, and thematic templates such as designs for restaurant menus and postcards. In order to make a new document using a template, do the following:

1. Select [File] - [New from Template] to open the New from Template dialog box.

2. Double-click on a folder and navigate to a template. Click [New].

3. Edit or draw in the template to create your artwork.

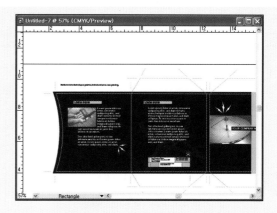

# Saving Documents

The File menu contains a number of commands for saving documents. The save commands can be used to create a file that is compatible with Illustrator CS, while the [File] - [Export] command can be used to create a file that is compatible with previous versions of Illustrator. Let's have a look at these commands.

## Using the Save and Save As commands

1. Click on [File] - [Save As] to open the Save As dialog box. Enter a file name, choose a file format, navigate to the desired save location, and then click [Save].

2. An Options dialog box will appear. In this case, choosing the Illustrator file format (*.ai) opens the Illustrator Options dialog box. Enter your desired settings and then click [OK]. More often than not, the default settings are used. See the note after this section for more information on the Illustrator Options dialog box.

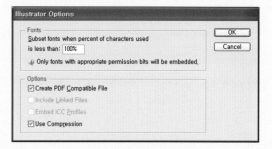

3. The file will be saved with the name you entered in the Save As dialog box. Notice that the document title has been changed to the new name. Moving forward, you'll be able to save your progress to the file using the [File] - [Save] command.

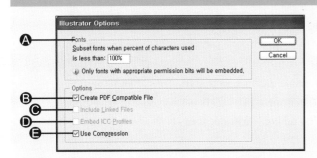

**Ⓐ Subset fonts when percent of characters used is less than**: When saving Illustrator files with unique fonts, you can choose to embed the entire font set with the file (i.e., all the characters), or only the characters that are used in the artwork. This option determines when the entire font should be embedded based on the percentage of characters used.

**Ⓑ Create PDF Compatible File**: Makes the file compatible with Adobe Acrobat.

**Ⓒ Include Linked Files**: Files, such as bitmap images, that are linked to the artwork will be embedded.

**Ⓓ Embed ICC Profiles**: ICC stands for International Color Consortium. It is a color management standard that makes sure an image's color remains the same from source to destination. Checking this option embeds the ICC profile with the artwork.

**Ⓔ Use Compression**: Determines whether PDF data will be compressed within the Illustrator file.

## Other Save Commands

• *Save a Copy*: Saves a copy of the file while the current document remains active.

• *Save as Template*: Use this command to save a file you created as a template.

• *Save for Web*: Saves an image as a graphic for the Web.

• *Save for Microsoft Office*: Saves the document in PNG format for use in Microsoft Office.

## Using the Export Command

The [File] - [Export] command can be used for saving files in a variety of file formats, including file formats for the Web and Microsoft Office. The advantage of using the Export command as opposed to using the save commands is that the Export command lets you adjust a variety of options before saving.

Depending on the file format chosen, options include resolution, opacity, and background color. Another advantage of using the [File] - [Export] command is that the command can be used to create a file that is compatible with previous versions of Illustrator.

Choosing a File Format ▶

47

# Common File Formats

Illustrator supports a wide variety of file formats, and the following is a list of the more commonly used ones:

## Adobe Illustrator (*.AI)

This is the basic Illustrator file format. It is advisable to work in this file format and only chose to save in another file format (if you wish) when the file is final. This is because you can only be certain that every aspect of your image is saved if you use the native Illustrator format.

## Illustrator Legacy (*.AI)

This option saves the file in a format compatible with previous Illustrator versions. Some of the effects used in Illustrator CS are not supported by older versions; such effects will automatically be rasterized when saved in the Illustrator legacy format. This process will limit your ability to edit your image.

## Illustrator EPS (*.EPS)

The EPS (Encapsulated PostScript) format is used for transferring image files across applications and platforms. For example, files created in Illustrator are saved in this format so that they can be imported into page layout programs Although this format can be used to save paths, it does not save alpha channels.

## Photoshop (*.PSD)

The PSD option exports the image as a Photoshop file while preserving layers. Photoshop is an image-editing program commonly used for creating and editing artwork, including photographs.

## Macromedia Flash (*.SWF)

Flash is a program used for creating animated graphics that can include sound. Flash movies are popular on the Web and you can use Illustrator to create images for these animations. Saving a file in the Macromedia Flash format converts the layers in Illustrator into Flash frames.

## BMP (*.BMP, *.RLE, *.DIB)

This is the native image file format for the Windows operating system. Bitmap formats support 24-bit color, but because they are not compressed, their file size is relatively large.

## Adobe PDF (*.PDF, *.PDP)

The Photoshop PDF (Portable Document Format) format was created for compatibility with Adobe Acrobat. It ensures that documents appear the same regardless of the operating system in which they are opened.

## CompuServe GIF (*.GIF)

The GIF (Graphic Interchange Format) format was developed as a compressed file format to reduce the size of image files sent over networks. It has since become a Web standard. The format supports animations, offers good compression without losing quality, and can be used to save transparent frames. The primary drawback to GIF images is that they can only contain up to 256 colors (8 bit).

### JPEG (*.JPG, *.JPEG *.JPE)

The JPEG (Joint Photographic Expert Group) format is a compressed file format used on the Internet for photographic or continuous-color images. This file format supports progressive viewing of images (i.e., the image will begin to appear before it's completely downloaded) and can display up to 24 bits of color. Users can configure the compression rate to reduce file size. However, higher compression rates result in lower image quality.

### PICT (*.PCT, *.PICT)

The PICT file format was created for use on Macintosh computers. RGB images saved as PICT files can be saved at a depths between 16 and 32 bits.

### PNG (*.PNG)

The PNG (Portable Network Graphic) format can be used to create transparent images for the Web in 8-bit or 24-bit color depth. PNG offers compression without a loss of quality but can result in larger file sizes compared with JPEGs. Because it is a relatively new file format, its use can cause problems with browser compatibility.

### TGA (*.TGA, *.VDA, *.ICB, *.VST)

The TGA (Targa) format was developed by Truevision for their Targa and Vista video boards. This format can be used on both PCs and Macs and supports 24-bit color, as well as 32-bit Web color.

### TIFF (*.TIF, *.TIFF)

The TIFF (Tagged Image File Format) format, like EPS, was developed for compatibility with editing programs. It can be used across different types of computers and most graphic software programs. The LZW compression option doesn't reduce quality and preserves channels. Compared with EPS files, TIFFs are faster and smaller. TIFF also supports ZIP compression and preserves transparent frames.

## Basic Color Concepts

Before you start using Illustrator or any other graphics program, you need to grasp some basic concepts related to the use of color in graphics software. In this section, you will learn about color models and color modes.

## Understanding Color Models and Color Modes

Color models and color modes affect the range of colors displayed on computer screens and printed files. Because colors appear differently on different computers and printers, it's important to put some thought into how you set up color in your images–to ensure maximum consistency.

## Color Models

Color models refer to a system of describing color. There are five color models in Illustrator–RGB, CMYK, Web Safe RGB, Grayscale, and HSB. To select a color model, click on the triangle button ( ⊙ ) in the Color palette and choose a color model from the palette menu.

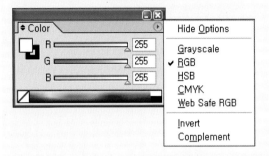

## Color Modes

Color modes determine how an image will be output to a printer, and there are two color modes available in Illustrator–RGB and CMYK. You can choose the color mode when you create a new document or change it anytime using the [File] - [Document Color Mode] command.

As a rule, it is not advisable to switch back and forth between different color models or color modes because each color model and color mode has its own unique color range. This means that some of the colors you use may get turned into other colors when you switch between color models or modes, and the more often you switch, the more often your color scheme will be skewed.

# RGB Color Model and Color Mode

The RGB color model describes the colors created by mixing red, blue, and green. This is the color system used by computer monitors and televisions. The three primary colors–red, green, and blue–create 16,800,000 colors when combined. You should use this color mode when creating or editing images on a computer. Note that mixing all three primary colors creates white light.

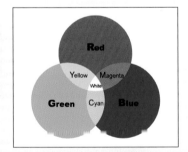

# CMYK Color Model and Color Mode

The CMYK color model is used to describe the colors created by mixing cyan, magenta, yellow, and black inks. Note that mixing all four colors creates black. In real life (on a printing press), mixing all four colors is likely to create a dark grayish color because of the impurities in the dye, so avoid overblending the four component colors. This color model is primarily used for printing.

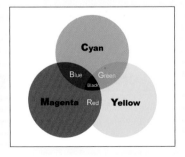

## Web Safe RGB Model

This color model is derived from the RGB mode and includes colors that can be used safely on the Web. When the Web Safe RGB model is selected, each of the RGB colors in the Color palette uses 16-bit colors between the 00 and FF color values. The RGB color range is limited to ensure that colors appear consistently on any of the computers that might visit your Web page.

## Grayscale Color Model

The Grayscale color model describes 256 shades of gray. In this mode, 0 represents black, 255 represents white, and all figures between 1 and 254 display increasingly dark shades of gray.

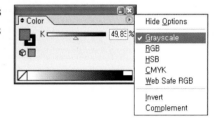

## HSB Color Model

The HSB color model describes color using hue, brightness, and saturation values.

- *Hue*: Represents a spectrum of colors that differ only in color–not in brightness or saturation.

- *Brightness*: Represents the brightness or darkness of a color.

- *Saturation*: Determines the strength or intensity of the color.

## Editing Stroke and Fill Attributes

Drawn objects are made up of a stroke (the line made by the object's path) and a fill (the area inside the path). The color of a stroke or fill can be changed either in the toolbox or by using the Swatches or Color palettes. The thickness and style of a stroke can be adjusted in the Stroke palette.

## Changing Stroke and Fill Colors

When a file is first opened or created, Illustrator will set the fill color to white and the stroke color to black by default. If you don't want to use any color, click the None icon (⬜) in the toolbox or the Color and Swatches palettes.

## Using the Toolbox

You can change the fill or stroke colors by double-clicking the Fill or Stroke color boxes in the toolbox to open the Color Picker and select a new color.

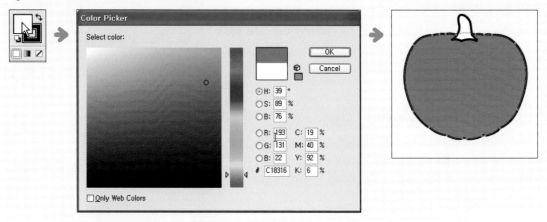

## Using the Color or Swatches Palette

Before you change a fill or stroke color, you will need to select the Fill or Stroke color box in the toolbox or Color palette. Pressing the [X] key toggles between the Fill and Stroke color boxes.

### Color Palette

The RGB color sliders in the Color palette can be adjusted to blend a color. You can also type in the color values directly or click on a color in the color spectrum. Clicking on the triangle icon ( ▶ ) opens the Color palette's pop-up menu, from which you can change the default RGB color mode to Grayscale, HSB, CMYK, or Web Safe RGB.

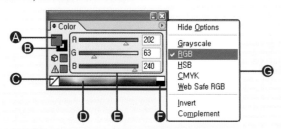

ⓐ **Fill Color**: Click to activate the fill color, then blend the color in the Color palette. Double-clicking it opens the Color Picker, which contains additional color options.

ⓑ **Stroke Color**: Click to activate the stroke color, then blend the color in the Color palette.

ⓒ **None**: Click to select no color.

ⓓ **Color Spectrum bar**: Click on this to select a color instantly.

ⓔ **Color Sliders**: Use the color sliders to alter the component color values.

ⓕ **White/Black**: Click to choose white or black.

ⓖ **Palette Menu**: Contains options for changing the color mode.

## Swatches Palette

You can select preset colors, gradients, and patterns from the Swatches palette; these can be used for both fills and strokes. Using the Swatches palette, you can select process colors, global process colors, nonglobal process colors, and spot colors. Choosing [Open Swatch Library] from the palette's pop-up menu allows you to add more swatch libraries.

You can save a color you mixed to the Swatches palette by clicking the New Swatch icon (⬜). If you create or modify a swatch library, you can save it by selecting [Save Swatch Library] from the pop-up menu. Saved swatch libraries can be accessed by selecting [Open Swatch Library].

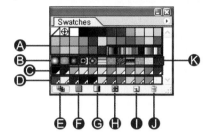

**Ⓐ Process Colors**: Process colors are mixed by combining one or more of these four colors: cyan (C), magenta (M), yellow (Y), and black (K). These colors represent the inks used in commercial printing, so this color system (CMYK) is suitable for print documents but not for Web images, which use the RGB (red, green, blue) color system.

**Ⓑ Gradients**: Gradients can only be used as fills. Gradients are created using the Gradient and Color palettes.

**Ⓒ Global Process Colors**: When you edit a global process color swatch, all objects using that color are updated. This way, you don't have to change the color for each of the objects separately.

**Ⓓ Spot Colors**: A spot color is a matched or exact color that is not created by mixing cyan, magenta, yellow, and black inks. A spot color is a premixed ink that you specify using a color matching system such as PANTONE. Unlike process colors, which can deviate from printer to printer, you can tell exactly how a spot color will look when printed by referring to a color book from PANTONE (or whichever color system you're using). When you update a Spot Color swatch, all objects using the color will be updated.

**Ⓔ Show All Swatches**: Show all swatches.

**Ⓕ Show Color Swatches**: Show only color swatches.

**Ⓖ Show Gradient Swatches**: Show only gradient swatches.

**Ⓗ Show Pattern Swatches**: Show only pattern swatches.

**Ⓘ New Swatch**: Make a new swatch.

**Ⓙ Delete Swatch**: Delete the selected swatch.

**Ⓚ Patterns**: Repeating patterns can be applied to both fill and stroke colors. To create a pattern swatch, create the pattern on the page and then drag it into the Swatches palette.

❶To apply a swatch color to an object, select the areas in the object to be changed and click on the desired swatch in the Swatches palette. In this example, the hat, scarf, and sack of the Santa piggy are selected and then the Global Red swatch in the Swatches palette is clicked to apply the color.

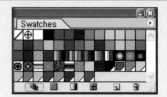

❷Double-clicking on a swatch opens the Swatch Options dialog box. In this case, we've double-clicked on the Global Red swatch to open the Swatch Options dialog box.

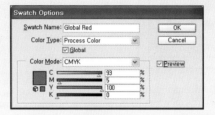

❸The new color is automatically applied to the areas containing the Global Red swatch.

## Changing Stroke Thickness and Style

The Stroke palette is used to adjust an object's stroke thickness and style.

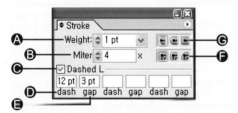

Ⓐ **Weight**: Adjusts the stroke thickness.

Ⓑ **Miter**: Sets the limit for when the stroke corners change from pointed corners to squared-off corners. For example, at the default miter limit of 4, a corner squares off when the length of the corner is 4 times the stroke thickness. A Miter value of 1 squares off all the corners.

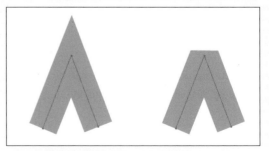

▲From Left to Right: Miter 4, Miter 2

**ⓒ Dashed Line**: Checking this option lets you create a dashed line by entering values for up to three dash and gap lengths.

**ⓓ Dash**: Sets the length of a dash.

**ⓔ Gap**: Adjusts the spacing between dashes. When using Butt Caps (⊟), the gap starts at the end. When using Round Caps (⊟) or Square Caps (⊟), the gap starts at the center of the dashed line and extends to the end.

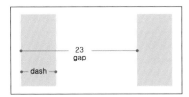
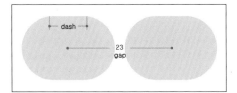

▲Using the Same Dash Value of 10 Points and Gap Value of 23 Points on a Line with Butt Caps (Left) and a Line with Round Caps (Right)

**ⓕ Join**: Select one of the corner styles—Miter Join (⊞), Round Join (⊞), or Bevel Join (⊞).

▲From Left to Right: Miter Join, Round Join, and Bevel Join

**ⓖ Cap**: Select a style for the end point—Butt Cap (⊟), Round Cap (⊟), and Projecting Cap (⊟).

▲From Left to Right: Butt Cap, Round Cap, and Projecting Cap

<< note

## Undo

You can use [Edit] - [Undo] to undo one or more previous steps. [Edit] - [Redo] reverses a previous Undo command.

<< note

## Eyedropper Tool and Paint Bucket Tool

The Eyedropper tool and the Paint Bucket tool can be used to copy the attributes of an object and apply them to another object. The Eyedropper tool affects all the paint attributes of an object. Double-click on the tool to access its dialog box and adjust the scope of the tool.

▲Use the Eyedropper tool to create a color sample.

▲Click the Paintbrush tool on another object to apply the color.

In the CS version of Illustrator, moving, scrolling, printing, and file saving are all much faster. Working across multiple artboards is also much speedier. In addition to these improvements, the following new features have been added.

## 3D Effects

Among all of the new features in Illustrator CS, the flashiest one has got to be the 3D effect option. The 3D submenu, which is found under the Effect menu, contains the Extrude and Bevel, Revolve, and Rotate commands. Using the Extrude and Bevel and Revolve commands, two-dimensional vector objects can be turned into three-dimensional objects. The Rotate command rotates two- and three-dimensional objects in three-dimensional space.

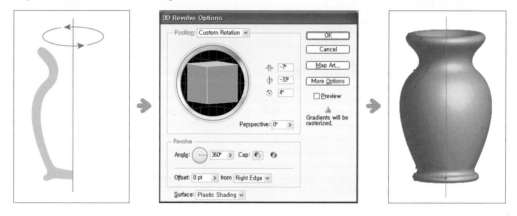

## New Type Options

One of the best improvements in Illustrator CS applies to typography. Let's look at the new typography features one by one:

### Type On a Path Submenu

There are more options now for positioning type on a path. The [Type] - [Type on a Path] submenu contains five preset alignment settings for placing type on a path. These preset alignment settings–named Rainbow, Skew, 3D Ribbon, Stair Step, and Gravity–are also found in the Type on a Path Options dialog box. The Type on a Path Options dialog box also contains options for adjusting spacing and alignment.

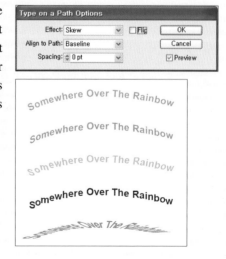

Type Effects (from Top to Bottom): Rainbow, Skew, 3D ▶
Ribbon, Stair Step, and Gravity

## Font Menu

The newly improved font menu displays a font name in the font face itself, making it much faster and easier to select your desired font.

## Every-line Composer Command

The new Every-line Composer command is found in the Paragraph palette's pop-up menu. When the command is selected, it automatically evens out the spacing between words and letters, and determines how best to break lines in a paragraph to minimize the use of hyphenation and maintain consistent line lengths.

The Single-line Composer command, which is not new to Illustrator CS, performs the same function as the Every-line Composer command, but does it line by line, rather than to the entire type area. Both of these commands work with the area type tools and the type on a path tools.

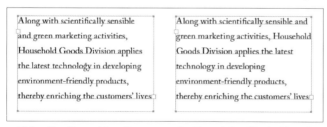

▲Using the Every-Line Composer (Left) and the Single-Line Composer (Right)

## Optical Kerning and Optical Margin Alignment

Both the Optical Kerning and Optical Margin Alignment commands are new and are used for adjusting spacing. The Optical Kerning command, which is found in the Character palette, automatically modifies the space between characters (i.e., kerning). In previous Illustrator versions, kerning had to be adjusted manually when the built-in kerning for character pairs in a given font did not create satisfactory results. To activate Optical Kerning, go to the [Set the kerning between two characters] option in the Character palette and select Optical.

"One of the interesting stories within the story of your domestic political scene is that there's a constitutional process and a rule of law that follows and that it remains business as usual both domestically and internationally"

"One of the interesting stories within the story of your domestic political scene is that there's a constitutional process and a rule of law that follows and that it remains business as usual both domestically and internationally"

▲The Default Kerning (Top) and Optical Kerning (Bottom)

▲Default type is shown on the left. The version on the right uses the Optical Margin Alignment command to align the left and right margins of the text area.

Another new kerning feature is the [Type] - [Optical Margin Alignment] command. The Optical Margin Alignment command is used for keeping the left and right margins of a text area aligned by changing the position of punctuation and characters at the edge.

## OpenType Font Support

With Illustrator CS, there is now support for the OpenType font format. OpenType fonts are compatible across Windows and Macintosh operating systems and they support a wider range of glyphs and characters. In addition, some OpenType fonts contain ligatures that can be activated in Illustrator to replace certain characters. Ligatures are character combinations that are designed as a single unit. For example, "1/2" can be turned into " $\frac{1}{2}$ " when the Fractions option is selected in the OpenType palette.

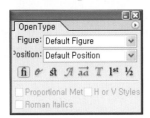

◄Original (top); Selecting the Swash option (𝒜) gives the letter p a nice flourish (bottom). The font used in this example is Adobe Garmond Pro.

◄Original (top); Selecting the Standard Ligatures option (fi) removes the dot from the letter i and joins the letters f and i (bottom). The font used in this example is Chaparral Pro.

◄Original (top); Selecting the Ordinals option (1st) allows for a stylistic flourish (bottom). The font used in this example is Minion Pro.

## Paragraph Styles and Character Styles Palettes

Commonly used paragraph and character settings can be saved in the Paragraph Styles and Character Styles palettes, respectively. These two new palettes make it possible to maintain a consistent style throughout your artwork when editing characters, lines, or entire paragraphs.

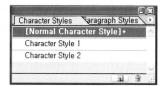

## Glyphs Palette

Earlier in this chapter, you learned that glyphs are special characters or symbols that are not found in the alphabet. Every font has its own set of glyphs, and with Illustrator CS you can now view and insert a glyph simply by double-clicking on it in the Glyphs palette.

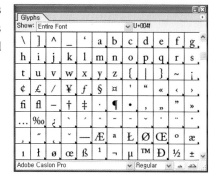

## Tab Leaders

Tab leaders are the dots and patterns that appear when the [Tab] key is hit. Tab leaders are created and edited in the Tabs palette. You can open this palette by selecting [Window] - [Type] - [Tabs].

## Improved Row and Column Features

After text has been entered into a text area, the text area can be split and the text distributed quickly into rows and columns. With the text area selected, choose [Type] - [Area Type Options] to open the Area Type Options dialog box and split the text area into rows and columns.

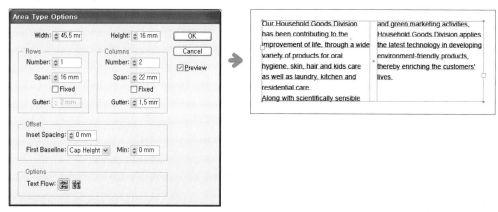

▲ Insert the number of rows and columns needed and click [OK] (left); the text will be distributed into two columns.

## Scribble Effect

The Scribble effect (the name says it all) creates artwork that looks scribbled. The casual, hand-drawn style is great for creating friendly, inviting designs. The command is found at [Effect] - [Stylize] - [Scribble].

## Enhanced Adobe PDF Support

PDF is the native file format for the Adobe Acrobat program. PDF files are widely used because they are compatible across many platforms and the Acrobat Reader program used for reading PDF files can be downloaded for free. In Illustrator CS, support for Adobe PDF has been enhanced to include compatibility with the Adobe Acrobat 6.0 program and the Adobe PDF 1.5 file format. This feature is useful for sharing artwork with clients or friends who lack the Illustrator program. Other new improvements include support for layers, printer marks and bleeds, and more security options.

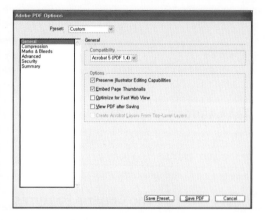

## Expanded Print Capabilities

The user interface for sending artwork to print has been streamlined to make the process smoother and faster. The Page Setup and Separations Setup dialog boxes have been removed and their functions consolidated into the Print dialog box. Using the Print dialog box, frequently used print settings can be saved as print presets which can be loaded when needed.

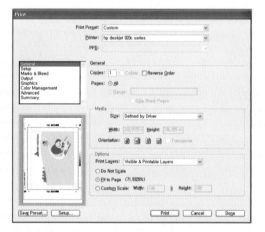

## Integration with Microsoft Office

The Save for Microsoft Office command can be used to save an Illustrator file so that the artwork can be opened in Microsoft Office applications such as Powerpoint, Excel, and Word. Files saved using this command work on both Windows and Macintosh operating systems.

# Templates

There are more than 200 different design templates in Illustrator CS. Templates are a great source of inspiration and can help you get started on a new project. All the elements in a template can be altered to create unique images. For example, if you need to create a CD label, you can use one of the CD templates just to get the CD label's dimensions right. The design of the CD can then be changed to suit your personal style.

Templates are opened as new files. Making changes to and saving these new files will not affect the original template in any way.

▲Stationery\Stationery 3 Business Card.ait

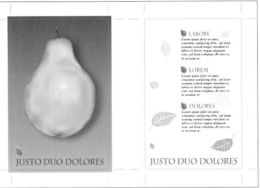

▲Cards and Post Cards\Post Card 3.ait

▲CD and DVD\CD ROM 1 Disc Label.ait

▲CD and DVD\DVD 3 Menu.ait

▲Restaurant\Restaurant 1 Menu Outside.ait

You can also save your own designs as templates, especially when working on a large project for which you need to maintain a consistent design.

Invitation 1.ait

◀A template saved by using the [File] - [Save As Template] command.

Chapter | 2

# Drawing Techniques

If you've explored the drawing tools found in most Office applications, you'll find that the drawing tools in Illustrator work pretty much the same way. Even if you have never used drawing tools before, you will find them easy to use soon enough.

In this chapter, you'll learn to use the line and grid tools, the shape tools, the selection tools, and the transform tools to create beautiful vector-based artwork.

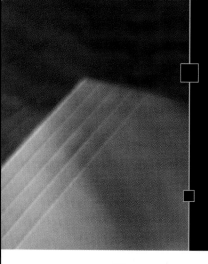

# Basic Drawing Tools

The basic drawing tools in Illustrator are the line, grid, and shape tools. Lines, arcs, and spirals are created easily with the line tools, while the grid tools make rectangular and polar grids a snap. Using the shape tools, a variety of shapes can be drawn. The selection and transform tools, which can be used to edit paths and shapes, are also covered in this chapter.

## Line and Grid Tools

There are three line tools and two grid tools in Illustrator. The line tools are the Line Segment tool, the Arc tool, and the Spiral tool. The grid tools are the Rectangular Grid tool and the Polar Grid tool.

In this section, you will learn to use all of these tools, whether on their own or together with keystrokes such as the [Ctrl], [Shift], and [Alt] keys. The properties of these tools can be modified by pressing these keys or by changing their options in the appropriate tool options dialog box.

### Line Segment Tool (◢), [\]

This tool is used to draw straight lines with a click-and-drag motion. To demonstrate, select the Line Segment tool and try it out on the artboard. If you press the [Alt] key while dragging, you will create a straight line that extends out in both directions from the point of origin. In other words, the point of origin becomes the center point of the line. If you press the [Shift] key while dragging, you will create vertical, horizontal, or 45° diagonal lines.

▲Drawing Lines in the Usual Way

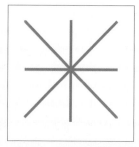

▲Drawing Lines by Pressing the [Alt]-[Shift] Keys and Dragging

If the Line Segment tool is selected and you click on the work space, the following options dialog box will appear.

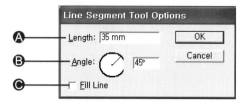

**Ⓐ Length**: Specifies the total length of the line.

**Ⓑ Angle**: Specifies the angle of the line. You can enter an angle in the text box or drag the angle preview dial. The dial shows the angle at which the line will be drawn.

**Ⓒ Fill Line**: By default, lines are drawn without a fill surface. Checking this option will fill the line with the current fill color.

To change the color of the line in the Color palette, the Stroke Color button (▢), and not the Fill Color button (▮), must first be activated in the toolbox. The Stroke Color button is the frame-like one that sits behind the solid color block of the Fill Color button.

 ◀Selecting the Fill Color Button

 ◀Selecting the Stroke Color Button

 ◀When Fill Line Is Not Selected in the Line Segment Tool Options Dialog Box

<< **note**

**Grave Accent Effect**

With the Line Segment tool selected, hold down the grave accent key [`] as you drag to create multiple lines emanating from the point of origin. Dragging slowly will create more lines than dragging quickly. To move the point of origin as you drag, hold down the spacebar. The grave accent effect can be applied using any of the line, grid, or shape tools by following the same steps.

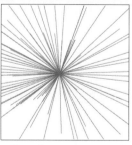

▲The Grave Accent [`] Effect with the Line Segment Tool

▲Using the grave accent [`] effect with the Ellipse tool (▢) produced the image shown here. This image was drawn using the [`] and [Spacebar] keys together.

# Arc Tool (⌐)

The Arc tool allows you to create a segment of a circle.

When using the Arc tool to draw convex or concave arcs, you can press the [ ↑ ] or [ ↓ ] keys to change the degree of the arc. While dragging, press the [Alt] key to extend the arc from both sides of the point of origin, the [Shift] key to create arcs at 45° angles, the [F] key to flip the arc, and the [C] key to alternate between open or closed arcs.

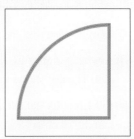

▲Press [ ↓ ] to make the arc less curvy.

▲Circle Drawn Using the [Alt]-[Shift] Keys

▲Press the [F] key to flip the arc.

▲Press the [C] key to turn an open arc into a closed arc and vice versa.

With the Arc tool selected, click anywhere on the artboard or double-click on the Arc tool to open the Arc Segment Tool Options dialog box.

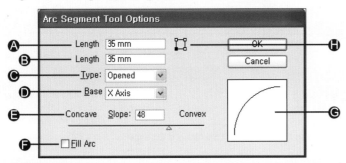

**Ⓐ Length**: Determines the width of the arc with respect to the point of origin.

**Ⓑ Length**: Determines the height of the arc with respect to the point of origin.

**Ⓒ Type**: Choose to create an opened or closed path.

**Ⓓ Base**: Choose whether to draw the base of the arc along the X axis or Y axis.

**Ⓔ Concave/Convex**: Enter a Slope value or use the slider (⌐) to adjust the angle and curvature of the arc. To draw a concave arc, enter a negative Slope value or drag the slider towards Concave (⌐). To draw a convex arc, enter a positive Slope value or drag the slider towards Convex (⌐).

**Ⓕ Fill Arc**: When the Fill Arc option is checked, the arc is filled with the current fill color.

**Ⓖ Preview**: Shows a preview of the arc. The preview window will only appear in the Arc Segment Tool Options dialog box if the dialog box was opened by double-clicking on the Arc tool in the toolbox.

**Ⓗ Reference Point Locator <⌐>**: Click on one of the four points to set the point from which the arc is drawn.

# Spiral Tool ( )

The Spiral tool is used to draw spiral shapes; the direction of the swirl can be adjusted in the tool's options dialog box. While dragging, press the [Ctrl] key to adjust the tightness of the swirl, the [ ↑ ] or [ ↓ ] keys to alter the number of spirals, the [R] key to flip the spiral, and the [Shift] key to constrain the spiral to a 45° angle. Also, holding down the [Alt] key while dragging outwards will increase the number of spirals. Conversely, dragging inwards while holding the [Alt] key will decrease the number of spirals.

▲A spiral drawn in the usual way.

▲A spiral drawn by pressing the [Ctrl] key and dragging outwards to create a loose spiral which is flipped by pressing the [R] key.

As with the other tools, select the Spiral tool and click anywhere to open its options dialog box.

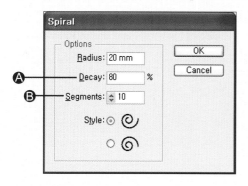

Ⓐ **Decay**: Determines the tightness of the spiral. A low percentage creates loose spirals and a high percentage creates tight spirals.

Ⓑ **Segments**: Sets the number of segments in a spiral. In other words, this determines the length of the spiral. One complete "wind" requires 4 segments.

# Rectangular Grid Tool ( )

This tool makes it easy to create grids on the artboard. While dragging with this tool, press the [ ↑ ] or [ ↓ ] keys to add or remove horizontal lines, and the [→] or [←] keys to add or remove vertical lines.

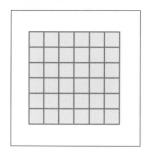

◄A Normal Grid

Pressing the [Alt] key while dragging with the Rectangular Grid tool will extend the grid from the origin point, while pressing the [Shift] key will constrain the grid to a square.

Pressing the [F] key pushes down the horizontal divisions, while pressing the [V] key pushes them up. Pressing the [C] key pushes the vertical divisions to the right, while pressing the [X] key pushes them to the left.

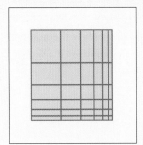

◀This grid was drawn by pressing the [F] and [C] keys while dragging.

# Polar Grid Tool ( ⊛ )

The Polar Grid tool makes a set of concentric rings to which radial lines can be added. This is useful for creating pie charts and other circular tables. While dragging, press the [ ↑ ] or [ ↓ ] keys to increase or decrease the number of concentric circles, and the [→] or [←] keys to increase or decrease the number of radial divisions. As you might expect, the [Alt] and [Shift] keys work with the Polar Grid tool as they do with other tools. Similarly, pressing the [V] key pushes the radial dividers clockwise, and the [F] key pushes them counterclockwise. The [C] key pushes the concentric circles outwards and the [X] key pushes them inwards.

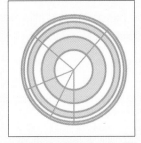

▲A Normal Concentric Circle     ▲Drawn by Pressing the [F] and [C] Keys

With the Polar Grid tool selected, click anywhere to open its options dialog box.

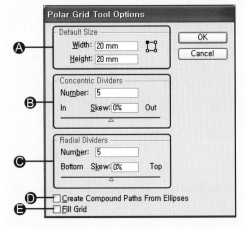

**Ⓐ Default Size**

*Width*: Determines the default width of the polar grid.

*Height*: Determines the default height of the polar grid.

⊞: Click on one of the four points to set the point of origin.

**Ⓑ Concentric Dividers**

*Number*: Sets the number of concentric circles.

*Skew*: A positive number pushes the concentric circles outwards, while a negative number pushes them inwards.

**Ⓒ Radial Dividers**

*Number*: Sets the number of radial dividers.

*Skew*: A positive number pushes the radial dividers clockwise, while a negative number pushes them counterclockwise.

**Ⓓ Create Compound Paths From Ellipses**: When this option is checked, alternating rings in the polar grid are colored with the fill color.

**Ⓔ Fill Grid**: When this option is checked, the grid is colored with the current fill color. Otherwise, it will not be filled with color.

## Shape Tools

The shape tools include the Rectangle tool, the Rounded Rectangle tool, the Ellipse tool, the Polygon tool, the Star tool, and the Flare tool. To draw shapes with one of these tools, select the desired shape tool and click-and-drag on the artboard. Except for the Flare tool, the click-and-drag motion lets you drag out a shape by one of its corner points. (With the Flare tool, the flare is dragged out from its center point.) Just like the Line and Grid tools, pressing keystrokes such as the [Shift] and [Alt] keys while dragging with a shape tool changes the properties of the tool. For all of the shape tools, pressing the [Alt] key sets the original point at the center of the shape.

Another way to adjust the properties of a shape tool is to change the options in the tool's options dialog box. To open a shape tool's options dialog box, click anywhere while the tool is selected.

## Rectangle Tool (▣), [M]

This tool is used to draw squares and rectangles. Pressing the [Shift] key while using the Rectangle tool creates a perfect square.

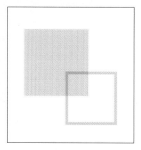

Drawing Rectangles ▶

## Rounded Rectangle Tool ()

This tool is used to draw squares or rectangles with rounded corners. The roundness of the corners is determined by the corner arc's radius. Press the [ ↑ ] key to make the corner rounder and the [ ↓ ] key for more angular corners. Hit the [→] key to maximize corner roundness and the [←] key to minimize it.

Drawing Rounded Rectangles ▶

## Ellipse Tool (), [L]

This tool is used to draw circles or ovals. Pressing the [Shift] key while using the Ellipse tool creates a perfect circle.

Drawing Ellipses ▶

## Polygon Tool (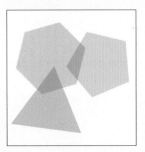)

This tool can be used to draw polygons with various numbers of sides. Dragging this tool over the artboard while pressing the [ ↑ ] key increases the number of sides in the polygon, while pressing the [ ↓ ] key reduces the number of sides.

Drawing Polygons ▶

## Star Tool ()

This tool is used to draw stars–you can fix the number of points and set the inner and outer radius of the resulting star. Dragging the Star tool while pressing the [ ↑ ] key increases the number of points in the star, while pressing the [ ↓ ] key reduces the number of points. If you press the [Ctrl] key while dragging inwards, you will fix the inner radius of the star; if you press it while dragging outwards, you'll fix the outer radius instead.

Drawing Stars ▶

# Flare Tool ( ⬚ )

This tool creates an effect that's similar to lens flare in a photograph–complete with a light source, halo, rays, and rings. With the Flare tool selected, click and drag on the artboard to determine the centers and intensity of the light source. While dragging, you can press the [ ↑ ] key to increase or the [ ↓ ] key to decrease the number of rays, and the [Shift] key to fix the rays at the current angle.

After you've fixed the light source, click and drag again to determine the length and direction of the flare. As you drag, you can press the [ ↑ ] or [ ↓ ] keys to increase or decrease the number of rings. Holding down the [Ctrl] key lets you adjust the size of the last ring of light. You can edit a flare you've created by double-clicking the Flare tool on it. You can also select [Object] - [Expand] to edit the flare like a normal object.

▲Creating the Flare

▲Creating a Light Ray Effect

The Flare tool options are as follows:

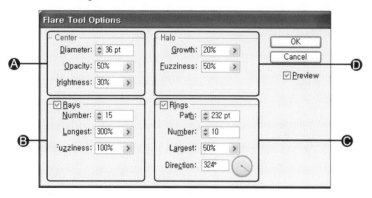

Ⓐ **Center**: Determines the center of the light source.
  *Diameter*: Sets the diameter of the light source.
  *Opacity*: Adjusts the opacity of the light.
  *Brightness*: Sets the brightness of the light source.

Ⓑ **Rays**: Check the Rays option to include rays in the flare.
  *Number*: Sets the number of rays.
  *Longest*: Sets the length of the rays.
  *Fuzziness*: Sets the sharpness of the rays.

Ⓒ **Rings**: Check the Rings option to include rings in the flare.
  *Path*: Determines the distance between the light source's center point and the farthest ring.
  *Number*: Sets the number of rings between the center point and farthest ring.
  *Largest*: Sets the size of the largest ring as a percentage of the average ring size.
  *Direction*: Sets the direction of the rings.

Ⓓ **Halo**: Alters the halo effect surrounding the light source.
  *Growth*: Used to determine the size of the halo.
  *Fuzziness*: Used to determine the sharpness of the halo.

Before you can use any of the editing tools in Illustrator, you must first select the item you wish to alter. The range of selection tools available in Illustrator makes it possible to select an object in several different ways, giving you more control over your artwork. As selection tools are used frequently, it's most convenient to simply press [Ctrl] to switch to the Selection tool (🔺), or press the [Ctrl]-[Tab] keys to switch between the Selection and Direct Selection tools. You can deselect the selection tools by clicking on an empty space in your work area or by pressing [Ctrl]-[Shift]-[A].

## Selection Tool (🔺), [V]

The standard Selection tool selects an entire object or group regardless of where you click the object or group. Because it selects objects in their entirety, the Selection tool is often used for moving objects from one point to another.

▲Click anywhere on an object to select it.

▲Drag over any region of an object to select it.

## Direct Selection Tool (🔺), [A]

Unlike the Selection tool, the Direct Selection tool selects only one object from a group of objects. When dragged, the tool selects only those anchor points enclosed in your selection. You can modify an object's shape by moving selected anchor points with the Direct Selection tool. In addition, you can also use the Direct Selection tool to select an anchor point's direction lines to adjust the curvature of the surrounding path. To select an entire object using this tool, drag over the entire object or click inside its fill area.

▲Moving an Anchor Point to Modify the Path

▲Moving a Direction Line to Modify the Path

\<\< **note**

## The Structure of Paths

In Illustrator, an object is made of paths. Paths, in turn, are made of anchor points and line segments. You can add, delete, or move anchor points, and their surrounding line segments can be either straight or curved. When an anchor point is selected, direction lines will appear on either side of the anchor point. You can move the direction points at the end of these direction lines to change the curvature of the surrounding path.

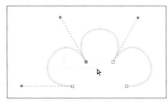
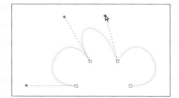

▲Selecting an Anchor Point     ▲Moving a Direction Point

# Group Selection Tool ()

The Group Selection tool is used to select and move individual objects within a group of objects. Click once on an object to select only the object within the group, and double-click to select the entire group of objects. In the image below, the stamens of the flower have been grouped together.

▲Click to Select a Single     ▲Double-Click to Select
  Object                        the Group of Objects

\<\< **note**

## Revealing Hidden Tools

Because there are so many tools in Illustrator, tools with similar functions are grouped together in the toolbox. For example, if you click and hold down the Direct Selection tool, you will see a hidden tool—the Group Selection tool. To select a hidden tool, drag the mouse over the desired tool and release the mouse button. Tools with hidden tools are identified by a triangle in the lower–right corner.

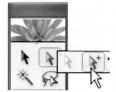

## Magic Wand Tool (), [Y]

The Magic Wand tool is used to select objects with similar properties such as fill color, stroke weight, stroke color, opacity, or blending mode. In the figure shown here, when the Magic Wand tool is used to select a red dot, all the other objects of the same color are also selected.

Making a Selection Using the Magic Wand Tool ▶

In this example, the Magic Wand tool was configured to select objects of the same color. To change the tool's parameters, double-click on its icon in the toolbox to open the Magic Wand dialog box, where you can choose to select objects based on similar fill color, stroke color, stroke weight, opacity, or which blending mode was applied. Click on the triangle icon on the top right if you do not see all the options shown here.

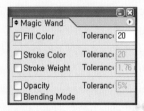

<< note

### Shortcut Keys Used with Selection Tools

If you drag a selected object while holding the [Alt] key, a duplicate of the object will be created when you release the mouse button. In addition, you can press the [Shift] key while dragging the selected object so that its movement is constrained to 45° angles. To select more than one object, hold down the [Shift] key while clicking other objects to add to the selection.

Creating a Copy of the Object by Pressing the [Alt] Key ▶

## Direct Select Lasso Tool (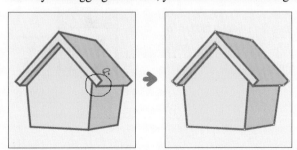), [Q]

Just like the Direct Selection tool, the Direct Select Lasso tool is used to select individual anchor points or line segments. But it differs in the way you use it to make a selection; instead of clicking on an anchor point directly or dragging out a box, you draw a line enclosing the area to be selected.

▲Selecting Part of an Object with the Direct Select Lasso Tool

▲All the anchor points and line segments within the lasso area are selected. If you select part of a line segment, the entire segment–including parts outside the lasso area–will be selected.

<< note

## Adding and Subtracting from a Selection

After making a selection, you can press the [Shift] key while dragging the Lasso tool to add to the selection, or press the [Alt] key to subtract from the selection.

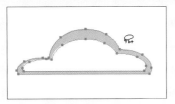
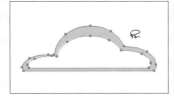

▲Adding to the Selection          ▲Subtracting from the Selection

# Transforming Objects

After you've drawn an object, you can edit the object using transformations such as scaling and rotating. The various transformation techniques available in Illustrator CS are reviewed below.

## Using the Bounding Box

When you select an object with a selection tool, a box appears around the selected object. This is called the bounding box; it has handles that look like hollow squares on every corner and side. You can drag these handles to transform the shape of the selected object.

You can hide or display the bounding box using the [View] - [Show/Hide Bounding Box] command or by pressing [Ctrl]-[Shift]-[B]. Holding down the [Shift] key while manipulating the bounding box maintains the object's proportions, while holding down the [Alt] key transforms the object from the center outward.

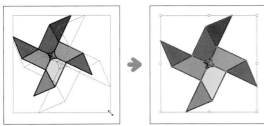
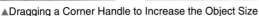
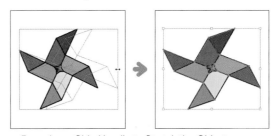

▲Dragging a Corner Handle to Increase the Object Size          ▲Dragging a Side Handle to Stretch the Object

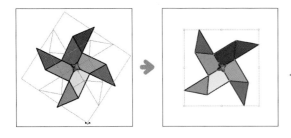

◄Placing your pointer slightly below a corner handle will turn it into a curved, double-headed arrow. In this state, you can rotate the object by dragging in both the clockwise and counterclockwise directions.

# Using the Free Transform Tool

The Free Transform tool (⌖) is like the handyman of transformation tools. You can use it to perform many different types of transformations quickly. These include scaling, rotating, reflecting, shearing, and distorting.

## Scaling

When your pointer is placed over a corner handle, it turns into a double-headed arrow, allowing you to increase or decrease the object's size. If you drag and hold down the [Shift] key at the same time, the object's proportions will be preserved. If you hold down the [Alt] key instead, the size will be transformed with respect to the center of the object.

## Rotating

You can rotate an object by clicking near the corners with the Free Transform tool (look for the curved, double-headed arrow). Holding down the [Shift] key as you drag restricts the object to 45° rotations.

## Shearing

You can shear (in other words, slant) an object by clicking on a side handle and holding down the [Ctrl] key as you drag. If you hold down the [Alt] key together with the [Ctrl] key, the object is transformed with respect to the center of the object.

## Distorting

Objects can be distorted by dragging a corner handle while holding down the [Ctrl] key. Hold down the [Alt] key as well to distort the object proportionately across the diagonal axis.

## Skewing to Add Perspective

To add perspective, drag a corner handle while pressing [Ctrl]-[Shift]-[Alt].

### Resetting the Bounding Box

When an object is rotated, its bounding box rotates with it. To return the bounding box to its original position in order to apply another transformation, select [Object] - [Transform] - [Reset Bounding Box].

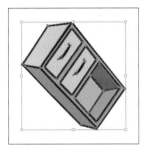

<< note

**Transform Again**

Use the [Object] - [Transform] - [Transform Again] command or the [Ctrl]-[D] keys to repeat the last transformation.

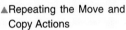

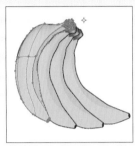

▲Repeating the Move and Copy Actions

▲Repeating the Rotate and Copy Actions

## Using Transform Tools

Using the transform tools, objects can be manipulated in ways that are only possible in vector-based applications such as Illustrator. The transform tools that will be covered in this section are the Rotate tool, the Reflect tool, the Scale tool, the Shear tool, the Reshape tool, and the Transform palette.

## Rotate Tool ( )

The Rotate tool is used to rotate an object clockwise or counterclockwise around a reference point (indicated by the icon). Regardless of which transformation tool is used, the reference point of an object is set by default as the center point of the object.

▲To rotate an object, the object should first be selected with the Selection tool. Then click on the Rotate tool. The object's wire frame will appear and your pointer changes to .

▲Click and drag clockwise or counterclockwise to rotate the object.

To change the reference point for the rotation, select the object then click the new reference point with the Rotate tool.

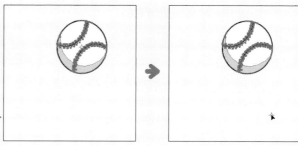

The Default Reference Point in the Center of the Ball ▶
(Left) and Setting a New Reference Point (Right)

Holding down certain keystrokes while dragging with the Rotate tool lets you create interesting effects and work more effectively. When used with the [Alt] key, for example, the Rotate tool lets you make a copy that is positioned along the rotation path. Before using any of the shortcuts, however, make sure you select the object and then activate the Rotate tool. Also, start dragging with the tool before you hold down the optional keystrokes.

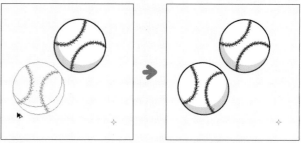

▲Click and drag to rotate the object around the reference point (shown here at the bottom right). Without releasing your mouse, hold down the [Alt] key. When the arrow pointer (▶) changes to a double-arrow pointer (▶), release the mouse button and the [Alt] key to create a copy of the object.

The [Shift] key constrains the rotation to intervals of 45°, while the [Alt]-[Shift] shortcut makes a copy on one of the 45° axes.

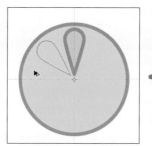

▲Rotating while holding down the [Alt]-[Shift] keys is used to make a copy at a 45° angle to the original. In this example, vertical and horizontal guides that intersect the reference point were created to highlight the 45° angle of the copy.

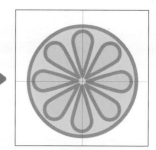

▲Choose [Object] - [Transform Again] to repeat the rotation and the copy for the other segments.

To set the angle of rotation precisely, double-click on the Rotate tool in the toolbox to open the Rotate dialog box. Entering a negative Angle value (-) rotates the object clockwise, while a positive Angle value (+) rotates the object counterclockwise.

Type in the desired Angle value and click the [Copy] button. ▶

A quick way to set a new reference point and rotate the object at the same time is to hold down the [Alt] key and click on a spot for the new reference point. When the Rotate dialog box appears, enter an Angle value and click [OK] to rotate the object around the new reference point. Clicking [Copy] instead of [OK] creates a copy that is rotated around the new reference point.

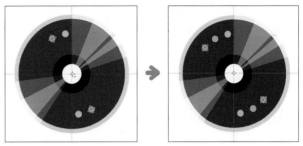

▲Hold down the [Alt] key and click on the vertex to open the dialog box for entering values. Type in the Angle value and click the Copy button.

<< tip

## Rotating Patterns

The Rotate dialog box contains the Patterns option. Checking the Patterns option < 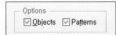 > will apply the selected rotation to any patterns used in the object.

▲A pattern is applied to the balloon.

▲After selecting the balloon object, double-click on the Rotate tool to rotate only the pattern 45°.

# Reflect Tool ( )

The Reflect tool flips an object across an invisible axis which is determined by setting one or two reference points.

▲With the object selected, activate the Reflect tool. When the arrow pointer changes to ⊕, click outside the object to set a new reference point.

▲Click and drag to flip the object. If the reference point is left at its default setting (the center point of the object), the object will flip with reference to its center point.

Just like the Scale tool, holding down certain keystrokes while dragging with the Reflect tool changes the properties of the Reflect tool. Holding down the [Shift] key reflects the object across an axis that is constrained by 45° increments and holding down the [Alt] key makes a copy at the new position. Holding down the [Alt]-[Shift] keys makes a copy that is reflected across an axis that is constrained by 45° increments.

▲Click on the shoreline to set a new reference point.

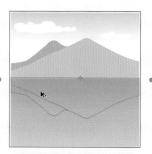

▲Click and drag while holding down the [Alt]-[Shift] keys to make a copy across the horizontal axis.

▲After making the copy, go to the Transparency palette and set the mode to Multiply to make the reflection more realistic looking.

Another way to create the reflection in the preceding example is to click on the shoreline while holding down the [Alt] key. This will set the new reference point and open the Rotate dialog box. In the dialog box, click the [Copy] button.

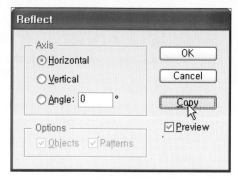

&lt;&lt; tip

## Reflect Dialog Box

To open the Reflect dialog box, double-click on the Reflect tool. In the Reflect dialog box, check Horizontal or Vertical to choose a horizontal or vertical axis. Checking the Angle option lets you set the angle of the axis. A negative angle value (-) reflects the object in a clockwise direction and a positive Angle value (+) reflects the object in a counterclockwise direction. The other options in the Reflect dialog box work the same way as those in the Rotate dialog box.

# Scale Tool (⬚)

The Scale tool changes the size of an object in relation to a reference point.

&lt;&lt; tip

## Default Reference Point

In order to move the reference point back to the center of an object, select the object, double-click on the Transform tool, and adjust the values. Alternatively, go to the Transform palette and select the center reference point (▦).

▲With the object selected, activate the Scale tool. Click and drag into or out of the object to scale the object relative to its reference point.

▲Hold down the [Shift] key to maintain the proportion of the object while scaling.

While dragging with the Scale tool, holding down the [Alt] key will make a copy of the object, and holding down the [Alt]-[Shift] keys will create a proportional copy of the object.

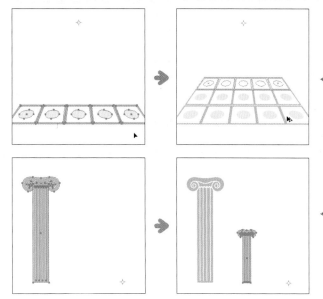

◀After selecting the Scale tool, drag the reference point to the top of the object as shown. Then hold down the [Alt]-[Shift] keys as you drag the object with the Scale tool. This creates progressively smaller copies of the object, giving the illusion of depth.

◀Select a column and activate the Scale tool. Holding down the [Alt] key, click on the center of the column's base to set a new reference point, then open the Scale dialog box. In the Scale dialog box, set Horizontal to 50% and Vertical to 50%. Click [Copy]. Click and drag the copy to the right.

To set the scale options, double-click on the Scale tool to open the Scale dialog box.

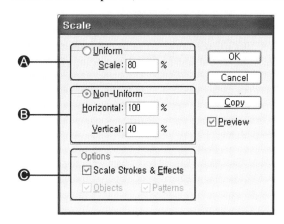

🅐 **Uniform**: Select Uniform to scale the object proportionally. At 100% the object's size will be unchanged. Values above 100% increase the size of the object and values below 100% decrease it.

🅑 **Non-Uniform**: This option lets you scale an object without maintaining the object's original proportions.

🅒 **Options**: Check the boxes to select the elements to be scaled–Strokes, Effects, Objects, or Patterns.

◀In this example, the stroke weight of the object's outline scales with the object; the outline gets thinner towards the top. This is achieved by scaling with the Scale Strokes & Effects option selected.

## Using the Scale Tool to Adjust Objects

It can be quite difficult to adjust objects using the Scale tool. To make the transformation easier, click on one of the four points that lie diagonally outside the object and drag it towards the center point.

Drag diagonally towards the ▶ center to make the object smaller.

# Shear Tool ( )

The Shear tool slants an object relative to a reference point or axis, making objects look three-dimensional.

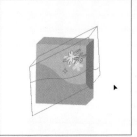

▲Select the object and activate the Shear tool. Click and drag up or down to slant the object along the vertical axis; drag left or right to slant along the horizontal axis.

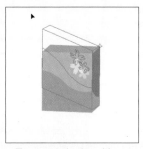

▲To constrain the object to its original height or width, hold down the [Shift] key while dragging with the Shear tool.

While dragging with the Shear tool, holding down the [Alt] key makes a copy of the sheared object. Holding the [Alt]-[Shift] keys restrains the shear angle and makes a copy.

▲Selecting only the page object and not the page contents, click to set the top-right corner as the new reference point. Drag while pressing the [Alt]-[Shift] keys to create a copy aligned vertically with the original page.

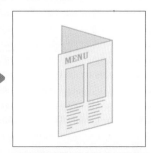

▲Press [Ctrl]-[Shift]-[[] to send the copy to the back and fill the copy with a darker color.

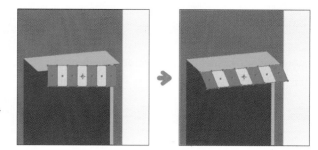

Double-click on the Shear tool to open the ▶
Shear dialog box, then set the Shear Angle to
-25° and the Angle to 30°.

To set the Shear options, double-click on the Shear tool to open the Shear dialog box.

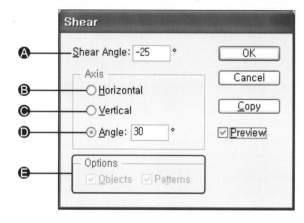

**Ⓐ Shear Angle**: An object can be sheared at any angle from -359° to 359°. The shear angle is entered after selecting an Axis option.

**Ⓑ Horizontal Axis**: To shear in the ◥ direction, enter a negative (-) value in the Shear Angle field and select Horizontal. To shear in the ▱ direction, enter a positive (+) value.

**Ⓒ Vertical Axis**: To shear in the ◳ direction, enter a negative (-) value in the Shear Angle field and select Vertical. To shear in the ▱ direction, enter a positive (+) value.

**Ⓓ Angle of Axis**: Enter an angle for a custom axis here.

**Ⓔ Options**: Select the elements to be sheared.

# Reshape Tool (  )

The Reshape tool is used to modify one or more anchor points or paths in an object at the same time.

▲First, the Direct Selection tool is used to select the anchor points to be reshaped. Holding down the [Shift] key lets you select more than one anchor point at a time.

▲The Reshape tool is then used to reshape the selected anchor points.

&lt;&lt; tip

## Transform Each Command

Selecting [Object] - [Transform] - [Transform Each] opens the Transform Each dialog box. The Transform Each dialog box has options for scaling, moving, rotating, and reflecting objects. Checking the Random option randomizes the transformation to create fun and interesting effects. Each time you check and uncheck the Random option, a different transformation is performed. Selecting [Object] - [Transform Again] allows you to repeat the last transformation used.

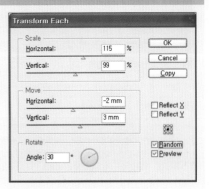

# Transform Palette

The Transform palette is used to adjust an object's coordinates, width, height, and degree of slant. Because absolute values can be entered into the Transform palette, the palette is useful for making exact transformations.

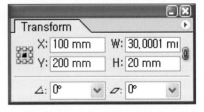

The pop-up menu of the Transform palette contains options for flipping, scaling strokes and effects, and transforming patterns.

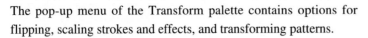

Flip Horizontal
Flip Vertical

✓ Scale Strokes & Effects

Transform Object Only
Transform Pattern Only
✓ Transform Both

# Making a Satellite Dish Using Shape and Selection Tools

In this tutorial, we'll draw a satellite dish to get familiar with the shape and selection tools. You will use the Rectangle, Ellipse, and Polygon tools to draw the required shapes. You will also use the selection tools and a few keystrokes to select and edit these shapes. By the end of this exercise, you'll have learned to copy, rotate, scale, arrange, and lock objects.

**Final File**
\Sample\Chapter02\figure_fin.ai

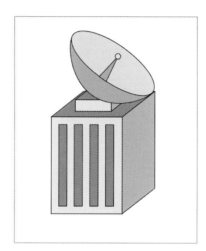

Final Image

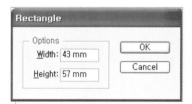

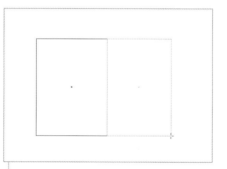

1 Press [Ctrl]-[N] and create an A4 document in CMYK mode. Let's start by drawing the pink building. Select the Rectangle tool (▢) from the toolbox and click on the artboard. In the Rectangle dialog box, set the Width to 43 mm and the Height to 57 mm and then click [OK].

2 You have created a white rectangle with a black border. This will be the facade of the building. Now, let's draw the facing side. You must pay close attention to this step because the side of the building must match up perfectly. First, select [View] - [Outline] to see the object as an outline. Next, click on the top-right corner of the rectangle and—without releasing the mouse—drag down to the lower-right corner to draw an identical, adjacent rectangle, as shown here.

<< tip

## Color and Stroke Defaults

The default fill color is white. The default stroke is black with the Weight set to 1 pt.

The Outline view, which displays artwork as paths and center points only, is useful for steps that require a high attention to detail. In this view, even paths or scattered points that are not visible on the screen (a white stroke on a white background, for example) will be shown. These paths can be selected using the selection tools. You can return to the normal view by selecting [View] - [Preview] or by pressing the shortcut keys, [Ctrl]-[Y].

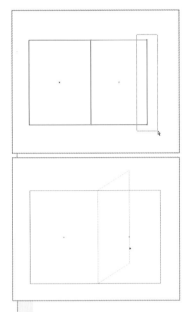

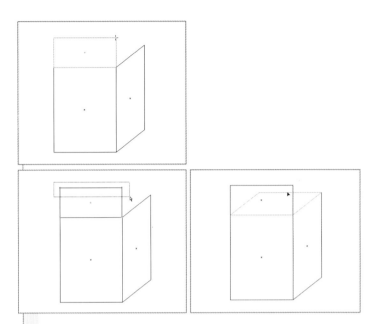

3 In order to move the facing side, choose the Direct Selection tool ( ) from the toolbox. Click and drag this tool over the two right corners to select the path as shown. Next, click on the path and drag it to the position shown.

4 To add a roof, select the Rectangle tool ( ) from the toolbox, click on the top-left corner of the facade, and drag it down and to the right. Select the Direct Selection tool ( ) and drag over the upper end of the "roof" rectangle to select the segment as shown. Click and drag the selected path to close the top of the building.

When selecting a path or an anchor point with the Direct Selection tool, check that the pointer is placed directly over the selection before clicking.

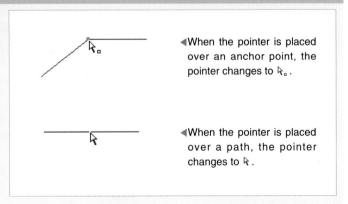

◀When the pointer is placed over an anchor point, the pointer changes to ▸.

◀When the pointer is placed over a path, the pointer changes to ▸.

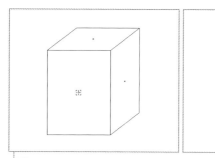
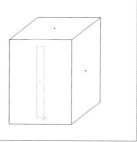

5 Select all the objects using the [Select] - [All] command from the menu bar, then group them together using [Object] - [Group]. Grouped objects can be selected as a group using the Selection tool. Now, it's time to add the windows. Select the Rectangle tool (▢) from the toolbox, position the pointer over the center of the facade, and drag it while holding down the [Alt] key to create vertical windows.

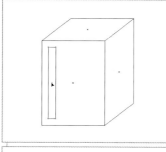
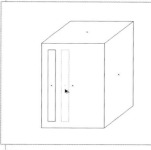
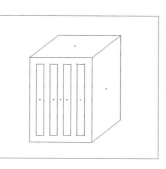
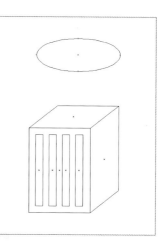

6 To properly position your window, click on the center point of the window using the Selection tool (▶) and drag the window to the left while holding down the [Shift] key. Holding down [Shift] locks the window to its horizontal axis while you move it into position. Now you can create copies of the window. Holding down the [Alt]-[Shift] keys, click on the center point and drag the window to the right to create a copy. Then, press [Ctrl]-[D] twice to repeat this step twice. Check to ensure that your windows are evenly spaced.

7 You will now use the Ellipse tool to make the satellite dish. Select the Ellipse tool (◯) from the toolbox and drag it diagonally over the top of the building to draw an ellipse, as shown here. Make a copy by pressing [Ctrl]-[C], then lock the shape using [Object] - [Lock] - [Selection]. Select [Edit] - [Paste in Back] to paste the copy behind the original ellipse. (Locking the original ellipse will facilitate modifying the pasted ellipse in the next step.)

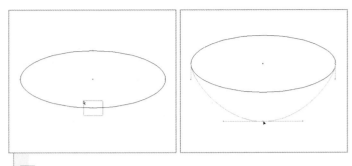

8 Select the Direct Selection tool (🔾) from the toolbox and drag it over the lower-middle anchor point. Click on this point to select it, then drag it down while holding down the [Shift] key to create the dish base.

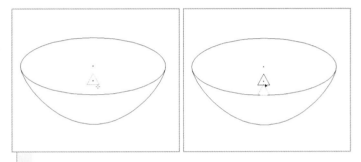

9 Select the Polygon tool (🔾) in the toolbox. Position the pointer over the center point of the ellipse and drag it down. Keep pressing the [ ↓ ] and [Shift] keys on the keyboard until you get a triangle, as shown here. Next, hold down the [Ctrl] key to switch to the Direct Selection tool (🔾). Click on the triangle and move it to the bottom of the dish while holding down the [Shift] key, as shown here. Holding down the [Shift] key will constrain the movement along a 45° angle.

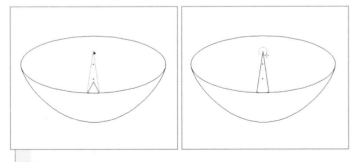

10 With the [Ctrl] key pressed down, click on the triangle's vertex and drag it up while holding down the [Shift] key. Next, select the Ellipse tool (🔾) from the toolbox and drag the vertex while holding down the [Alt]-[Shift] keys to draw a small circle, as shown. You have finished drawing the outline of the satellite dish.

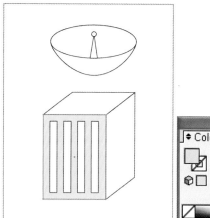

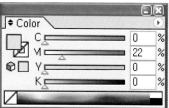

## Applying Color

At the bottom of the toolbox, you will find the Fill and Stroke boxes. To change the fill color of an object, you must first check that you have selected the Fill box in the toolbox before choosing a color in the Color palette. To change the line color instead, just click on the Stroke box.

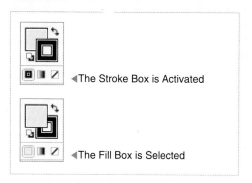

◀The Stroke Box is Activated

◀The Fill Box is Selected

11 Now you'll need to color the building. Select [View] - [Preview] so that you can see the artwork in color. With the Direct Selection tool ( ) selected, click on the facade and set the M (magenta) value to 22% in the Color palette. In this step, use either the Direct Selection tool ( ) or the Group Selection tool ( ) to select only the facade and not the entire group to which it belongs.

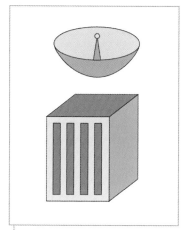

12 Select [Object] - [Unlock All] to unlock the ellipse. Next, color the objects as follows:

*Facing side - M: 50%*

*Roof and windows - M: 62%, K: 12%*

*Antenna and dish exterior - C: 50%, M: 25%*

*Antenna Tip - Y: 100%*

*Dish interior - C: 25%, M: 12.5%*

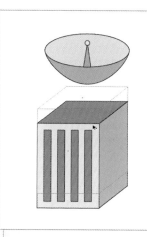 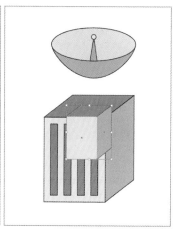

13 Let's copy the building to create a platform for the satellite dish. Click on the building using the Selection tool ( ) and drag it up while holding down the [Alt]-[Shift] keys. This will create a copy. Select [Object] - [Arrange] - [Bring to Front] so that the copy is shuffled in front of the other objects. To scale down the copy, select the Free Transform tool ( ) from the toolbox. Click and drag a handle on the object's bounding box inwards while holding down the [Alt]-[Shift] keys to reduce the copy's size.

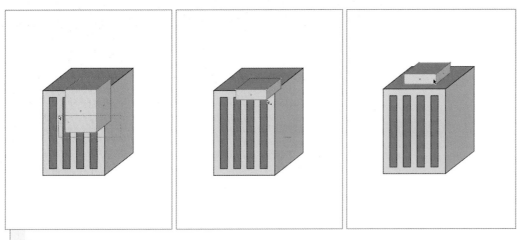

14 Let's make the copy shorter. Lock all the other objects by pressing [Ctrl]-[Alt]-[Shift]-[2]. Drag the Direct Selection tool (⬚) over the bottom of the copy as shown. Click on the anchor points, and—without releasing the mouse button—hold down the [Shift] key and drag upwards to shorten the copy. Next, select the entire object and position it as shown.

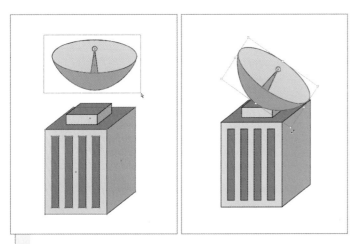

15 In this final step, you will place the satellite dish on top of the platform and tilt it to the right. Unlock all the objects by selecting [Object] - [Unlock All]. Select the satellite dish, place it on the platform, and then rotate it using the Free Transform tool (⬚). If the satellite dish is blocked by the other objects, right–click on it and select [Arrange] - [Bring to Front]. You have completed this exercise.

# 2 Making a Dartboard Using the Polar Grid Tool and the Pathfinder Palette

If you need to draw an object that is made up of concentric circles and radial lines, you will find the Polar Grid tool very useful. In this section, let's use the Polar Grid tool to draw a circular grid on a dartboard. Then we'll split it up with the Pathfinder's Divide option so that we can apply alternating colors.

**Start File**
\Sample\Chapter02\dart_board.ai

**Final File**
\Sample\Chapter02\dart_board_fin.ai

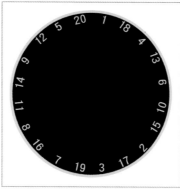
Original Image

Final Image

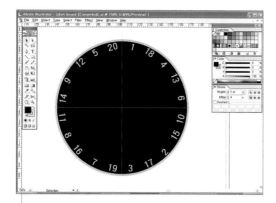

1 Open the dart_board.ai file from the \Sample\Chapter02 folder. You will now create guidelines on the artboard to help you center the polar grid on the dartboard. With the Selection tool ( ) activated, click on the dartboard to display its bounding box. Then, select [View] - [Show Rulers] to display the rulers on top and at the left of the screen. Click on the top ruler and–without releasing the mouse button–drag a guide that passes through the center of the dartboard. Repeat the step on the left ruler. To better distinguish the lines, go to [Edit] - [Preferences] - [Guides & Grid], set the color to Light Blue, and set the style to Dots.

2 Press [Ctrl]-[A] to select all the objects. Then, select [Object] - [Lock] - [Selection] to prevent the dartboard from being edited. When this is done, you will insert a polar grid over the dartboard. Double-click on the Polar Grid tool ( ) in the toolbox. When the Polar Grid Tool Options dialog box appears, leave the Width and Height settings as they are. Simply enter the number of concentric and radial dividers as shown above and check the Fill Grid option to fill the grid with the current fill color.

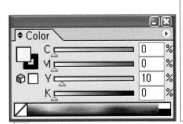

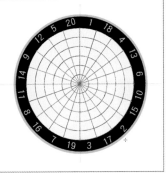

3 Set the fill color to 10% yellow. While holding down the [Alt]-[Shift] keys, click on the center of the circle and drag outwards until the grid is the size shown here. You may notice that the grid is filled with light yellow. As you have selected the Fill Grid option, you can change the fill color should you decide that you don't like this color.

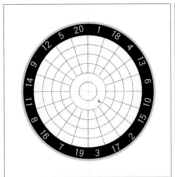

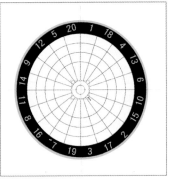

4 With the Group Selection tool ( ) activated, click on the innermost circle on the grid and then, holding down the [Shift] key, click on the next circle and select [Object] - [Arrange] - [Bring to Front]. Select the Free Transform tool ( ), then click and drag a bounding box handle towards the center while holding down the [Alt]-[Shift] keys. Shrink the circles to the size shown here.

5 Let's make the third circle a little larger. Select the Group Selection tool ( ) and click on the third circle. Next, select the Free Transform tool ( ) and, holding down the [Alt]-[Shift] keys, expand the circle to the size shown here.

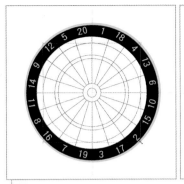 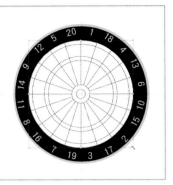

6 | In the same way, expand the fifth circle to the size shown in the figure above. Next, reduce the size of the sixth circle slightly, and we're done with the circles.

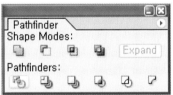

7 | Let's split the grid into closed paths so that you can fill it with color. With the Group Selection tool (🔲) activated, double-click on one of the "rays" to select them all. Then, holding down the [Shift] key, select the third through sixth circles to add them to the selection. Select [Window] - [Pathfinder] to open the Pathfinder palette. Click on the Divide icon (🔲) in the Pathfinder palette to divide the grid into closed sections.

8 | Let's color the grid now. Using the Selection tool (🔲), hold down the [Shift] key and select the sections shown in black above. Next, set the K value to 100% in the Color palette.

 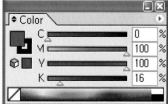

9  Now you'll color the red parts. Observe the figure above, then select the appropriate sections and choose a red color from the Color palette.

 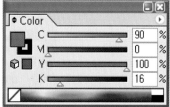

10  In the same way, color the green segments to complete this exercise.

# 3 Creating an Oil Lamp Using the Rectangular Grid and Free Transform Tools

In this exercise, you will create the glass panels for an oil lamp, making use of the Rectangular Grid tool to draw the glass lattice and the Free Transform tool to modify the shape of the lattice for the different sides of the lantern. You will also learn to use the Opacity setting in the Transparency palette to control the transparency of the panels and create lighting effects.

**Start File**
\Sample\Chapter02\lamp.ai

**Final File**
\Sample\Chapter02\lamp_fin.ai

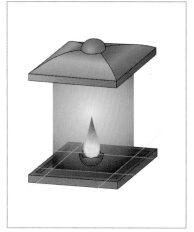

Original Image

Final Image

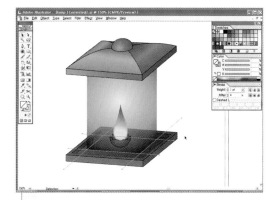

1 Open the lamp.ai file located in the \Sample\Chapter02 folder. As you can see, some sky blue lines appear at the base of the lamp. You can turn these into guidelines which will help you position the lattice later on. Use the Selection tool ( ) to select the sky blue lines and then select [View] - [Guides] - [Make Guides] to turn them into guidelines.

&lt;&lt; tip

## Using Guidelines

I find guidelines very useful when working on all sorts of artwork, so I would urge you to make good use of them. In any case, guidelines will not appear when printed or when the artwork is used as a Web image. As shown in the exercise, you can select [View] - [Guides] - [Make Guides] to turn lines (or, for that matter, any object) into guidelines. To turn them back, first select [View] - [Guides] - [Lock Guides] to unlock all the guidelines. Notice that the check mark beside the Lock Guides command disappears. Next, select [View] - [Guides] - [Release Guides].

Guideline preferences such as color can be changed by clicking [Edit] - [Preferences] - [Guides & Grid] and changing the settings in the dialog box that appears.

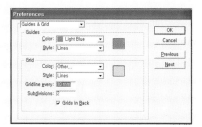

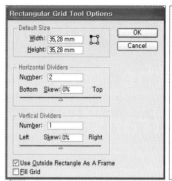

2 The top of the lamp is blocking our view of the lamp body, so let's hide it from view. First, select it using the Selection tool (⬆), then select [Object] - [Hide] - [Selection].

3 Let's use the Rectangular Grid tool (▦) to make semi-transparent glass panels for the lamp. First, double-click on the Rectangular Grid tool (▦) to open the Rectangular Grid Tool Options dialog box. Leave the Width and Height values as they are and enter the number of horizontal and vertical dividers as shown. Click [OK]. Next, double-click on the Fill color box in the toolbox and set yellow to 25% in the Color Picker dialog box. Click and drag from the top-left corner of the lamp to the lower-right corner to draw the lattice as shown here.

<< tip

## Coloring a Grid

To make it possible to fill a grid with color, check the Use Outside Rectangle As A Frame option in the Rectangular Grid Tool Options dialog box.

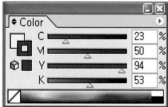

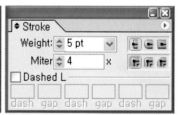

4 Click on the Stroke color box in the toolbox and change the stroke color in the Color palette to the values shown above. Change the line thickness to 5 pt in the Stroke palette.

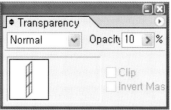

5 Let's transform the lattice so that it'll fit on the left side of the lamp. Select the Free Transform tool (🔳) and click on the middle-right handle of the bounding box. Then, while holding down the [Ctrl] key, drag it to the left so that it is slightly slanted, as shown in the image above. Select [Window] - [Transparency] and enter 10% for the Opacity value. This value is very important because it determines the amount of light that passes through the glass lattice.

6 Let's create the back panel that will show faintly through the front panel. Copy the left panel by pressing [Ctrl]-[C] and paste it in front by pressing [Ctrl]-[F]. Click the middle-left handle of the bounding box, hold down the [Ctrl] key, and move the copy to the back, as shown.

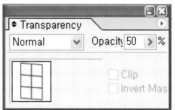

7 Let's make the front panel now. Select the Rectangular Grid tool (🔳) from the toolbox. Click and drag from the top-left corner of the lamp to the lower-right corner, as shown here. Select the Free Transform tool (🔳). Click on the middle-right handle on the bounding box and–while holding down the [Ctrl] key–drag it downwards so that the base of the panel is aligned with the guideline. In the Transparency palette, set the Opacity to 50% to see a yellowish glow from the light source behind.

8 The right panel is all that remains, now. Copy the front panel by pressing [Ctrl]-[C] and paste it in front by pressing [Ctrl]-[F]. Click on the middle-left handle of the bounding box, hold down the [Ctrl] key, and position it as shown. When you have completed this step, deselect the Free Transform tool (🔳).

9 Press [Ctrl]-[Alt]-[3] to show all the objects and unhide the top of the lamp.

10 Select the top of the lamp, then choose [Object] - [Arrange] - [Bring to Front] to place it in front of the lamp body. Then select [View] - [Guides] - [Hide Guides] to hide the guidelines add view your final image.

# A Cartoon Postcard - Simplifying and Adding Anchor Points

In this section, you will learn how to draw cartoon characters using a wide variety of tools and commands. Some of the steps will seem familiar to you as you reinforce your knowledge of tools you're already familiar with, such as the Ellipse tool. Other techniques will be new to you. As you progress through the pages of this book, the exercises will become more complex. In creating this postcard, you will learn to simplify paths, add anchor points to your objects, apply the Zig Zag filter, and use the Spiral tool.

**Final File**
\Sample\Chapter02\post_card_fin.ai

Final Image

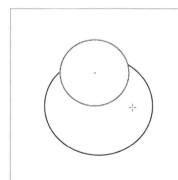 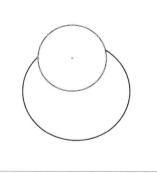 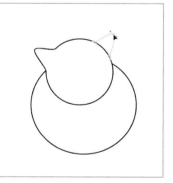

1 Open a new document. Let's start off by drawing a lion. Select the Ellipse tool (⬭) from the toolbox, draw a large circle for the body, and draw a smaller one on top for the head. Select [Object] - [Path] - [Add Anchor Points] twice to add anchor points to the smaller circle. Click on an empty spot to deselect the object, then select the Direct Selection tool (▷). Click on the smaller circle to reveal the anchor points. Click on an anchor point and drag it outwards to create a ear, as shown in the image on the right. Repeat the step on the other side of the circle.

Instead of using the Add or Delete Anchor Point tools in the toolbox to add and delete anchor points one by one, use the Simplify or Add Anchor Points commands in the [Object] - [Path] submenu. This makes editing object shapes much easier and faster.

## ■ Adding Anchor Points

When you choose the [Object] - [Path] - [Add Anchor Points] command, a new anchor point is automatically inserted between every two existing anchor points in the selected object. You can adjust the position of the new and existing anchor points using the Direct Selection tool ( ) or by transforming them with filters.

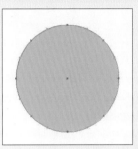

▲Circle with Four Anchor Points

▲Add Anchor Points is applied twice. The pink anchor points are added in the first round and the green ones in the second.

## ■ Removing Anchor Points to Simply a Path

If you need to simplify (i.e., reduce the detail) your shapes, you can use the Simplify command to reduce the number of anchor points without changing the overall shape of the path too much. The command also reduces the file size of the image.

▲Original Image

▲Simplified Image

To apply the Simplify command, select [Object] - [Path] - [Simplify] to open the Simplify dialog box. Let's have a look at the options in the Simplify dialog box.

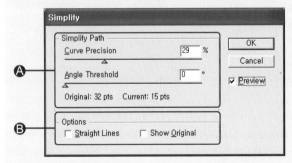

### Ⓐ Simplify Path

*Curve Precision*: Determines how closely the simplified paths follow the original curves. The higher the percentage, the more similar it is to the original (with fewer anchor points being removed).

*Angle Threshold*: Determines how closely the new corners follow their original angles. Corners with angles below the angle threshold–you can enter an angle between 0° and 180°–are left unchanged. Therefore, the higher the threshold, the more detail will be maintained in your objects/paths.

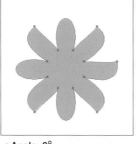

▲Original ▲Angle: 0° ▲Angle: 90°

*Original*: Displays the number of anchor points in the original object.

*Current*: Displays the number of anchor points in the modified object (subject to the set values).

### Ⓑ Options

*Straight Lines*: Changes curves into straight lines.

*Show Original*: Displays the original paths in red so that adjustments can be made in comparison.

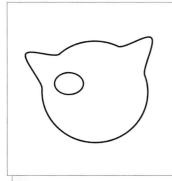
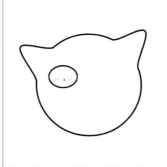
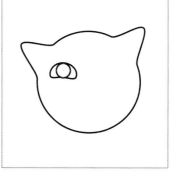

2  Let's add a pair of eyes to the face. Select the Ellipse tool (🔘) from the toolbox and draw two ellipses on the face. Select the Direct Selection tool (🔲) and click on the left ellipse to display its anchor points. Click on its bottom anchor point and move it up slightly. Select the Ellipse tool (🔘) and–while holding down the [Alt]-[Shift] keys–draw a perfect circle inside the left eye to make the pupil. Repeat these steps to form the right eye.

3 Let's move on to the nose. Select the Polygon tool (⬤) from the toolbox. Click and drag on the nose area and keep pressing the [↓] key until you get a triangle.

4 Let's use the Spiral tool (⬤) to draw the mouth. Select the Fill button in the toolbox and then click on the None button below it. With this done, the spiral you draw will only have lines–no fills. Select the Spiral tool (⬤). Click and–without releasing the mouse button–drag from the end of the nose while holding down the [Ctrl] key to create a loose spiral, as shown on the left. To shorten the spiral without changing its complexity, release the [Ctrl] key and move the mouse back toward the nose until the spiral looks similar to the one shown on the right, above. With the mouse button still pressed, hold down the [Spacebar] and move the spiral into position, as shown.

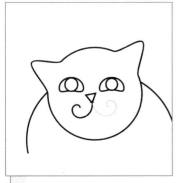

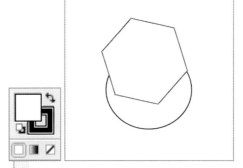

5 The Spiral tool (⬤) will remember the last spiral's properties so there is no need to change its settings (or hold the [Ctrl] key) when drawing the other side of the mouth. All you need to do is to change the direction and position. Hold down the [R] key when drawing the other side of the mouth to create a mirror reflection and, after adjusting the size, and hold down the [Spacebar] to position the spiral beneath the nose, as shown.

6 You will now use the Polygon tool (⬤) and Zig Zag filter to create the mane. Let's change the fill and stroke settings back to their defaults (white fill and black stroke) by clicking on the [Default Fill and Stroke] button (⬒) in the toolbox. Next, select the Polygon tool (⬤) and draw a polygon that covers the entire face. Press the [↑] key while dragging to increase the number of sides in the polygon.

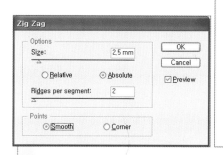

7  Let's apply the Zig Zag filter to the mane to make it look more natural. Select [Filter] - [Distort] - [Zig Zag] and adjust the settings as shown. After applying the filter, move the mane to the back by holding down the [Ctrl] key and hitting the [ key until the entire face appears.

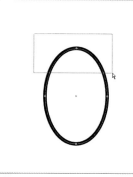

8  Set the fill color to None in the toolbox and select the Spiral tool (⊚) again. Draw the tail as shown.

9  Now let's make the paws. First, click on the [Default Fill and Stroke] button (▣) and select the Ellipse tool (◯). Draw a vertical ellipse as shown. Drag over the top of the ellipse using the Direct Selection tool (▷) and press [Delete]. Place the remaining half below the body to make the left paw and then, holding down the [Alt] key, drag a copy to the right to make the right paw.

10  This is the fun part: let's color our lion. Use the Selection tool (▶) to select the objects and color them according to these color values: Face, eye whites, nose, body, and paw color - Y: 50%; Mane color - M: 24%, Y: 100%, K: 8%; Pupil color - C: 32%, Y: 100%, K: 55%. Note that I chose to have no outlines for the pupils, as I find the lion's eyes more aesthetically pleasing this way. I did this by setting Stroke to None in the toolbox. In order to change the color and thickness of the lion's outlines, drag over the entire lion and then—holding down the [Shift] key—click on the eye outlines so that they are not part of the selection. Then, in the Stroke palette, set the line thickness to 2 pt. With the selection still active, change the stroke color to C: 32%, Y: 100%, K: 55%.

11 Let's tilt the lion's head slightly to make the character look more expressive. Hold down the [Shift] key and select only the face and its elements with the Selection tool (🔺). Next, select the Free Transform tool (▦) and rotate the head slightly to the left. It is a good idea to group these elements by pressing [Ctrl]-[G].

12 Let's use a copy of the lion to create the lioness. With the Selection tool (🔺) activated, select the lion, hold down the [Alt] key, and drag a copy to the right, as shown here. After that, select the Free Transform tool (▦), hold down the [Shift] key, and drag the top-left handle diagonally down to the right. By pressing the [Shift] key, the image will be reduced proportionately. Deselect the Free Transform tool (▦) and switch to the Selection tool (🔺). Select the mane and press [Delete].

13 Select the lioness' face and rotate it slightly clockwise, as shown here.

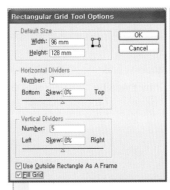

14 Select the Rectangular Grid tool (▦) from the toolbox and click on the artboard. When the Rectangular Grid Tool Options dialog box appears, set the options as shown and click [OK].

<< tip

## Line Thickness

If an object among a group you selected is set to have no outline, you won't be able to change the line thickness of the entire group at once.

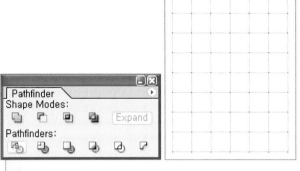

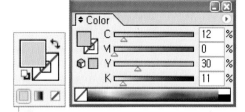

15 To create a checker pattern on this grid, let's make use of the Pathfinder palette's Divide filter. Select [Window] - [Pathfinder] and click on the Divide icon ( ).

16 With the grid still selected, let's create a checker pattern for the background. Click on the Fill button in the Color palette and select the values shown here.

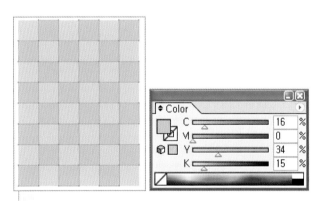

17 You will now isolate alternating boxes on the grid to change them into a darker shade of green. Select the Group Selection tool ( ) and click on alternating boxes while holding down the [Shift] key. Then change the color in the Color palette to the values shown here.

18 Press [Ctrl]-[Shift]-[[] to send the background to the back. Center the characters on the background and complete the image by using the Star and Spiral tools to add flourishes to the background.

# Creating a 3D Gift Box

There will be times when you'll need to position or line up the objects in your artwork with great precision. In this exercise, you will use smart guides to help you line up the sides of a box. Smart guides show you where any paths and anchor points are as you move the mouse over an object. These guides also show relative positions, angles, and intersections when moving objects or drawing with the Pen tool. This makes your work much easier!

**Start File**
> \Sample\Chapter05\lavender.ai

**Final File**
> \Sample\Chapter05\lavender_fin.ai

Original Image

Final Image

1   Open the lavender.ai file. The file contains the artwork for three sides (top, left, and right) of a box.

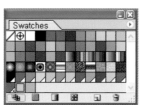

2   To create the box in this exercise, you will only need three sides. The top surface is already completed, so you will only need to work on the left and right sides of the box. Go to the Swatches palette and select New Color Swatch 1 (▢) for the fill color. Set the stroke color to None in the toolbox.

3 Choose the Pen tool ( ) from the toolbox. Select [View] - [Smart Guides] to turn on smart guides. Place your cursor on the bottom-left corner of the top surface. Click when you see the word, "anchor".

4 Move the mouse straight down and click when you see the word, "intersect".

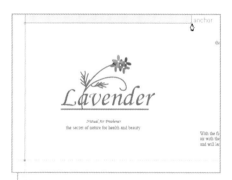

5 Before clicking on the right corner of the bottom side, you need to find the correct point of intersection. Start by moving the mouse in the upper-right corner until the anchor note appears. Do not click the mouse, yet.

6 Next, move the mouse pointer to the right corner of the bottom side. When you see the point of intersection, click the mouse. This will draw the bottom side of the box front.

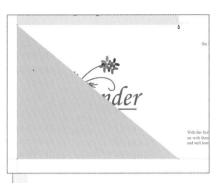

7  Again, move vertically back to the top. When the anchor appears between the top side and the point of intersection, click the mouse.

8  Move the mouse horizontally to the left and, again, click when the anchor appears.

9  Press [Ctrl]-[Shift]-[[] to move the rectangle to the back. This completes the front plane. When drawing the side plane, press [Ctrl]-[2] so that the front plane is not selected.

10  Let's make the side plane. Select New Color Swatch 2 (■) from the Swatches palette. Place the mouse on the top-right corner of the front plane and click when the anchor appears. This will begin your new shape.

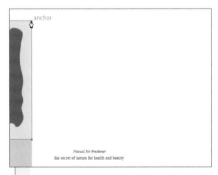

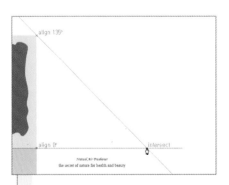

11  Place the mouse at the top-right corner of the box top. Feel around until you get the anchor note, but do not click the mouse button.

12  Continue moving the mouse until a point of intersection appears at the top-right corner of the side plane. Click the mouse to form the top of the side panel.

13 Move the mouse down towards the bottom and place it where the guideline intersects. Click when you see the intersect note.

14 Move the mouse horizontally to the left until you see the anchor note and click the mouse button.

15 Move the mouse vertically towards the top and click when the anchor note appears.

16 Press [Ctrl]-[Shift]-[[] to move the rectangle to the back of the artboard. This completes the side plane.

17 Let's now fill in the empty side surface with flowers. Holding down the [Shift] key, select the flowers on the front panel using the Selection tool ( ).

18 Drag the flowers to the middle of the side surface while holding down the [Alt] key to make a copy.

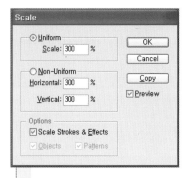

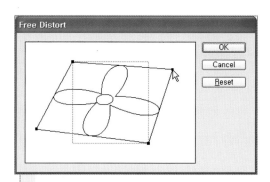

19 Double-click on the Scale tool ( ), check Uniform, and scale up to 300%.

20 Now let's use filters to distort the shape. Selecting one of the duplicated flowers, choose [Filter] - [Distort] - [Free Distort]. Drag the anchors to distort the shape. Selecting another flower, choose [Filter] - [Distort] - [Free Distort]. You will see that the previous settings remain. Click [Reset] to clear the settings, then drag the anchor points to distort the shape of the second flower.

21 Do the same for the remaining flowers to produce something like the image shown above.

22 Before transforming each surface, you need to convert the text into path-based objects. In addition to ensuring the font will display correctly on any system, this will allow you to distort, shear, and transform the text. Select one letter using the Selection tool ( ). Choose [Select] - [Object] - [Text Objects] to select all the text and then choose [Type] - [Create Outlines]. Group the text together. Next, press [Ctrl]-[Alt]-[2] to unlock all locked objects. Drag the mouse over one side of the box and press [Ctrl]-[G] to group the objects on that surface. Repeat this step for the other sides.

23 Let's now begin the transformation for each surface. Select the top surface and choose the Free Transform tool ( ![icon] ). Clicking the tool on the middle anchor point on the left side, hold down the [Ctrl] key and drag it downwards. The more you shear the side, the more of the front of the box you will see in the final image.

24 Selecting the Rotate tool ( ![icon] ) from the toolbox, click on the edge where the three box sides meet to create an anchor point. Holding down the [Shift] key, rotate it 45° clockwise.

25 Now we'll match the front and side surfaces to the top surface. Hold down the [Ctrl] key and select the front surface. Click the Free Transform tool ( ![icon] ) on the middle anchor point on the left side and drag it up toward the box top while holding the [Ctrl] key.

26 Finally, select the middle anchor point on the right side of the final box panel. Holding the [Ctrl] key, drag it up until the side aligns with the box top. The image is now complete.

Chapter | 3

# Drawing Paths

To create elaborate drawings that cannot be assembled using geometric shapes, you'll need to master the Pen tool, which allows you to make smooth, flowing curves using paths. The Pen tool can be frustrating at first, but with practice and patience you'll realize just how important paths are to the Illustrator CS environment. In Chapter 3, we'll introduce you to drawing paths so that you can implement some of the more complex operations the program has to offer.

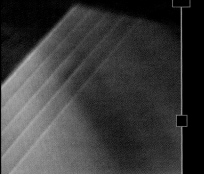

# Drawing and Editing Paths

I n this chapter, we'll start by exploring the basic concepts related to drawing paths. We'll learn to make paths, then edit them by adding, deleting, and converting anchor points. Next, we'll discuss the Pencil tool, which is required for freehand drawing; the shearing tools, which are used for editing shapes; and several other features found in the [Object] - [Path] menu and Pathfinder palette.

## Pen and Anchor Point Tools

The Pen and anchor point tools are found on the same tab in the toolbox; this provides an obvious clue regarding the close relationship between these tools. The Pen tool is used for drawing paths, while the Add Anchor Point, Delete Anchor Point, and Convert Anchor Point tools are used for editing paths by manipulating anchor points.

### Pen Tool (🖊), [P]

The Pen tool can be used to draw any shape through a combination of straight lines and curves. Of all the tools in Illustrator, the one used most often for drawing curves is the Pen tool. That's why using the Pen tool, which allows users to draw precise curves, is one of the most fundamental skills required of Illustrator CS.

With the Pen tool selected, click on the artboard to create anchor points for your path. Holding down the [Shift] key when you click your anchor points will limit your lines to 45° increments.

Clicking and dragging when you place your anchor points allows you to determine the line segment curvature on either side of your anchor points. Experimentation is key to understanding how this works. In this case, holding down the [Shift] key allows you to make very precise, regular curves (see the example below).

Placing the Pen tool on an existing line segment converts it into the Add Anchor Point tool, while placing it over an existing anchor point converts it to the Delete Anchor Point tool. To change it to the Convert Anchor Point tool, press the [Alt] key.

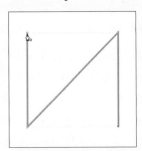

▲Holding Down the [Shift] Key and Clicking to Draw a Straight Line

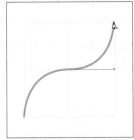

▲Holding Down the [Shift] Key and Dragging to Draw Precise Curves

# Add Anchor Point Tool (⊞), [+]

This tool adds a new anchor point to an existing path. Adding anchor points allows you to change the shape of a path dramatically. The Add Anchor Point tool can be used to reshape objects or fix curves that make your drawings look awkward. You can toggle between the Add Anchor Point tool and the Delete Anchor Point tool by pressing the [Alt] key.

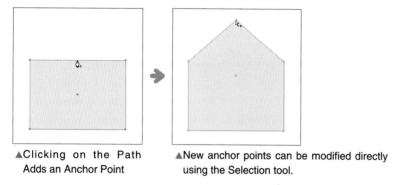

▲Clicking on the Path
Adds an Anchor Point

▲New anchor points can be modified directly
using the Selection tool.

# Delete Anchor Point Tool (⊟), [-]

This tool deletes existing anchor points and is used to simplify a path or to change the shape of an object. As mentioned above, pressing the [Alt] key toggles the tool with the Add Anchor Point tool.

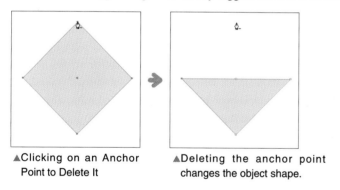

▲Clicking on an Anchor
Point to Delete It

▲Deleting the anchor point
changes the object shape.

# Convert Anchor Point Tool (⌐), [Shift]-[C]

There are two types of anchor points: smooth points with direction lines and corner points without direction lines. Smooth points are found on continuous curves, while corner points are found on corners and paths that bend sharply.

The Convert Anchor Point tool lets you change from one type of point to the other. To turn a corner point into a smooth point, click on the corner point and drag out the direction lines to your liking. To turn a smooth point into a corner point, simply click once on the smooth point.

You can also use this tool to adjust the curvature of a smooth path by clicking and dragging the direction lines; simply select the path to make the direction lines appear then drag them to suit your needs. Basically, this is the tool for editing paths.

▲Clicking on a Corner Point and Dragging Out Direction Lines to Make a Curve

▲Clicking on a Smooth Point to Turn It into a Corner Point

## Drawing Lines

In this section, let's concentrate on using the Pen tool to draw both straight lines and curves. We'll draw open and closed paths, convert anchor points to modify existing paths, and draw smooth curves. As in the preceding pages, we'll also go through the shortcut keys associated with the Pen tool that allow you to access other functions quickly.

### Bezier Curves

The lines or curves that you draw in Illustrator are known as bezier curves. Developed by the french mathematician, Pierre Bezier, a bezier curve is defined by a simple cubic equation from which the program derives the two-dimensional coordinates for the curve. Bezier curves are in fact constructed using a series of dots placed very close together–so close they appear as a solid line on-screen. Because of the mathematical nature of bezier curves, you can magnify an image drawn in Illustrator to any size without affecting the image quality. As with all vector-based programs, you do not have to specify a resolution.

When drawing curves in Illustrator, you need at least two anchor points to form a line. With the Pen tool selected, click on the artboard to specify the starting anchor point, then click and drag out direction lines on another position to specify the ending point. As you drag out the direction lines, you can adjust the angle and height of the resulting line segment's curvature. See the following figure for a better understanding of bezier curves.

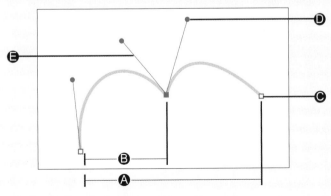

**Ⓐ Path**

A path consists of one or more straight or curved segments connected by anchor points; they can be open or closed to form shapes.

**Ⓑ Segment**

A segment is the line between one anchor point and the next. When the Direct Selection tool is activated, you can click and drag a segment directly to change the object shape.

**Ⓒ Anchor Point**

An anchor point connects segments to form a path. With fewer anchor points, you get smoother curves, but this is not necessarily a good thing; intricate drawings require numerous anchor points. Bear in mind that additional anchor points create bigger file sizes that affect almost every aspect of your user experience–program slowdown, slow file transfers, and longer print times.

**Ⓓ Selected Anchor Point**

As you can see, a selected anchor point appears as a filled square while an unselected anchor point appears as a hollow square.

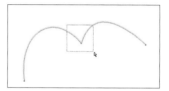

**Ⓔ Direction Line**

A smooth point has two direction lines; adjusting their lengths and angles controls the shape of the resulting curve. These direction lines are displayed when you click and drag on a smooth point or a segment with the Direct Selection tool.

▲It's difficult to adjust a curve using only a single direction line.

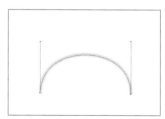

▲It is much easier when you use the direction lines at both the surrounding anchor points.

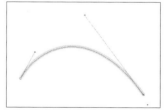

▲The length and angle of the direction lines determines the shape of the curve.

**Ⓕ Direction Point**

To drag a direction line, click and drag on the direction point located at the end of the line.

# Using the Pen Tool to Draw

By now, you should have an idea of how to draw with the Pen tool. But there's more to drawing in Illustrator than what has been covered so far. In this section, we'll go into greater detail so that–by the end of this chapter–you'll know how to draw numerous combinations of lines and curves.

## Drawing Straight Lines

When the Pen tool is selected, the pointer changes to ✎, and you can click on the work space to draw straight lines. You can draw vertical and horizontal lines by holding down the [Shift] key as you click to place your anchor points. When drawing an object, remember that you can close a path by placing the pointer on the starting anchor point; simply click when the pointer changes to ✎.

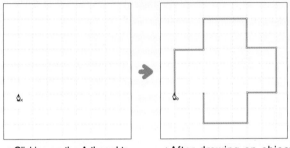

▲Clicking on the Artboard to Start a Path

▲After drawing an object, click on the starting anchor point to close its path.

<< tip

## Drawing Separate Lines

After using the Pen tool to draw a line, hold down the [Ctrl] key and click on an empty spot to complete the current action. This will reset the Pen tool, and the next anchor point you place will start a new line.

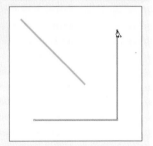

## Drawing Curves

Drawing curves with the Pen tool requires a clicking and dragging technique. To better control the curve of a segment, don't simply click when drawing the first anchor point (this will produce a corner point, not a smooth point); click and drag so that your starting point has its own direction lines.

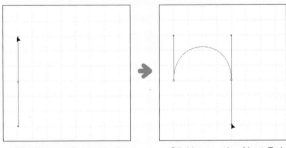

▲Clicking and Dragging the Starting Point to Determine the Resulting Curve

▲Clicking on the Next Point and Dragging Out Direction Lines to Complete the Curve

## Drawing a Straight Line from a Curved Line

When you draw curves, direction lines appear on both sides of each smooth point. In order to draw a straight line that extends from a curved segment, you need to delete one of the direction lines from your last anchor point. Place the Pen tool on a smooth point and, after the cursor changes to ◊, click to automatically delete the appropriate direction line.

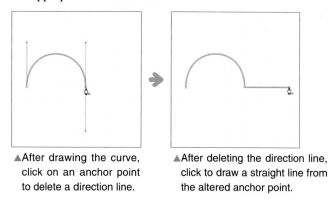

▲After drawing the curve, click on an anchor point to delete a direction line.

▲After deleting the direction line, click to draw a straight line from the altered anchor point.

## Drawing Open Curves in Succession

Drawing open curves in succession is problematic because the anchor point that completes one curve produces direction lines that interfere with the start of the next curve. To get around this, place the Pen tool pointer on the first curve's end point and—when the cursor changes to ◊ —click to remove the offending direction line. Then click and drag on another position to draw the next curve.

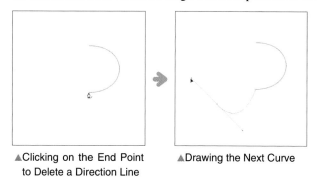

▲Clicking on the End Point to Delete a Direction Line

▲Drawing the Next Curve

## Joining Open Curves

To join open curves, click on the first curve's end point to remove the offending direction line, then click on the other curve's end point to make the connection.

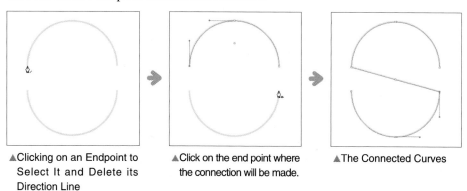

▲Clicking on an Endpoint to Select It and Delete its Direction Line

▲Click on the end point where the connection will be made.

▲The Connected Curves

**119**

## Drawing a Curved Line from a Straight Line

If you want to draw a curved line from a straight line, you will need to create a direction line for manipulating the curve. You can do this by clicking on the line's end point and dragging out a direction line.

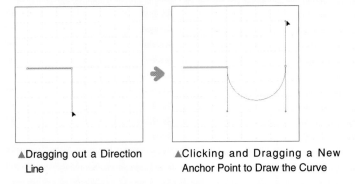

▲Dragging out a Direction Line　　　▲Clicking and Dragging a New Anchor Point to Draw the Curve

## Drawing an Angular Curve

To create an angular curve, you must first adjust the direction line of your starting line segment. There are two ways to do this:

- One option is to first click the end point to delete a direction line and then–holding down the [Alt] key–click on the end point again to drag out a direction line in the direction of the new curve segment.

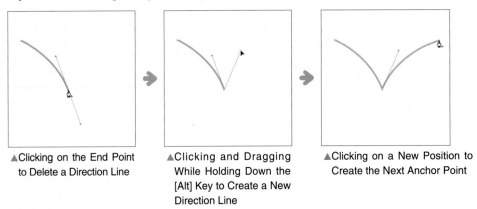

▲Clicking on the End Point to Delete a Direction Line　　　▲Clicking and Dragging While Holding Down the [Alt] Key to Create a New Direction Line　　　▲Clicking on a New Position to Create the Next Anchor Point

- Alternatively, hold the [Alt] key to switch to the Convert Anchor Point tool, then click on the direction point and drag it in the direction of the new curve.

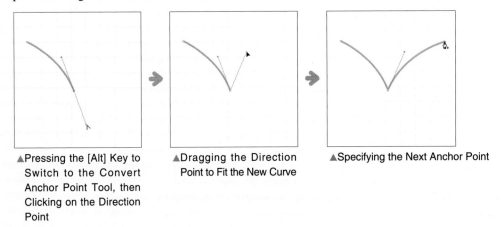

▲Pressing the [Alt] Key to Switch to the Convert Anchor Point Tool, then Clicking on the Direction Point　　　▲Dragging the Direction Point to Fit the New Curve　　　▲Specifying the Next Anchor Point

## Drawing a Freehand Curve

The Pencil tool lets you create drawings in Illustrator without having to draw segment-by-segment or manipulate direction lines. Drawing with the Pencil tool in Illustrator is similar to drawing on paper with a pencil. Unlike bezier curves, freehand lines are very intuitive, and they are very common in Illustrator artwork. For touching up drawings created by hand with the Pencil tool, you can use the Smooth and Eraser tools.

## Pencil Tool ( 🖉 ), [N]

With the Pencil tool selected, simply click and drag on the artboard to draw an object. When drawing a new object, the Pencil tool icon changes to 🖉 . After drawing a shape, if you place the pointer near the path, the icon changes to 🖉 . In this form, the Pencil tool allows you to edit an object's path and anchor points simply by redrawing them. Pressing the [Alt] key switches to the Smooth tool.

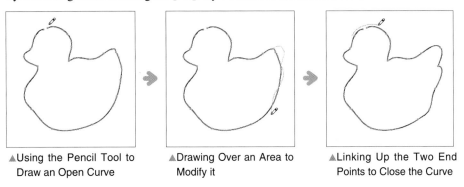

▲Using the Pencil Tool to
Draw an Open Curve

▲Drawing Over an Area to
Modify it

▲Linking Up the Two End
Points to Close the Curve

Double-clicking on the work space will open the Pencil Tool Preferences dialog box.

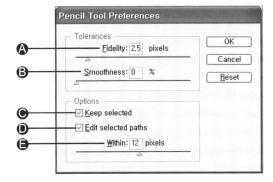

Ⓐ **Fidelity**: Determines how far you have to move your mouse before an anchor point is added to the path. A higher value creates a path with fewer anchor points.

Ⓑ **Smoothness**: Determines the smoothness of the path.

Ⓒ **Keep selected**: Check the Keep selected option to keep the anchor points selected after the path has been drawn.

Ⓓ **Edit selected paths**: Check the Edit selected paths option to enable the Pencil tool to edit existing paths.

Ⓔ **Within __ pixels**: The Within __ pixels option is only active when the Edit selected paths option is selected. This option determines how close your mouse has to be to an existing path before the path can be edited.

**121**

# Smooth Tool (✏)

The Smooth tool, as the name suggests, smoothes curves. After drawing a curve using the Pen or Pencil tool, drag the Smooth tool over the path. The anchor points will be rearranged to create a smoother path.

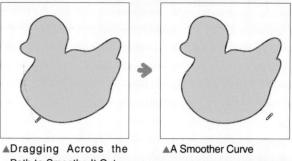

▲Dragging Across the Path to Smoothe It Out       ▲A Smoother Curve

Double-clicking the Smooth tool on the work space will open its preferences dialog box.

Ⓐ **Fidelity**: Determines how far you have to move your mouse before a path will be smoothed. A higher value creates a path with fewer anchor points.

Ⓑ **Smoothness**: Sets the smoothness of the path.

**Smooth Tool Preferences**

Tolerances
Ⓐ — Fidelity: 2.5 pixels
Ⓑ — Smoothness: 25 %

OK
Cancel
Reset

# Erase Tool (✏)

The Erase tool can be used to delete a section of an image. It has the same effect as selecting a section using the Direct Selection tool and pressing the [Delete] key.

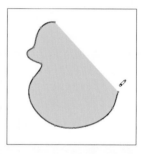

Dragging the Erase Tool Across a Section of the ▶ Image to Delete It

<< note

## Info Palette

The Info palette shows you information on your active tool and selection as you work in Illustrator. The information displayed can be useful in a number of situations, such as when you need to place an object in an extremely precise location. For the sake of example, the information shown when the Pen tool is selected is reviewed below.

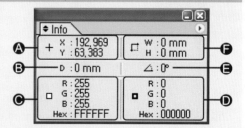

Ⓐ **X, Y**: The X and Y coordinates of the pointer. The value of (0,0) refers to the bottom-left corner of the artboard.
Ⓑ **D**: Shows the displacement distance as you move an object on the artboard.
Ⓒ **Fill**: Shows the fill color.
Ⓓ **Stroke**: Shows the stroke color.
Ⓔ **Angle**: Shows the displacement angle as you move an object on the artboard.
Ⓕ **W, H**: Shows the width and height of the selected object, or the horizontal and vertical displacement as you move the selected object on the artboard.

## Cutting Paths

Tools used to cut paths include the Scissors tool and the Knife tool. These tools are used to turn a section of an object into an open or closed curve.

## Scissors Tool (✂), [C]

To cut a path, click on an anchor point or a segment with the Scissors tool. If you click on a closed path, an end point appears automatically at the "cut" to turn it into an open path. Cut the open path again and you'll get two separate paths. Pressing the [Alt] key turns this tool into the Add Anchor Point tool.

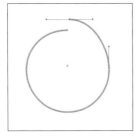 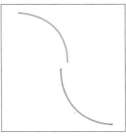 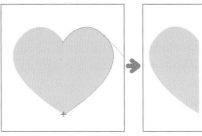

▲After cutting a closed path, move the end point using the Direct Selection tool to reveal the cut.

▲When cutting an open path, move one segment to reveal the cut.

▲You can also use the Scissors tool to divide filled shapes.

## Knife Tool (🔪)

The Knife tool separates an object into two closed paths when you click and drag through the object's path. When an object is selected using this tool, only the selected object is cut. If no objects are selected, any shapes in the Knife tool's path will be cut. You can press the [Alt]-[Shift] key to cut an object with a straight line vertically, horizontally, or at a 45° angle.

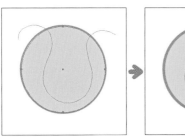 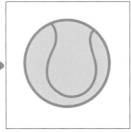 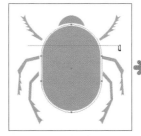 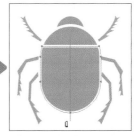

▲Clicking and Dragging the Knife Tool through the Selected Object

▲The result is two closed paths.

▲Select the object and press the [Shift]-[Alt] keys to cut horizontally.

▲You can cut an object vertically using the same technique.

The Pathfinder palette is used to combine two or more paths or objects to create totally new paths and shapes. Access this palette by selecting [Window] - [Pathfinder].

## Shape Modes

The Shape Modes feature is used to combine objects in different ways to create new shapes. After combining the objects, you can use the Direct Selection tool to edit the resulting shape. You can also click the [Expand] button to remove the properties of the original paths (for instance, if the "extra" segments and points interfere with your work). Hold down [Alt] while pressing the desired mode button to apply the Expand command at the same time. To undo a shape mode, press the triangle button (⯈) on the top-right side of the Pathfinder palette and select [Release Compound Shape] from the shortcut menu that appears.

### Add to Shape Area (⬜)

After selecting two or more objects, click this button to combine the objects to produce a new object with the color of the topmost object.

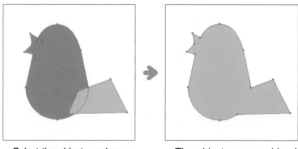

▲Select the objects and press the [Add to shape area] button.

▲The objects are combined as shown.

### Subtract from Shape Area (⬜)

This button cuts out the shape of the underlying object from the object on top.

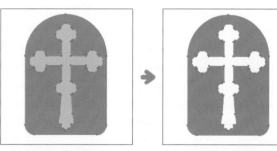

▲Select the objects and press the [Subtract from shape area] button.

▲This cuts out the bottom object from the top object.

### Intersect Shape Areas ( ▣ )

This button leaves behind only the overlapping region of two or more objects, deleting the rest. The color of the topmost object is maintained.

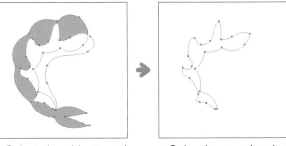

▲Select the objects and press the button.

▲Only the overlapping areas remain.

### Exclude Overlapping Shape Areas ( ▣ )

The overlapping areas of the objects are deleted and the color of the topmost object is used.

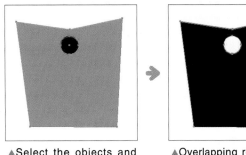

▲Select the objects and press the button.

▲Overlapping regions are deleted.

## Pathfinders

Pathfinders are used to combine paths in a variety of different ways. After any of the pathfinder effects is applied, the objects are automatically grouped together and can be ungrouped by selecting [Object] - [Ungroup] from the menu bar.

### Divide ( ▣ )

This button divides an object into individual filled areas. After applying the command, you can use the Direct Selection ( ▶ ) or Group Selection ( ▶ ) tools to manipulate these areas independently.

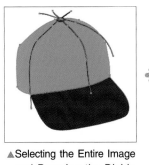

▲Selecting the Entire Image and Pressing the Divide Button

▲Selecting the Divided Surfaces One at a Time Using the Group Selection Tool to Fill Them with Different Colors

<< note

## [Effect] - [Pathfinder]

The pathfinders found in the Pathfinder palette are the same as the Pathfinder filters found in the Effect menu, but the Effect menu can only be applied to objects that are grouped together.

## Trim (⬚)

The Trim pathfinder removes the hidden parts of a filled object without merging objects of the same color.

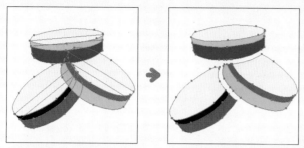

▲Selecting the Entire Image

▲After applying the Trim pathfinder, you can ungroup the objects and move them using the Selection tool.

## Merge (⬚)

Similar to the Trim pathfinder, the Merge option removes the hidden parts of a filled object while merging objects of the same color.

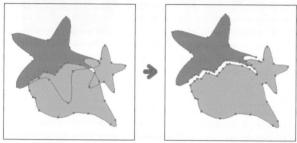

▲Selecting the Entire Image

▲After applying the Merge pathfinder, you can ungroup the objects and move them using the Selection tool.

## Crop (⬚)

This pathfinder divides an image into individual filled areas, then deletes anything that falls outside the topmost shape. This pathfinder is similar to the [Object] - [Clipping Mask] - [Make] command.

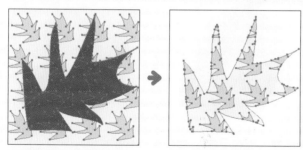

▲Selecting the Entire Image

▲All areas outside the leaf are deleted.

## Outline (⊡)

The Outline pathfinder simplifies an image by deleting the fill colors and showing only the object outlines. The stroke color is replaced by the fill color. After applying this effect, the stroke weight is set to 0 pt and must be changed in the Stroke palette; otherwise, it will remain invisible.

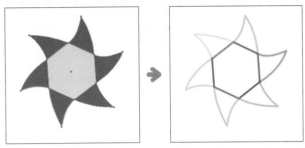

▲Selecting the Entire Image ▲After setting a stroke weight for the separated paths, a different color is applied to each of them.

## Minus Back (⊡)

Similar to the Outline pathfinder, the Minus Back option removes the hidden parts of a filled object while merging objects of the same color.

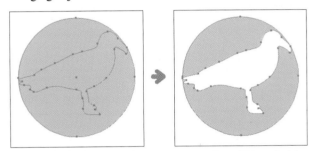

▲Selecting the Entire Image ▲An outline of the underlying object is cut from the overlying object.

# Drawing Illustrations Using the Pen Tool

Although it is more difficult to draw with the Pen tool, it allows you to make more precise drawings than either the Pencil or Shape tools. In this example, you will use the Pen tool to trace the outline of an image and then edit its shape using the Convert Anchor Point tool. Following this, you will apply transformation filters to create a background. This example focuses on drawing lines and curves, selecting and manipulating lines, and using the Outline Stroke feature.

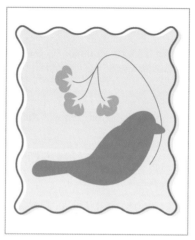

Final Image

**Start File**
　\Sample\Chapter03\drawing.ai

**Final File**
　\Sample\Chapter03\drawing_fin.ai

<< tip
### Hiding the Palette

In order to maximize the workspace, you can use shortcut keys to hide or show the palettes and toolbox. The [Shift]-[Tab] shortcut hides or shows only the palettes, while the [Tab] key hides or shows both the palettes and the toolbox.

1 Open the drawing.ai file from the \Sample\Chapter03 folder. The sketch of a bird appears on the left of the two-page artboard. On the right, a sketch shows this file's objects in their proper locations. Let's begin by tracing the bird on the left with the Pen tool. Holding down [Ctrl]-[Spacebar], click on the bird a few times to magnify the screen to 300%. Still holding down the [Spacebar], drag the view to center it on the screen. Click on the [Default Fill and Stroke] icon (⊡) in the toolbox and select None for the fill color. Next, select the Pen tool (✎) from the toolbox and click on point A. Click on point B and drag a direction line towards the right until it's the same length as the direction line in the sketch. You should now see a curve and two direction lines.

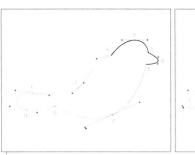

**2** Now click on point C. Since the curve drawn is exactly what is needed, you don't have to drag out direction lines at this point. Next, click on point D and drag out a direction line downwards to adjust the curvature of the segment as shown.

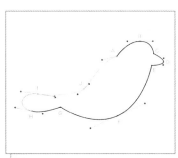
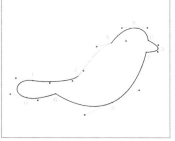

**3** After clicking on point E, click on point F and drag diagonally towards the left, as shown. After clicking (without dragging) on point G, click on point H and drag to the left, as shown. Up until now, you have created anchor points with two equal direction lines, but for greater control you'll sometimes need to adjust the direction lines on both sides differently on either side of an anchor point. To do this, start by holding down the [Alt] key to switch to the Direct Selection tool. Next, click and drag the left direction point of point H as shown.

**4** As before, create the curves at points I and J. Finally, move the mouse to point A. When the pointer changes to ♦₀ , this means that this is the starting anchor point for the path, and you can click on it to close the path. So, click on point A and drag towards the right to close the path.

<< tip

## Manipulating the Direction Line at the Origin Point

When closing a path, it can get tricky adjusting the curvature of the new segment. This is because when you click on the origin point to close the path the direction lines of that point affect the resulting line segment. It short, it's hard to know what you're going to get. To draw the ending segment without moving the starting segment, hold down the [Alt] key while clicking and dragging on the origin point.

1. Create an origin point.

2. After creating a starting curve segment, clicking and dragging on the origin point to close the path causes both segments to shift.

3. Clicking and dragging on the origin point while holding down the [Alt] key keeps the starting segment from shifting.

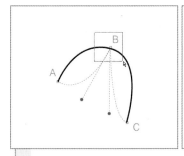 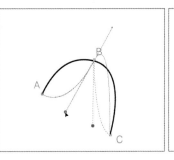 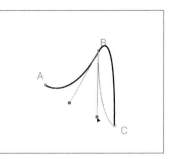

5  Let's use the Direct Selection tool (🔍) and the Convert Anchor Point tool (◺) to make the stalk. Holding down the [Spacebar], drag the view up so that the stalk is centered on the screen. Select the Direct Selection tool (🔍) from the toolbox and click on point B to display its direction lines. Click on the left direction point and drag it downwards to the position shown in the sketch. The direction line on the other side moves at the same time, changing the shape of the curve. After positioning the left direction line, select the Convert Anchor Point tool (◺) from the toolbox to manipulate the right direction line. Drag the right direction point downwards to the position shown.

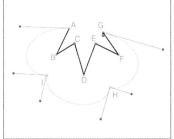 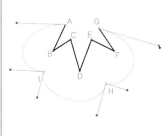 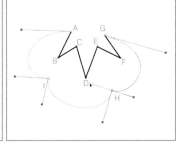

6  Holding down the [Spacebar], move the view up until the flower appears on the screen. Let's try to draw a path that has both lines and curves. Select the Pen tool (✒) and click on points A through G to connect them with lines. You will now create a direction line on point G in order to draw a curve from it. Click and drag out a direction line from point G, matching it to the sketch position. Then, click on point H and drag towards the left, as shown in the image on the right.

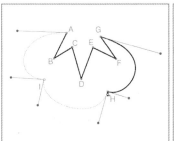 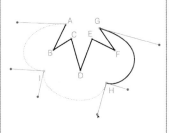

7  To move point H's left direction line in place, hold down the [Alt] key and drag the left direction point as shown.

<< tip

## Making Direction Lines

You can create direction lines for corner points by clicking on and dragging from the point. But for smooth points that have a direction line, you need to hold down the [Alt] key to keep the existing direction line in place before clicking and dragging to create a new direction line.

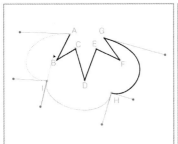 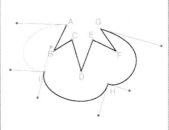 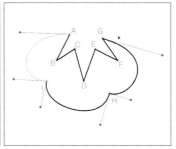

8 Click on point I and drag the direction line upwards, as shown. To move the direction line, click on the direction point at the top while holding down the [Alt] key, then move it to the position shown in the sketch. Finally, click on point A and drag towards the right to close the curve.

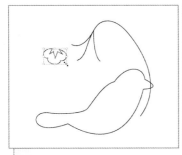 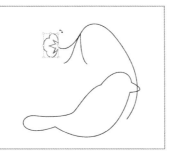

9 You are now finished with the drawing stage of this example. Now choose the Selection tool ( ) from the toolbox and position the bird and stalk over the sketch on the next page. As for the flower, reduce its size with the Free Transform tool ( ) and rotate it clockwise while holding down the [Shift] key until it's perpendicular to the page. Position it as shown.

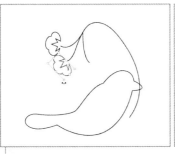 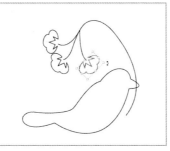 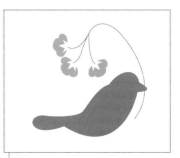

10 Hold down the [Ctrl]-[Alt] keys and drag the flower downwards to make a copy. Rotate the image counterclockwise while holding down the [Shift] key until it lines up with the stem perfectly. Repeat this step for the last flower.

11 Next, let's select each of the objects and color them. The following colors were used in this exercise:

*Bird - C: 75%, M: 37%*

*Flower - C: 50%, M: 25%*

*Stalk - C: 100%, M: 50%*

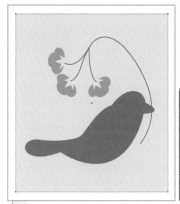  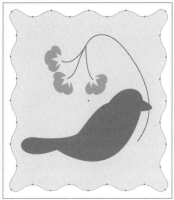

**12** It's time to create the background. Select the Rectangle tool ( ) from the toolbox. Click on the [Default Stroke and Fill Color] icon and set the stroke color to none and the fill color to C: 16%, M: 8%. Draw a rectangle like the one shown on the left and hit [Ctrl]-[Shift]-[[] to send it to the back. To make the background look like a frame, select [Filter] - [Distort] - [Zig Zag] and set the Size to 2 mm, Ridges per segment to 7, and the Points to Smooth. Then click [OK].

<< tip

**Outline Stroke Gradient Fill**

After you convert an object's border into a filled object with the [Object] - [Path] - [Outline Stroke] command, you can apply a gradient to it.

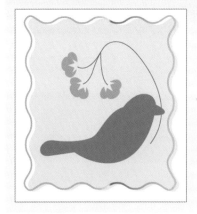

**13** Click on the Stroke box and set it to C: 100%, M: 50%. Next, select a stroke weight of 3 pt in the Stroke palette. Let's convert the stroke to a filled object in order to move it slightly off the main picture. Select [Object] - [Path] - [Outline Stroke] and move the border slightly using the Selection tool ( ). The image is now complete.

# 2

# Drawing a Drum Using the Pen Tool and the Pathfinder Palette

In this exercise, you will draw a drum using the Pen tool and the shape modes in the Pathfinder palette. Looking at the final image of the drum, you may think that this is a rather simple, straightforward task. But this is not the case. Notice that the drawing can be split into separate, non-standard objects such as the circular band on the drum shell and the outline of the drum. These objects are deceptively difficult to create.

Final Image

**Final File**
\Sample\Chapter02\drum_fin.ai

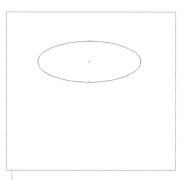

1 Select the Ellipse tool (  ) from the toolbox, draw an oval, and press [Ctrl]-[C] to make a copy. You will paste the copy, which will be used to make the drum head, in a later step. Let's leave it on the clipboard for now.

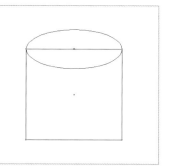

2 Press [Ctrl]-[Y] to switch to Outline view in order to draw with more precision. Select the Rectangle tool ( ) from the toolbox, then click and drag from the center point on the left of the ellipse to the lower-right corner, as shown in the figure here.

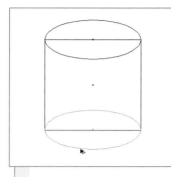

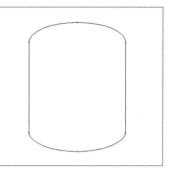

3 Using the Selection tool (⬉), drag the oval down while pressing the [Shift]-[Alt] keys until the center of the ellipse lines up with the bottom of the rectangle. In order to make an outline of the drum, you will combine these shapes. Use the Selection tool (⬉) to select both the ellipses and the rectangle and then click on the [Add to shape area] button (🔲) in the Pathfinder palette while holding down the [Alt] key.

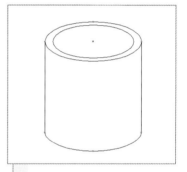

4 Press [Ctrl]-[F] to paste the oval copy from step 1 in front. Select the Free Transform tool (📐) and, while pressing the [Alt]-[Shift] keys, drag a corner handle toward the middle to make the oval smaller. Then, press [Ctrl]-[2] to lock this shape to protect it from being edited in the following steps.

5 Press [Ctrl]-[F] to paste the oval in front again. As you will be editing the cylinder to create a circular band for the drum shell in the next two steps, you need to keep a copy of the original cylinder. Select the cylinder with the Selection tool (⬉) and copy it by pressing [Ctrl]-[C]. Leave the copy on the clipboard for now.

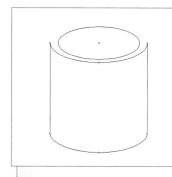

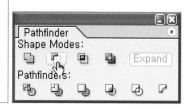

6 Select the oval copy (the one that isn't locked) and the cylinder and press the [Subtract from shape area] button ( ▣ ) in the Pathfinder palette while holding down the [Alt] key.

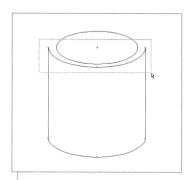
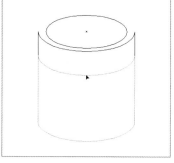

7 Select the Direct Selection tool ( ▶ ) from the toolbox, select the paths in the upper part of the drum as shown, and drag down while holding down the [Shift] key until your image matches the one shown above.

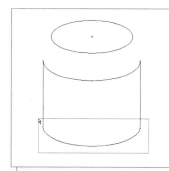

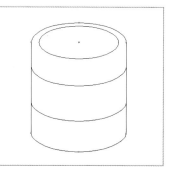

8 In the same way, select the lower portion of the drum and drag it upwards while holding down the [Shift] key. When you are done, press the [Ctrl]-[B] keys to paste the cylinder copy in the back.

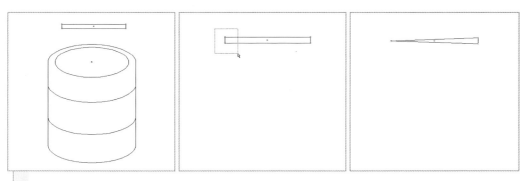

9 It is time to make the drumsticks. Select the Rectangle tool (▢) from the toolbox and draw the shape as shown here. Use the Direct Selection tool (▶) to select the two corner points on the left. Then select [Object] - [Path] - [Av___ check the Both option when the Average dialog box appears.

## Averaging And

The Average command lets you move two or more anchor points to a position that reresents the average of their locations. To use this command, select the anchor points and select [Object] - [Path] - [Average]. In the Average dialog box, you can choose to average along the horizontal or vertical axis—or both. The shortcut keys for this function are [Ctrl]-[Alt]-[J].

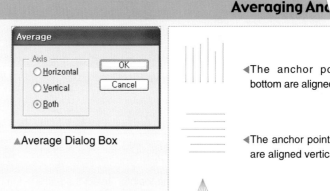

▲Average Dialog Box

◀The anchor point
bottom are aligned ho..zontally.

◀The anchor points on the right
are aligned vertically.

◀The anchor points are moved
to a single average point.

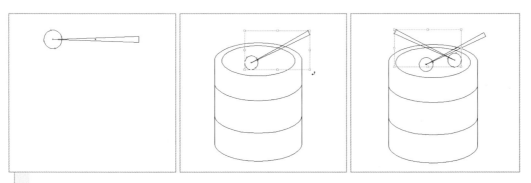

10 Let's add a rounded tip to the drumstick. Select the Ellipse tool (◯) from the toolbox. Then, place your pointer over the sharp end of the drumstick and click–while holding down the [Alt]-[Shift] keys–to draw a small circle. Press the [Ctrl] key to convert to the Selection tool (▶) and select the entire stick. Then press [Ctrl]-[G] to group the objects together. Holding down the [Ctrl] key, drag the drumstick to the top of the drum and then, with the Free Transform tool (▦) selected, rotate the stick as shown. Press the [Ctrl]-[Alt] keys and drag out a copy of the drumstick. Next, select the Free Transform tool and rotate the copy so that both drumsticks appear as shown. Next, place the drumsticks so that they match the image above.

11 Let's color the drum. First, press [Ctrl]-[Y] to return to Preview view. Next, use the Direct Selection tool (▶) to select the objects and color them as shown here. These are the colors used:

*Circular band - M: 100%, Y: 100%, K: 36%*
*Drum head - K: 20%*
*Drum sticks - M: 24%, Y: 100%, K: 8%*
*Outline - M: 100%, Y: 100%, K: 71%*

12 You'll add stars to the drum in this step. Set the fill color to K: 20% and the stroke color to None. Then, select the Star tool (⭐) from the toolbox and draw stars on the drum shell in a zig-zag fashion, as shown here.

13 Let's add some line flourishes to the drum. Select the Pen tool (✒) from the toolbox and set the fill color to None and the stroke color to white. Draw a curve at the position shown. Press the [Alt] key to change to the Convert Anchor Point tool (⊾). Move the direction line of the curve segment's end point in order to draw the next curve at an acute angle, as shown.

14 Click to draw the next curve. As in the preceding step, you need to move the direction line of the curve's end point. Press the [Alt] key to use the Convert Anchor Point tool (⊾) and move the direction line upwards. Repeat the steps until you've drawn lines across the entire drum. The exercise is now complete.

# Chapter 4

# Coloring, Blending, and Masking Objects

There are many ways to apply color to objects or groups of objects in Illustrator. Using the preset colors, patterns, and gradient swatches in the Swatches palette, objects can be filled with color easily and quickly. In this chapter, you will learn additional methods for filling objects, with a focus placed on more advanced gradient techniques. In addition, you will learn to blend objects to create morphing effects, and to apply a clipping mask to change the shape of an object.

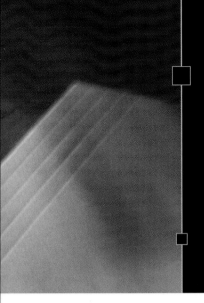

# Using Gradients, Blends, and Clipping Masks

Large areas of flat color can leave an image looking fairly mundane. Using gradients and blends, depth and contrast can be introduced, allowing for softer, more three-dimensional artwork. Another way to create interesting images in Illustrator is to use a clipping mask to generate unique shapes. These techniques and more are covered extensively in the following sections.

## Working with Gradients

A gradient is a gradual transition between two or more colors. Gradients can be used to make smooth color transitions, and they are especially useful for making objects appear more three-dimensional. Gradients are often used to create highlights and shadows, giving objects a sense of depth.

### Applying Gradients

There are a number of ways to apply a gradient. You can use the preset gradients found in the Swatches palette or create your own gradients using the Gradient palette.

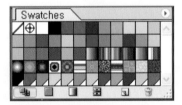

To create and apply your own gradient, you need to use the Gradient palette, the Color palette, and the Gradient tool ( ).

◀Select an object and apply a gradient from the Swatches palette.

The Gradient palette is used for editing the form and color of a gradient. The Color palette is used for editing the color of a gradient, and the Gradient tool ( ) is used to adjust the direction of the gradient to create different effects. Gradients can be applied in a straight line or in a circular pattern, but they can only be used to fill closed paths.

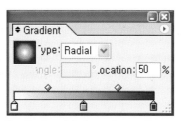
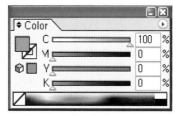

▲Create a gradient using the Gradient and Color palettes, then use the Gradient tool (▣) to adjust the direction of the gradient.

You can save a gradient you've created as a preset gradient in the Swatches palette, or edit a preset gradient using the Gradient and Color palettes.

## Gradient Palette

Whether you are editing a preset gradient or creating your own gradient, you need to do it in the Gradient palette. To hide or show the Gradient palette, hit the [F9] key. Now, let's have a look at the options in the Gradient palette.

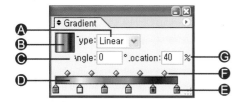

Ⓐ **Type**: Selects the type of gradient to apply-Linear (side-to-side) or Radial (from the center out).

Ⓑ **Gradient Fill**: Shows a preview of the selected gradient.

Ⓒ **Angle**: Determines the direction of the gradient (only applies to linear gradients).

Ⓓ **Gradient Slider**: The slider is your primary work area for constructing gradients.

Ⓔ **Gradient Stop**: Stops are used to select colors and position their locations in the gradient spectrum.

Ⓕ **Diamond Icon**: Determines the transition point between two surrounding stops.

Ⓖ **Location**: Use the Location field to enter location values for the stops and diamonds on the slider.

<< tip

## Gradient Angle

When applying a linear gradient, negative angle values produce a clockwise rotation, and positive angle values produce a counterclockwise rotation. The figure to the right shows you how the gradation changes with respect to the gradient angle.

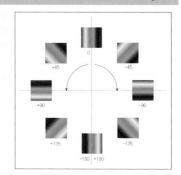

## Editing Gradients

A gradient is edited by modifying the gradient stops on the gradient slider. Potential modifications include changing the color of an existing gradient stop or adding or removing gradient stops.

There are four ways to change the color of a gradient stop. The most common way is to click on the gradient stop in the Gradient palette and select a color for the gradient stop in the Color palette. To apply a preset color from the Swatches palette to a gradient stop, select the gradient stop and click on a swatch color while holding down the [Alt] key. If the gradient stops are not shown on the spectrum bar, click once on the slider to bring them up.

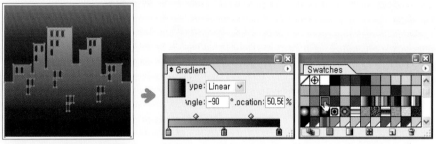

▲After selecting the gradient stop, hold down the [Alt] key and click on a preset color in the Swatches palette.

To apply color from the document window to a gradient stop, select the gradient stop and click on the color using the Eyedropper tool ( ) while holding down the [Shift] key.

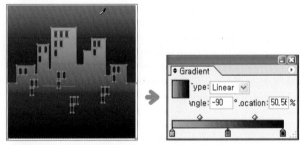

▲With the gradient stop selected, activate the Eyedropper tool, hold down the [Shift] key, and click on a color in the document.

To choose a color from the color spectrum bar in the Color palette, select the gradient stop and click on a color in the spectrum.

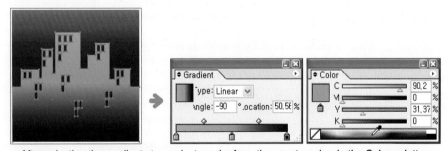

▲After selecting the gradient stop, select a color from the spectrum bar in the Color palette.

To move a gradient stop, just drag it along the gradient slider. To delete a gradient stop, drag it down and out of the Gradient palette. To add a gradient stop, just click at the bottom of the gradient slider. To make a copy of a gradient stop, select the gradient stop and drag out a copy sideways while holding down the [Alt] key.

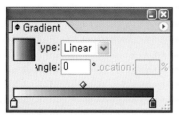

◀Select the gradient stop and drag down to delete it.

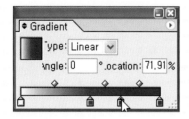

◀Click on the bottom of the gradient slider to add a gradient stop.

## Saving Gradients

To reuse a gradient you've created, you should save the gradient as a preset gradient in the Swatches palette. This can be done in two ways. One option is to go to the toolbox or Gradient palette and drag the selected fill or gradient fill swatch to the Swatches palette. The gradient will be added to the Swatches palette.

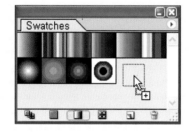

◀Select a fill from the toolbox and
drag it to the Swatches palette.

Another way to select a gradient is to click the Gradient button in the toolbox and–with the desired gradient selected in the Gradient palette–click on the New Swatch button (⬛) in the Swatches palette.

# Gradient Tool (⬛), [G]

The Gradient tool is used to adjust the direction of a gradient that has been applied to an object. All gradients have a beginning point (the left gradient stop) and an ending point (the right gradient stop); how the colors at these two points are applied depends on whether a linear or radial gradient is selected in the Gradient palette.

Dragging the Gradient tool across linear gradients will create a straight gradation across the shape. The length of the line you drag will determine the progression of the gradient across the object. In radial gradients, however, the gradation moves from a central point outward. Dragging the Gradient tool across radial gradients relocates this central point, and the length of your line determines the rate of the gradient's progress.

Dragging the tool while holding down the [Shift] key allows you to constrict the angle of the gradient to multiples of 45°.

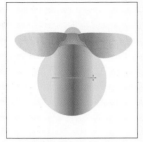
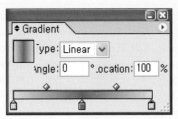

▲Hold down the [Shift] key while dragging the Gradient tool from left to right to create a perfectly flat gradient.

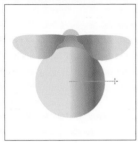

▲If the endpoint is dragged beyond the edge of the object, only part of the gradient will appear in the fill.

To apply a gradient that extends across several objects, first select all the objects by clicking on them with the Direct Selection tool (▨) while holding down the [Shift] key. Next, drag the Gradient tool across the objects.

▲Selecting and Applying a Gradient to the Objects One at a Time

▲Dragging the Gradient Tool to Create a Gradient that Extends across All the Objects

<< tip

## Applying Gradients to Borders and Text

Gradients cannot be applied directly to strokes or text. You must first apply the [Object] - [Path] - [Outline Stroke] command to strokes and the [Type] - [Create Outline] command to text before applying the gradient. These commands convert these objects into closed paths so they can be filled.

▲Convert the text into a closed path before applying the gradient.

▲Convert the border into a closed path before applying the gradient.

144

**<< tip**

## Combining Several Objects into One

If there are several objects that you need to work with as a whole, you can combine these objects into a single entity instead of using the Direct Selection tool (⬚) and the [Shift] key to select all of these objects repeatedly. To do so, select the objects using the Direct Selection tool (⬚) and the [Shift] key, then select [Object] - [Compound Path] - [Make].

# Blending Objects

Blending objects in Illustrator creates the effect of one object transitioning into another. Using the Blend tool or Blend command, intermediate shapes–known as blended objects–are automatically created. Because the color and shape of the objects are automatically blended, this makes it much easier to create transitions between objects. In this section, let's learn to use the Blend tool and the Blend command. We'll also cover editing blends and setting the blend options.

## Blend Tool (⬚), [W]

To apply a blend with the Blend tool, simply click the Blend tool on an anchor point from each of the objects to be blended. For a more accurate blending, you should set up the blend options before you use the Blend tool. To set up the blend options, double-click the Blend tool to open the Blend Options dialog box. Instructions for doing this follow:

You'll need at least two objects in order to use the Blend command. The general procedure is to double-click the Blend tool to bring up the options window, select your options, and then click reference points (either a shape or anchor point) in the work area to indicate which items you wish to blend, and how you wish to blend them.

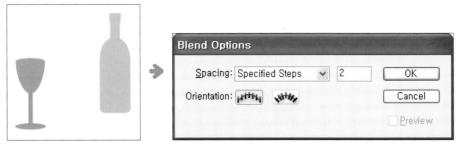

▲The Objects to be Blended    ▲Double-click on the Blend tool. In the Blend Options dialog box, enter the number of blended objects that you want to create.

- You do not have to select the objects before applying the blend. However, selecting the objects beforehand creates anchor points, which make it easier to choose a precise reference point.

- To create a natural blend, click on the same or similar reference points in the objects to be blended.

- An offset reference point creates an unnatural and awkward blend.

▲For a more natural blending effect, click with the Blend tool on the red dots shown.

▲On the other hand, selecting an awkward pair of points with the Blend tool will create unnatural objects.

<< tip

## [Object] – [Blend] – [Make]

The [Object] - [Blend] - [Make] command allows you to apply a blend without using the Blend tool. To set up the blending options before applying the command, click [Object] - [Blend] - [Blend Options]. Note that the Blend tool is more useful than the Blend command because the Blend tool lets you decide on the anchor points to be used as a reference for blending. This will give you more control over the blended objects.

The Blend Options dialog box lets you adjust the spacing and orientation of the blended objects generated by the Blend tool or command.

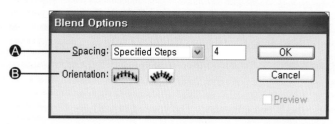

Ⓐ **Spacing**: Determines the blend Style–Smooth Color, Specified Steps, or Specified Distance. (These options are discussed more thoroughly later in the chapter.)

Ⓑ **Orientation**: Determines the orientation of the blended objects if the path of the blend is curved.

*Align to Page* (▯): Maintains the orientation of the objects as they are blended.

*Align to Path* (▯): Transforms objects to fit the path of the blend.

## Blending Grouped Objects

Applying a blend to grouped objects will always give you naturally blended objects no matter which anchor points you click with the Blend tool. The following steps will demonstrate how this is done.

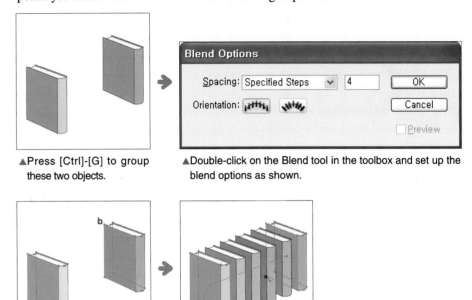

▲Press [Ctrl]-[G] to group these two objects.

▲Double-click on the Blend tool in the toolbox and set up the blend options as shown.

▲After grouping the two objects, select the Blend tool and click on an anchor point from each of the two objects. A natural blend results.

# Blend Styles

There are three blend Styles–Smooth Color, Specified Steps, and Specified Distance. You can choose one of these options by clicking on the Spacing pop-up menu in the Blend Options dialog box. Let's find out more about each of these three options.

## Smooth Color

This option is used to create smooth color transitions.

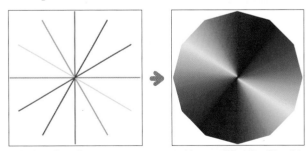

▲Before Blending

▲After applying the Blend tool with the Spacing set to Smooth Color, the result is a polygon with smooth transitions.

## Specified Steps

The Specified Steps option lets you decide the number of blended objects. This option is particularly useful when you want to create copies of an object in varying colors and sizes.

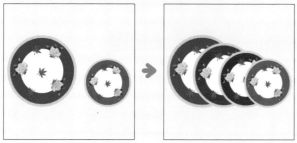

▲These two objects, which have the same design but are different in size and color, will be used for blending.

▲After blending the objects with Specified Steps set to 2.

## Specified Distance

Instead of deciding on the number of blended objects, the Specified Distance option lets you decide the distance between the blended objects and automatically creates the indicated number of transitions.

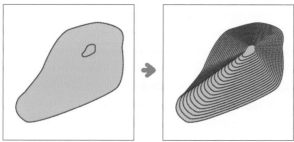

▲These two contours of different sizes will be used to create a three-dimensional image.

▲A detailed contour is created after setting the Specified Distance to 2 mm.

# Editing Blends

After applying a Blend, you can use the Selection tool ( ), Path tool ( ), and shortcut keys to edit the color, shape, or path of the blend. You can also make detailed modifications using the [Object] - [Blend] menu.

## Changing Color and Shape within Blends

The color or shape of blended objects is changed automatically when the color or shape of the objects used for their blend is changed. To edit the original objects, start by using the Direct Selection tool ( ) or Group Selection tool ( ) to select them.

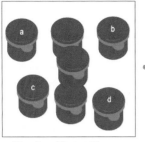

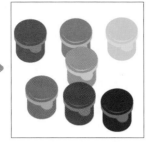

▲Blending objects of the same size and color: The objects have been blended in the following order: a, b, c, d.

▲The colors of the a, b, c, and d objects have been changed to create color transitions.

▲The size and shape of the a, b, c, and d objects have been changed to create shape transitions.

## Changing Positions and Making Copies within Blends

The Direct Selection tool (⬚) or Group Selection tool (⬚) can be used to drag the objects used in a blend to new positions. When an object used for a blend is moved, the spacing of the blended objects changes to match the new position of the object.

Dragging an object while holding down the [Alt] key creates a copy of the object and inserts blended objects between the copy and the object; this effectively extends your blend to include an additional object.

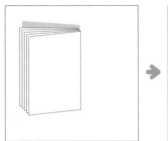

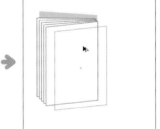

▲This book is created by blending two pages.

▲Using the Direction Selection tool to drag the last page while holding down the [Alt] key creates a copy of the page.

▲Pages are created between the original page and the new copy. The last page can be repositioned to create a more natural-looking path for the pages.

## Modifying the Blend Path

Blended objects are positioned along a path which can be modified to change the position of the blended objects. This path can be edited like any other path. You can add or delete anchor points and modify the shape of the path.

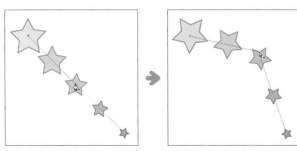

◀Finally, the Direct Selection tool (⬚) is used to move the anchor point and reconfigure the blend shape.

▲A path appears when the two stars are blended. The Add Anchor Point tool is then used at the center of the path.

You can also use the [Object] - [Blend] - [Replace Spine] command to replace the original path with a path that you've drawn.

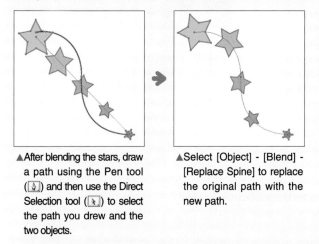

▲ After blending the stars, draw a path using the Pen tool (　) and then use the Direct Selection tool (　) to select the path you drew and the two objects.

▲ Select [Object] - [Blend] - [Replace Spine] to replace the original path with the new path.

## Reversing Position and Stacking Order within Blends

The Reverse Spine command reverses the position of the original objects, while the Reverse Front to Back command reverses the stacking order of all the objects used in the blend. Both these commands are found in the [Object] - [Blend] menu.

▲ Selecting [Object] - [Blend] - [Reverse Spine] reverses the positions of the objects on the path.

▲ Selecting [Object] - [Blend] - [Reverse Front to Back] reverses the stacking order of the objects. An object that was previously right in front will be placed at the bottom, and vice versa.

## Ungrouping Blended Objects

Blended objects are grouped together by default. To ungroup blended objects, select the [Object] - [Blend] - [Expand] command. This lets you select and modify the blended objects individually.

▲Applying the [Object] - [Blend] - [Expand] command will ungroup blended objects.

<< note

### Expanding Objects

The [Object] - [Expand] command can also be used to expand ordinary objects. In this case, expanding does not mean to make an object bigger. The Expand command instead splits an object into the individual objects that make up the whole. In short, it sections your object into its basic parts.

Sometimes complex objects created in Illustrator—such as those with gradients, blends, and patterns—cannot be recognized in other applications. Or, they may have problems printing. Such problems can be solved by using the Expand command to reduce the complexity of the equations that define the object.

Ⓐ **Expand**: Choose to split the object, fill, or stroke into individual shapes.

Ⓑ **Expand Gradient To**: These options determine how gradients will be turned into regular objects.

Ⓒ **Gradient Mesh**: Changes a gradient object into a gradient mesh.

Ⓓ **Specify**: Splits a gradient object into the specified number of shapes.

A clipping mask is used to clip away or mask sections of an image so that only some sections of the image remain visible. Essentially, the shape of one object is used to determine which areas of an underlying object are visible onscreen. Clipping masks are useful for changing the shape of your artwork.

## Applying or Removing Clipping Masks

A clipping mask can be created using an object or an entire layer. For a clipping mask to work, it has to be on top of the object(s) to be masked. After an object is turned into a clipping mask, it will automatically lose its fill and stroke properties, leaving only a path outline. The Group Selection tool () or Direct Selection tool () can then be used to add lines or fill colors to the clipping mask.

◀ Select the fish object, which will be used as the clipping mask, and move it in front of the other objects by selecting [Object] - [Arrange] - [Bring to Front].

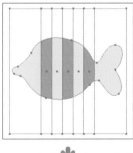

◀ Holding down the [Shift] key, select the objects to be masked. Check that the clipping mask is also selected and apply [Object] - [Clipping Mask] - [Make] to create a striped fish.

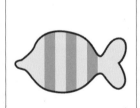

◀ Using the Direct Selection tool (), or the Group Selection tool (), add an orange stroke color to the fish clipping mask. The fish object used for the clipping mask originally had a blue fill and no stroke.

A clipping mask can be removed by selecting [Object] - [Clipping mask] - [Release]. After applying this command, an object that was used as a clipping mask will lose its masking properties. Note that the object's original fill and stroke properties are not retained.

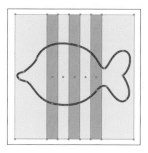

◀Use the [Object] - [Clipping mask] - [Release] command to remove the clipping mask. The stroke color remains orange, but the fish is now an object and not a clipping mask.

## Compound Paths

The Compound Path command groups two or more objects as one, then deletes any overlapping areas. Compound paths can be very useful for creating unique shapes and clipping masks. As you might have guessed, the Compound Path command achieves the same effect as the Exclude function in the Pathfinder palette.

▲Overlapping Objects of Different Colors

▲Selecting [Object] - [Compound Path] - [Make] applies the color of the object underneath to both objects, and a hole is created where the two objects overlap.

▲Select the objects to be used as a clipping mask and apply the Compound Path command.

▲Select both the new object and the background.

▲Select [Object] - [Clipping Mask] - [Make] to turn the compound path into a clipping mask.

# Using the Blend Command to Create Animation

Blend is a tool that conveniently creates intermediate stages between two objects. It is especially useful for creating animation, which calls for several repeating intermediate frames. After applying the Blend command, we'll use the Release to Layers option in the Layers palette to break up the blended objects into separate layers. Finally, we'll use [File] - [Export] to export the file as an SWF animation file.

**Start File**
\Sample\Chapter04\ani_swf.ai

**Final File**
\Sample\Chapter04\ani_swf_fin.ai

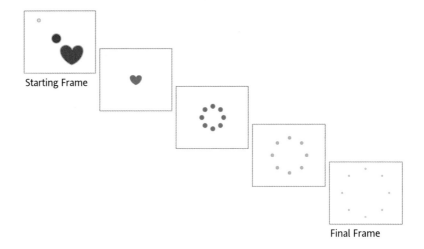

Starting Frame

Final Frame

1 Load \Sample\Chapter04\ani_swf.ai.

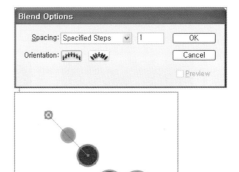

2 Start by blending the small and large circles, which are grouped together. Double-click on the Blend tool ( ) and, when the Blend Options dialog box appears, select Specified Steps for spacing and enter 1 in the text field. Click [OK]. Click on one of the circles and then click on the remaining circle to create a blend.

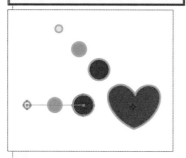

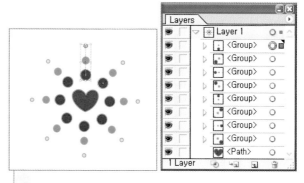

3 | Use the ruler and the guidelines to find the center of the heart. Then use the Rotate tool ( ⟲ ) to rotate the blended objects 45° using the heart's center point as the pivot point. Hold down the [Alt] key to make a copy as you rotate the objects.

4 | With your new copy selected, press [Ctrl]-[D] to make additional copies as shown.

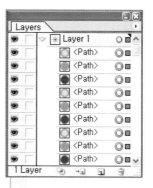

5 | Select everything and then choose [Object] - [Blend] - [Expand] to undo the blend.

6 | Since the objects for which we canceled the blend are grouped together, select [Object] - [Ungroup] to ungroup them.

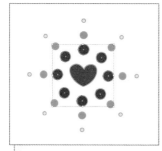

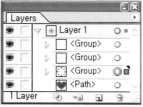

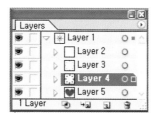

7 | Group the circles into sets according to their sizes.

8 | Choose [Release to Layers (Sequence)] from the Layers palette pop-up menu to release the objects into separate layers.

9　Choose [File] - [Export] to save the file as an SWF file. In the Options dialog box, set [Export Options] - [Export As] to 'AI Layers to SWF Frames', check 'Preserve Editability Where Possible', and then click [OK].

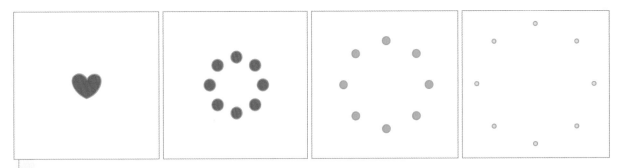

10　This creates an SWF and an HTML file. Try playing the animation by opening the HTML file in your Web browser.

<< note

## Editing SWF Files

SWF files can be edited in their native program: Macromedia Flash. If you have Flash on your system, choose [File] - [Import] - [Import to Stage] within Flash to edit SWF files.

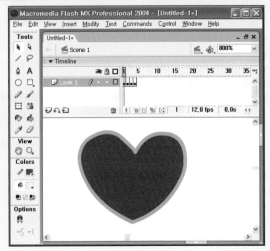

# Jazzing Up a Book Illustration

In this section, you will learn to create an illustration that will be used in a book. You will learn to apply linear and radial gradients, color objects using the Gradient tool, edit gradients, and blend two objects using the Blend tool.

**Start File**
\Sample\Chapter04\illust_01.ai

**Final File**
\Sample\Chapter04\illust_01_fin.ai

Original Image

Final Image

1 Load the illust_01.ai file from the sample folder. Select the Selection tool ( ) and click on the sky, as shown. In the next few steps, you will blend the stars in the sky and fill the pond and lotus leaf with a gradient.

2 Click on the Gradient button ( ) in the toolbox.

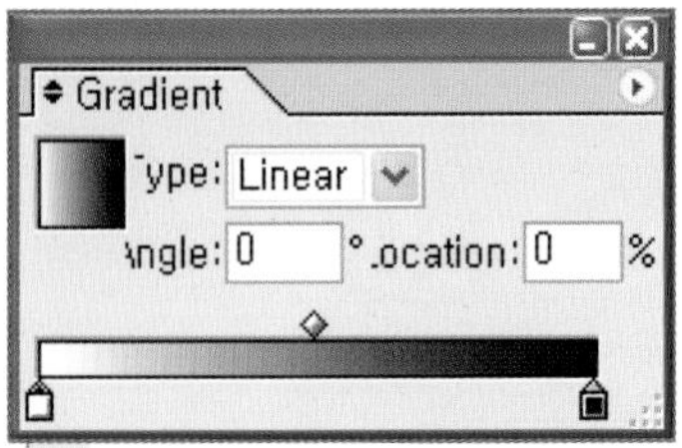


3 In the Gradient palette, let's edit the gradient and use it to color the sky. Click on the gradient stop (  ) on the left of the gradient slider.

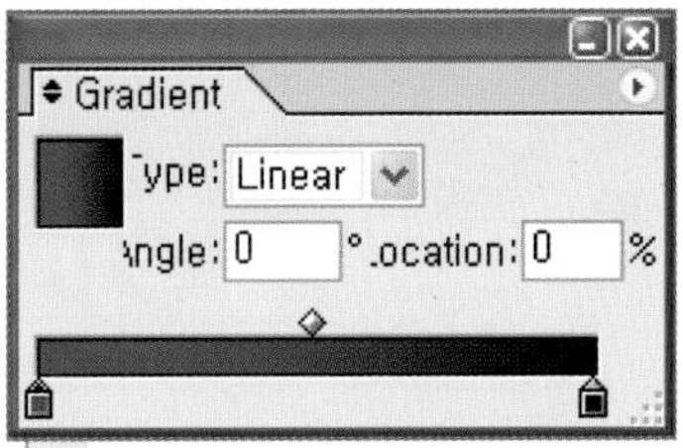


4 In the Color palette, click on the triangle button (  ) to display the palette menu. If your Color palette is not expanded, click Show Options. Check that CMYK is selected in the palette menu. Enter the following values: C: 93%, M: 50%, Y: 2%.

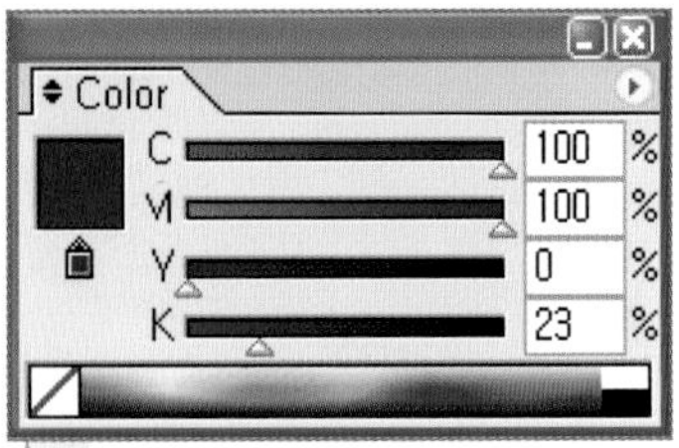


5 Repeat steps 3 and 4 on the right gradient stop. In the Color palette, enter C: 100%, M: 100%, K: 23%.

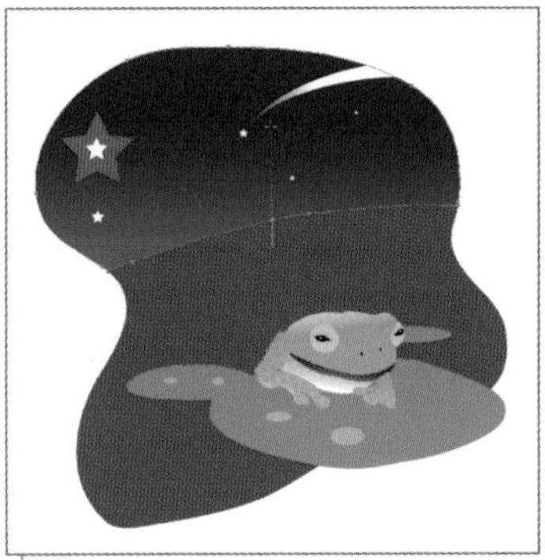

6 Selecting the Gradient tool (  ) from the toolbox, hold down the [Shift] key and drag the tool from the bottom to the top of the sky, as shown.

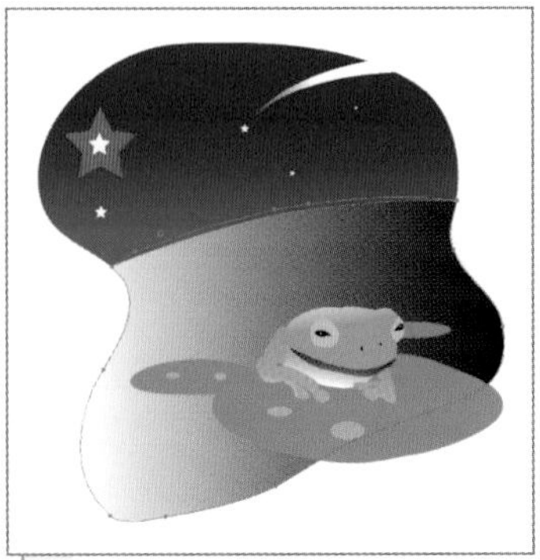

7 Let's color the pond. Select the pond using the Selection tool (  ) from the toolbox and then click on the White, Black gradient (  ) in the Swatches palette. The pond will be filled with a white-to-black gradient from left to right.

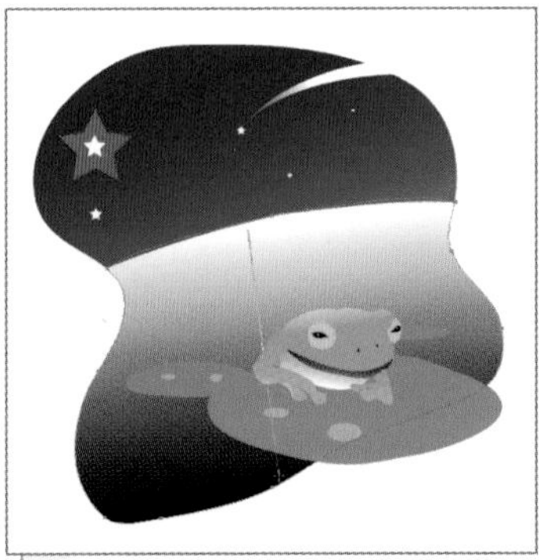

8 Selecting the Gradient tool (  ) from the toolbox, drag the tool from the top of the pond to the bottom, as shown.

## Defining Gradient Directions

A gradient from the Swatches palette is applied according to its predefined direction, as shown in the Swatches palette. To edit such a gradient, click on the Gradient tool (⬛) and drag out a direction line.

9 Let's make the light reflecting off the pond a little more striking by changing it to a light yellow color. Click on the left gradient stop in the Gradient palette. Notice that the Color palette is in grayscale mode. Click on the triangle button (▶) and change it to CMYK mode. Next, change the color to Y: 21% in the Color palette.

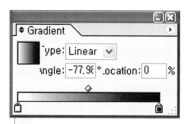

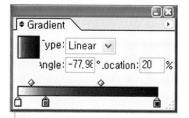

10 Repeat steps 3 and 4 on the right gradient stop. In the Color palette, enter C: 100%, M: 100%, K: 7%.

11 Click on the bottom of the gradient slider to create a new stop. Set the Location to 20%. Then, go to the Color palette and change the color to C: 37% and M: 73%.

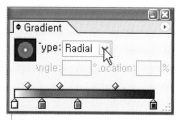

12 Click on the bottom of the gradient slider again, set the Location to 45%, and change the color in the Color palette to C: 63% and M: 54%. To save the gradient, click on the New Swatch button (⬛).

13 Let's color the water droplets on the lotus leaf. Click on one of the water droplets using the Selection tool (🔺). In the Gradient palette, set the Type to Radial.

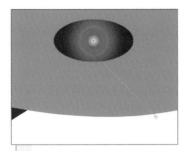

14 To change the direction of the gradient, select the Gradient tool (▣) from the toolbox. Click on the top, left-hand side of the water droplet and drag the tool diagonally to the bottom-right side, beyond the water droplet's boundary. This will prevent the middle and final gradient colors from showing up.

15 Color all the remaining water droplets in the same way.

16 Let's color the lotus leaf using the gradient swatch you created earlier. Using the Selection tool (▶) to select the bigger leaf, go to the Swatches palette and click on New Gradient Swatch 1 (▮).

17 Selecting the Gradient tool (▣) from the toolbox, start dragging downwards from a point that is slightly above the top edge of the leaf toward an endpoint that extends beyond the lower edges of the leaf. Refer to the image above for a demonstration of this motion.

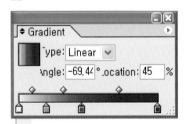

18 Click on the second gradient stop in the Gradient palette and then, holding down the [Alt] key, click on Green (▮) in the Swatches palette to change the color. Click on the third gradient stop and click on Forest (▮) in the Swatches palette–again, while holding down the [Alt] key.

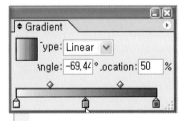

19 Click on the rightmost gradient stop and drag it downwards to remove it. Drag the third gradient stop to the right corner of the gradient slider and drag the second gradient stop to the middle of the slider (or you can set the Location for the second gradient stop to 50%). You should end up with something like the image shown above.

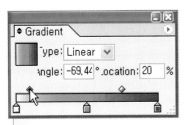

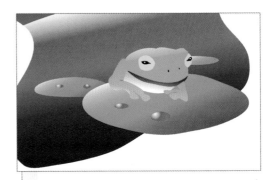

20 Drag the left diamond icon on the gradient slider farther to the left to reduce the yellow area.

21 Click on the New Swatch button ( ) in the Swatches palette to save the gradient. Select one of the smaller leaves and click on the swatch you just saved to apply the gradient to the leaf. Repeat this step for the last leaf.

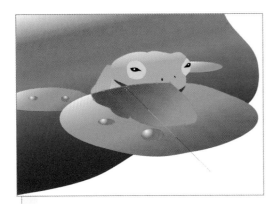

22 Let's create the frog's shadow. Use the Pen tool ( ) to draw the shape of the shadow, as shown above. Select the gradient used on the lotus leaf from the Swatches palette and then drag the Gradient tool from the bottom to the upper left to fill in the shadow.

23 Use the Selection tool ( ) to select the frog and choose [Object] - [Arrange] - [Bring to Front] to bring the frog to the front.

24 You will now blend the stars in the sky. Before applying the blend, double-click on the Blend tool ( ) or select [Object] - [Blend] - [Blend Options] and set the Spacing to Specified Steps, 8.

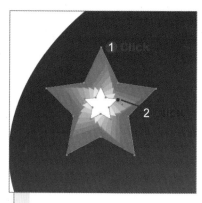

25 In order to see the anchor points, hold down the [Shift] key. Then use the Selection tool (🔺) to select the large star and then the small star. Next, use the Blend tool (🔧) to click on the two anchor points indicated above.

26 Holding down the [Alt] key, use the Selection tool (🔺) to drag the star to make a copy. You can add a little diversity by using the Free Transform tool (🔲) to rotate the stars and vary their sizes.

&lt;&lt; tip
### Using the Selection Tools

Clicking the Group Selection tool (🔺) twice on a blended object will select all the objects used in the blend. Use the Direct Selection tool (🔺) to edit the blend path.

27 Let's change the blend color of the duplicated stars. Click the Group Selection tool (🔺) on the center of a star. In the Color palette, select: (M=60%, Y=100%). Change the colors of the other stars to (M=20%, Y=100%), (C=80%, Y=75%), (C=88%, M=46%), and (C=50%, M=90%). This will give each star a different color. The image is now complete.

# Creating an Event Poster

In this section, you will create a poster using the Blend tool, the Divide pathfinder effect, and a clipping mask. To create the background, a clipping mask will be used and a pair of dancing girls will be blended and edited to create additional dancing girls.

**Start File**
\Sample\Chapter04\festival.ai

**Final File**
\Sample\Chapter04\festival _fin.ai

Original Image

Final Image

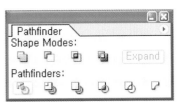

1 Load the festival.ai file from the sample folder. Note that the radiating lines on the poster are grouped.

2 Let's first prepare the background for the stage. You will be using the Divide pathfinder to divide the beige background using the radiating lines. Select the beige-colored background using the Selection tool (⬉) from the toolbox and press [Ctrl]-[C] to copy it to the clipboard. Holding down the [Shift] key, select the radiating lines. In the Pathfinder palette, hold down the [Alt] key and click on the Divide button (⬚).

3 This will divide the beige background into several fill faces (or shapes). Note that the radiating lines are no longer individual lines and are instead part of the resulting shapes.

4 The fill faces are automatically grouped. Let's change the color of some of the fill faces. Click outside the fill faces to deselect them and then choose the Group Selection tool ( ). Hold down the [Shift] key as you click, from left to right, on the second, fourth, and sixth fill surfaces. All three surfaces will be selected.

5 Click on the Yellow swatch ( ) in the Swatches palette to color the selected surfaces yellow.

6 Let's apply a reddish gradient to the stage floor. Choose the Selection tool ( ) and click on the line demarcating the stage floor. Click on the Sensual Red gradient ( ) in the Swatches palette to apply the gradient to the stage floor.

7 Then, selecting the Gradient tool ( ) from the toolbox, click and drag across the stage to adjust the gradient color. You should drag along the slant of the stage, as shown here.

8 Selecting the Stroke button ( ) in the toolbox, click on the None button ( ) to remove the black outline from the stage.

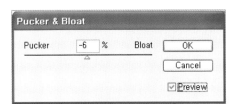

9 You now need to apply a mask to clean up the edges of the stage. Press [Ctrl]-[F] to paste the beige background you copied earlier and then select [Filter] - [Distort] - [Pucker & Bloat] and set the value to -6%. Click [OK].

10 To fan out the objects so that they are slightly overlapping each other, double-click on the Selection tool ( ) in the toolbox to open the Move dialog box. Set the Horizontal to -3, the Vertical to 3, and then click [OK].

11 Double-click on the Selection tool (⟨⟩) in the toolbox, then set the Horizontal to 6 and the Vertical to 6. Click [Copy].

12 Let's now separate the two objects. Since only one of the background objects is selected, hold down the [Shift] key and click on the other one to select both objects at the same time. In the Pathfinder palette, click the Divide button (⟨⟩) while holding down the [Alt] key.

13 We are going to create a clipping mask in the poster. First, choose [Object] - [Ungroup] to ungroup the objects. Next, drag the Selection tool (⟨⟩) over the objects that form a rectangle in the center. See the screenshot above for guidance. If you accidentally selected the dancing girl or the L-shaped edges framing the rectangle, hold down the [Shift] key and click on these objects to deselect them.

14 Choose [Object] - [Clipping Mask] - [Make] to activate the mask. Press [Ctrl]-[2] to lock the mask.

15 Use the Selection tool (⟨⟩) to select the frame on the edge, then set the fill color to M: 2%. Y: 20% in the Color palette. Press [Ctrl]-[2] to lock the object.

16 Let's make the text more three-dimensional. Drag the Selection tool (⬉) over the text to select it, then press [Ctrl]-[C] to make a copy. Deselect the text and select only the word, Festival. In the toolbox, drag the Fill button (⬛) over to the Stroke button (⬜) so that the text outline has the same color as the fill.

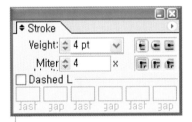

17 Go to the Stroke palette and set the line thickness to 4 pt.

18 Change the stroke color and size of the 2003 text in the same way. Deselect the 2003 text when you are done.

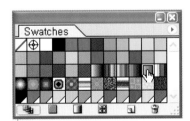

19 Press [Ctrl]-[F] to paste the copy of the text (from step 16) in front. With the Fill Color button selected, set the fill color of the Festival text to M: 25%. Choose the Midday Sky gradient (⬛) from the Swatches palette for the fill color of the 2003 text.

20 Selecting the Gradient tool (⬛) from the toolbox, hold down the [Shift] key and drag the tool from the top to the bottom, as shown.

**167**

21 Select the 2003 text using the Selection tool (🔺) and move the text slightly to the top left. This will create a drop shadow effect with the copy underneath.

22 Now, you will blend the image of the dancing girl to create a few more dancing girls. First, let's make a copy. Select the dancing girl using the Selection tool (🔺) and then, holding down the [Alt] key, drag a copy to the upper-left corner of the stage.

23 To blend the two images, you need to select them both. Then, double-click on the Blend tool (🔧) to adjust the blend options and set the Spacing to Specified Steps, 5. The Orientation must be set to Align to Page. Click [OK].

24 Click on a point in each of the two objects.

25 If the high-kicking legs of the girls are hidden, you need to reverse the positions of the girls. Select [Object] - [Blend] - [Reverse Spine] to reverse their positions. Next, we'll draw a curved line that we can use to replace the spine of the blend. Start by selecting the Pen tool (🖊) from the toolbox, then draw a line as shown above.

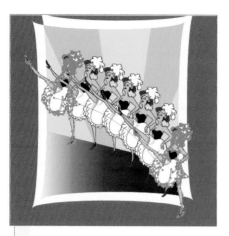

26 Use the Selection tool ( ) to place the curved line on top of the dancing girls and then, holding down the [Shift] key, click on the dancing girls so that they are selected as well. Then choose [Object] - [Blend] - [Replace Spine] to modify the blend path.

27 Next, choose [Object] - [Blend] - [Expand] so that the girls can be modified individually.

28 Click the Group Selection tool ( ). Holding down the [Shift] key, click on the tops of the second, fourth, and sixth dancing girl so that all three girls are selected. Click the Eyedropper tool ( ) on the shoes of one of the girls. The image is now complete.

# Creating Neon Text and Simulating Motion

In this section, you will use blend options to make a gradually changing image. The balls will be given a motion effect using transparency and blend commands.The neon text effect will use line color and thickness techniques. This example will give you an opportunity to become familiar with editing blends and using transparent masks.

Original Image

Final Image

1 Load the circus.ai file from the sample folder.

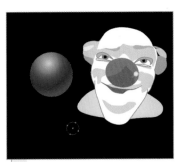

2 Let's start by blending the blue ball and the white circle. Note that the blue ball is filled with a gradient. In the following steps we'll use the Blend command to go from a semi-transparent object (the white circle) to one with full opacity (the blue ball).

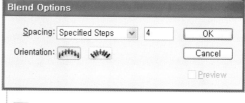

**3** First, select the white circle using the Selection tool ( ) from the toolbox. In the Transparency palette, set the Opacity to 0%.

**4** Double-click on the Blend tool ( ) and set the Spacing to Specified Steps, 4.

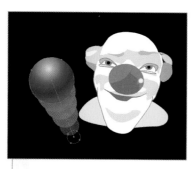

**5** Click on the midpoints of the ball and the circle to blend them. You should see blended objects created along a linear path, as shown.

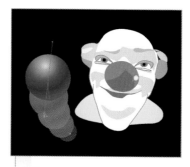

**6** Let's modify the blend path. Select the Convert Anchor Point tool ( ). Click on the anchor point of the path (the one at the center of the blue ball) and drag downwards to turn the linear path into a curved path.

**7** Let's copy the blue ball and its trail of blended objects. Select the blended objects using the Selection tool ( ) and, holding down the [Alt] key, drag out a copy. Use the Free Transform tool ( ) to rotate it slightly in the clockwise direction. When you're done, place it above the clown as shown above.

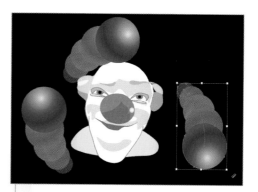

**8** Make a copy for the right side and rotate it as shown.

**171**

9 Let's change the color of the blended object copies that you made. Using the Group Selection tool (🔍) to select the balls above the clown's head, click on New Gradient Swatch 1 (⬛) in the Swatches palette to apply a red radial gradient to the balls. Then use the Gradient tool (⬛) to adjust the direction so that highlights are created in the top center area, as shown above.

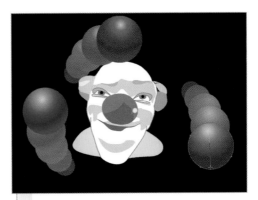

10 In a similar way, apply a green radial gradient to the balls on the right by selecting New Gradient Swatch 2 (⬛). Again, adjust the direction of the gradient so that the highlights appear as shown.

11 To add dimension to the circus text, you will first have to make the text larger. Drag the Selection tool (🔍) over the text so that the entire word is selected and press [Ctrl]-[C] to make a copy.

12 Select [Object] - [Path] - [Offset Path] and set the Offset to 2 mm in the Offset Path dialog box. The Offset Path command creates a copy of the selected path and places the copy at a specified distance from the original.

13 Click on the Swap Fill and Stroke icon (⤴) in the toolbox to switch the fill and stroke properties.

14 Double-click on the Gradient tool (⬛), then select New Gradient Swatch 4 (⬛) in the Swatches palette for the fill color.

**15** With the Selection tool () selected, use the arrow keys on the keyboard to move the text slightly to the left.

**16** Holding down the [Shift] key, drag the Gradient tool () from the top to the bottom, as shown. Then press [Ctrl]-[2] to lock the object.

**17** Let's create a glow for the text. Drag the Selection tool () over the red text to select it, choose [Effect] - [Blur] - [Gaussian Blur], and set the Radius to 5.

**18** After selecting the Stroke, click on New Color Swatch 1 () in the Swatches palette. Press [Ctrl]-[2] to lock it in place.

**19** You are now going to use the Blend feature to create neon text. Press [Ctrl]-[F] to paste the copy of the text you made in step 11. Repeat this step to paste another copy.

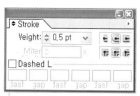

**20** For the stroke color, apply New Color Swatch 2 () from the Swatches palette and set the line thickness to 0.5 pt in the Stroke palette. This creates a light yellow text outline.

**173**

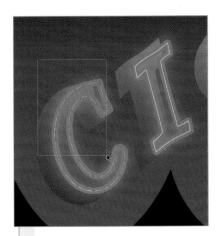

21 Let's apply a blend. Drag the Selection tool ( ) over the letter C to select both C outlines. Double-click on the Blend tool ( ) and set the Spacing to Specified Steps, 3.

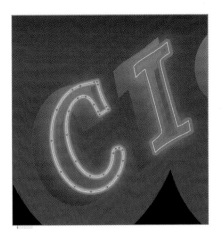

22 Since both C objects are aligned right on top of one another, you cannot click points on the objects, so apply [Object] - [Blend] - [Make] instead.

23 Repeat steps 21 and 22 for the remaining letters. Don't forget to apply [Object] - [Blend] - [Make]. Now, before moving onto the next step, press [Ctrl]-[A] to select all the objects and then press [Ctrl]-[2] to lock them.

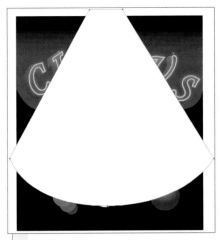

24 Now it's time to create a soft spotlight. First, you need to use the Pen tool ( ) to draw in the path of the light. Use the image above as a guide. Set the fill color to white ( ) in the toolbox.

25 Next, we'll soften the edges of the fan shape. Select [Effect] - [Stylize] - [Feather] and set the Feather Radius to 6 mm. Then go to the Transparency palette and set the Opacity to 50%.

26 An opacity mask is used to hide the light at the bottom. Use the Rectangular Selection tool ( ) to draw in a square over the area that will be covered by the spotlight. Then, select the White, Black gradient ( ) from the Swatches palette for the fill and, holding down the [Shift] key, drag the Gradient tool ( ) from top to bottom so that the gradient moves from white at the top to black at the bottom.

27 Use the Selection tool ( ) to select both the conical, fan-shaped object and the square object to which the White, Black gradient was applied. Then, click on the triangle button ( ) in the Transparency palette and select Make Opacity Mask.

<< tip

## Color Determines Transparency

When using opacity masks, black is 100% opaque and white is 100% transparent. If you've applied a gradient fill, the areas in-between these extremes display varying degrees of semi-transparency.

Chapter | 5

# Using Layers and Filters

The ability to separate your work into layers is one of the most important features of Illustrator CS. Layers can assist greatly with the organization of complicated or elaborate projects. Layers can also prove effective for creating unique effects, such as those involving creative use of transparency. Such effects can be further complimented by the use of Illustrator's suite of filters, which can be implemented to create any number of artistic details. Using layers and filters will greatly benefit your creative work in Illustrator, and both concepts are covered in depth in the following chapter.

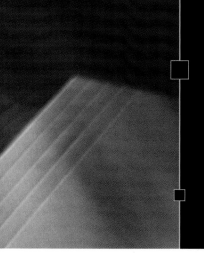

# What Are Layers and Filters?

Y ou can think of layers as transparent sheets with which you can "stack" objects to create the whole of your artwork. Filters are commands that allow you to apply various effects to your artwork. In this chapter, we'll introduce you to layers, review the options available in the Layers palette, and review the many filters that Illustrator places at your disposal.

## Understanding Layers

Though we've yet to cover layers explicitly, you should already be familiar with the general idea. As you know, the objects in your work space are "stacked" as you create them, which is why commands such as Bring to Front are constantly required as you arrange shapes in the work space. Layers simply allow you to place these stacked objects on their own dedicated "sheets" so that you can isolate them and take greater control over their use in your artwork.

### Layers Palette

The Layers palette, which can be opened by clicking on the Layers tab in the palette window or by selecting [Window] - [Layers], is where layers can be manipulated. In this section, let's learn to use or manipulate layers in the Layers palette.

▲An Image Created Using Multiple Layers

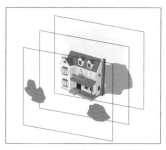

▲The Image Separated into Individual Layers

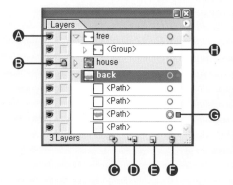

Ⓐ **Toggles Visibility**: Hides/shows the layer.
- *Outline* (🔲): Shows layer in outline form.
- *Preview* (👁): Gives a preview of the layer. Click on the eye icon to hide the layer.

Ⓑ **Toggles Lock**: Locks the layer so that it can't be edited. Click on the (🔒) icon to unlock the layer.

Ⓒ **Make/Release Clipping Mask**: Activates or deactivates clipping masks.

Ⓓ **Create New Sublayer**: Creates a new sublayer.

Ⓔ **Create New Layer**: Creates a new layer.

Ⓕ **Delete Selection**: Deletes the selected layer.

**Ⓖ Indicates Selected Art**: Used to select just one object for copying or moving.

**Ⓗ Click to target**: Click to select an object. Determines how it will be depicted (◎/●) when an opacity, effect, appearance, or graphic style is applied. Also used to move or copy attributes.

## Displaying Sublayers

Clicking the triangle icon (▷) to the left of a layer will display its sublayers, comprised of objects or grouped objects. Every ungrouped object is placed on a separate sublayer marked <Path>, while grouped objects are placed together on a sublayer named <Group>. Clicking on the triangle icon on a <Group> layer displays that group's sublayers.

## Selecting Objects in a Layer

On the right of every layer listing is the target icon (◎). Clicking on the target icon allows you to select all the objects in that layer. Clicking on the target icon of a sublayer selects only the object on that sublayer. You can also select all the objects on a layer by clicking on the layer listing while holding down the [Alt] key.

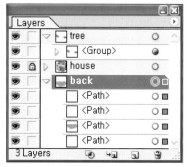

▲Clicking on the target icon of the "back" layer in the Layers palette selects all the objects in the layer.

## The Target Icon As a Status Indicator

A glance at the target icons in the Layers palette will tell you whether the objects on a layer are selected, and whether the selected layer has any appearance attributes aside from a single fill and/or stroke. Appearance attributes include characteristics such as effects and transparency. See the examples below for more info:

○
▲Not Selected;
   No Appearance Attributes

◎
▲Selected; No Appearance Attributes

●
▲Not Selected; with
   Appearance Attributes

◉
▲Selected; with
   Appearance Attributes

〈〈 tip

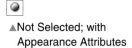

**Shortcut Keys in the Layers Palette**

Clicking on the target icon while holding down the [Ctrl] key will deselect all the objects. After clicking on the target icon of one layer, hold down the [Shift] key and click on the target icon of another layer to select both layers simultaneously.

## Locking and Hiding Layers

When you are working only on a specific layer, the other layers can get in the way. Using the Layers palette, you can lock or hide layers to make it easier to work. To hide a layer from view, click on the eye icon (◉) of the layer to hide all the objects contained in that layer. Click on the empty box (☐) to see all the hidden objects again.

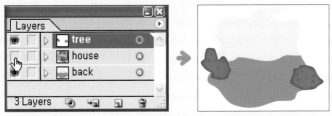

▲Click the eye icon to hide the layer.

Holding down certain keystrokes while clicking an eye icon will hide or display the objects on a layer in different ways. Clicking on the eye icon of a layer while holding down the [Alt] key will hide all the other layers except for the one selected. Holding down the [Alt] key and clicking on the eye icon again will display all the layers.

On the other hand, clicking on the eye icon while holding down the [Ctrl] key will display an outline drawing of the object. Clicking on the eye icon again will return you to the Preview view for that object.

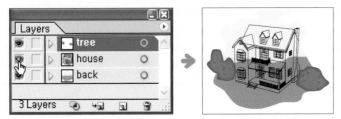

▲Click on the eye icon while holding down the [Ctrl] key to see an outline drawing of the objects in the selected layer.

Clicking on the eye icon while holding down [Ctrl]-[Alt] will show an outline view of all the layers other than the one selected. Click again to see all of the layers in Preview mode.

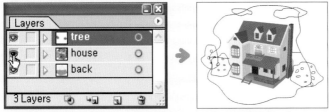

▲Click on the eye icon while holding down [Ctrl]-[Alt] to display an outline view of all the layers other than the one selected.

To avoid making changes to other layers, click on the Toggles Lock button (☐) next to an eye icon to lock all the objects in that layer. Clicking on the Toggles Lock button while holding down the [Alt] key will lock all the layers–excluding the selected layer. Click again to unlock all the layers.

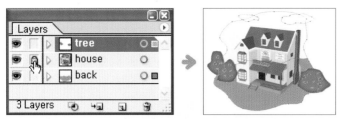

▲Click on the Toggles Lock button to lock the objects in a layer.

## Creating Layers

To create a new layer, click on the Create New Layer button ( ▣ ) at the bottom of the Layers palette. A new layer will be created right above the current layer.

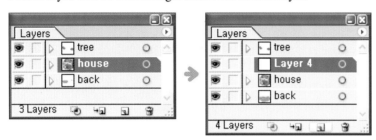

◀Select the house layer and click on the Create New Layer icon.

Some layer properties can be changed in the Layer Options dialog box. Double-clicking on a layer name in the Layers palette opens the Layer Options dialog box. In addition, clicking on the Create New Layer button ( ▣ ) while holding down the [Alt] key will open the Layer Options dialog box while creating a new layer.

Using the Layer Options dialog box, you can change the name of a layer, specify a selection color mark for a layer, and set other options. A selection color mark doesn't affect the actual artwork in any way. When an object is selected, a bounding box appears around the object. The color of the bounding box can be customized by setting the selection color mark of the layer in which the object is found. The selection color mark is shown as a colored square ( ▣ ) to the right of the layer in the Layers palette. The square only appears if an object on the layer is selected. A new layer will automatically be given its own selection color mark, so it is not really necessary for you to set this manually.

◀Double-click on a layer name to open the Layer Options dialog box, then enter a new name for the layer.

To create a new sublayer, select a layer and click on the Create New Sublayer icon ( ▣ ) at the bottom of the Layers palette.

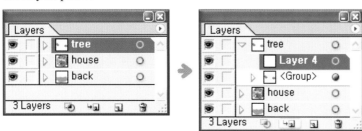

◀Creating a New Sublayer

**181**

## Copying Layers

To copy a layer, drag and drop a layer onto the Create New Layer icon (⊞) at the bottom of the Layers palette. Duplicating a layer will also duplicate all the objects contained within the layer. Making a layer copy is useful for making changes to artwork without having to commit to the changes permanently. The changes can be made on a copy while the original layer is locked and saved as a backup.

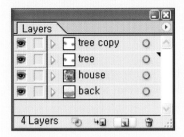

◀Drag and drop the tree layer onto the Create New Layer icon to create the tree copy layer.

## Deleting Layers

To delete a layer, drag it to the Delete Selection icon (🗑) at the bottom of the Layers palette. Alternatively, select the layer and click the Delete Selection icon (🗑) to delete it.

## Positioning Layers

When creating an image, it is important to know which layer you are working on, as well as that layer's position or stacking order in your document. A layer at the bottom of a stack of layers will be covered in the work area by the layers that fall above it in the stack. As a result, the order in which you stack your layers will be a crucial factor in the final appearance of your artwork.

To change the stacking order of a layer, click on the layer's name in the Layers palette. The layer will be highlighted and the current layer indicator will appear to the right of the layer to indicate that it is selected. Click and drag the layer to another position in the stack–it's as simple as that.

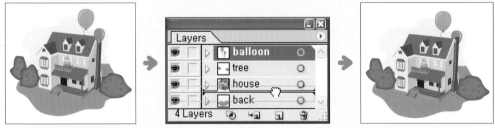

▲Move the balloon layer below the house layer so that the smaller, red balloon is hidden by the house.

A sublayer's stacking order can also be changed. A sublayer can be repositioned within a layer or moved to another layer. A layer can also be turned into a sublayer for another layer.

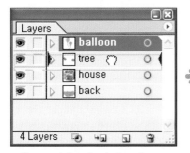

▲Drag and drop the balloon layer on the tree layer to turn the balloon layer into a sublayer of the tree layer.

▲Note that this method inserts the balloon sublayer right at the top of the stack of sublayers in the tree layer.

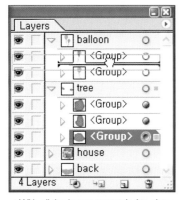

▲With all the layers expanded to show the sublayers, drag a <Group> sublayer from the tree layer to the balloon layer, placing it between the sublayers of the balloon layer.

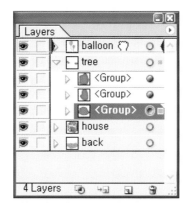

▲Alternately, dragging the <Group> sublayer from the tree layer directly to the balloon layer (not between its sublayers) will insert the sublayer at the very top of the balloon sublayers.

## Moving Objects to a Different Layer

Using keyboard shortcuts or menu commands, you can copy or cut objects from one layer and paste them on a different layer. Selecting an object, press [Ctrl]-[C] to copy or press [Ctrl]-[X] to cut, then select the layer on which to paste the object. Next, press [Ctrl]-[V] to paste or select a paste command from the Edit menu. Select [Edit] - [Paste in Front] to paste the object on the top of the layer, or [Edit] - [Paste in Back] to paste it right at the bottom.

▲Press [Ctrl]-[X] to cut out the image of the car from its layer.

▲Selecting the tree layer, press [Ctrl]-[F] to paste the image right at the top of the tree layer.

You can also move objects between layers using only the Layers palette. First, select the object by clicking on the target icon of the layer or sublayer where the object is placed. Then click and drag the selection color mark of the layer to the layer where you want to paste the object.

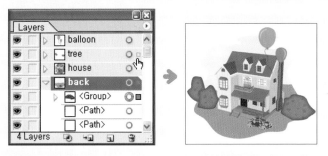

◀Click on the <Group> sublayer's target icon to select the car image, then drag the layer's selection color mark to the tree layer to move the car image there.

## Merging Layers

Layers can be merged into one layer using the Merge Selected command. First the layers to be merged have to be selected. To select a group of consecutive layers from the Layers palette, hold down the [Shift] key and click on the first, then last layer you wish to select. To select layers that are not adjacent in the Layers palette, hold down the [Ctrl] key and click on the layers one at a time. To remove a layer that was selected by mistake, click on it again while holding down the [Ctrl] key. After selecting a group of layers, select Merge Selected from the pop-up menu of the Layers palette to merge the selected layers. Selecting Flatten Artwork from the pop-up menu will merge all the layers together, except for any hidden layers.

◀Hold down the [Shift] key to select the adjacent layers and then choose Merge Selected from the pop-up menu.

## Making a Clipping Mask with Layers

In Chapter 4, you learned to create clipping masks using objects. In this section, you will learn to create a clipping mask using layers. Unlike clipping masks created from objects, layer masks are applied to all objects in the same layer whether the objects are selected or not. To apply a layer mask to the sublayers in a layer, the sublayer to be used as a mask must be placed at the top of the sublayers in the layer. Then, with the layer selected, clicking on the Make/Release Clipping Mask icon ( 🔾 ) at the bottom of the Layers palette will turn the sublayer into a mask. You should note that the mask will only be applied to the objects in the layer and not to the objects on other layers. Clicking on the icon again will release the mask.

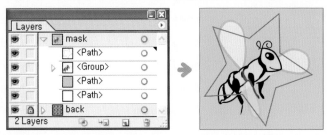

◀Move the <Path> layer containing the star to the top of the mask sublayers. This sublayer will be used as a layer mask.

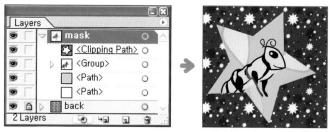

▲Select the mask layer and then click on the Make/Release Clipping Mask icon at the bottom of the Layers palette.

## Template Layers

A template layer is used for placing an image that you wish to trace over. A template layer behaves just like any other layer, except it cannot be printed or exported.

1. Choose [File] - [Place] to load a bitmap image.

2. Double-click on the layer's thumbnail in the Layers palette and check Template when the Layer Options dialog box appears. Enter a value in the Dim Images to option to adjust the image's opacity. Another way to turn a layer into a template is to choose [Template] from the Layers palette pop-up menu, but this method will lock the resulting template layer.

3. After a layer has been turned into a template, the eye icon (👁) will be replaced by the template icon (🖼) in the Layers palette. To turn a template layer back into a regular layer, uncheck the [Template] option from the Layers palette menu.

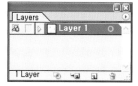

Filters are effects or commands that allow you to alter objects or shapes in countless ways. Most filters are practical, fun, and easy to use. A primary advantage of using filters is that you can create complicated artwork in just a few simple steps. Examples of filter sets include the Colors filters, the Distort filters, and the Stylize filters.

Filters can be applied to an object, a group of objects, or an entire layer. Before applying a filter, a selection has to be made. To apply a filter to an object or a group of objects, select the object or group in the artboard. To apply a filter to a layer, click on the target icon (⬤) of the layer.

After a selection is made, choose a filter from the Filter menu. If an options dialog box for the filter appears, adjust the settings, click Preview to preview the results, and then click [OK] to apply the filter.

## Filter Menu

There are many filters available in Illustrator, and all of the filters are applied using the Filter menu.

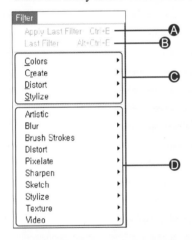

<< tip

**Bitmap Images**

There are two ways to create bitmap images. Bitmap images can be imported using the [File] - [Place] command or created by rasterizing a vector image using the [Object] - [Rasterize] selection.

Ⓐ **Apply Last Filter ([Ctrl]-[E])**: After applying a filter, the words "Last Filter" in this menu option change to the name of the last filter used. You can then click the command to apply the filter again. For example, if the Drop Shadow filter was the last filter to be applied, clicking this command will apply it again to any selected objects.

Ⓑ **Last Filter ([Alt]-[Ctrl]-[E])**: Opens the dialog box of the last filter that was applied. After setting the options in the dialog box, you can click [OK] to apply the filter. Use this option if you want to use the last filter, but with different settings.

Ⓒ **Colors through Stylize Filters**: With the exception of the Object Mosaic filter, all of the filters found in the top section of the Filter menu can be applied to vector images. In addition, some of the Create and Colors filters can be applied to bitmap images.

Ⓓ **Artistic through Video Filters**: The filters found in the bottom section of the Filter menu can be applied only to color bitmap images. In addition, these filters cannot be applied to multiple objects, groups, or layers.

## Vector-Based Filters

This section covers the Colors, Create, Distort, and Stylize filter submenus. Because Illustrator is primarily used for working with vector images and not bitmap images, the Artistic through Video subgroupings will not be covered in this section.

## Colors Submenu

The Colors submenu contains many filters for restoring, correcting, or manipulating color.

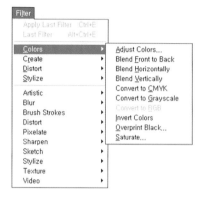

### Adjust Colors Filter

Using the Adjust Colors filter is similar to using the Color palette to adjust color. The main difference is that the Adjust Colors filter lets you adjust the colors of the selection's fill and stroke at the same time.

#### Adjust Colors Dialog Box

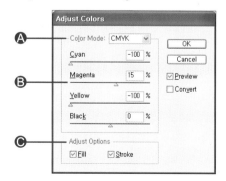

**A Color Mode:** If your document's color mode is CMYK, you can choose the CMYK or Grayscale color modes. If your document's color mode is RGB, you can choose the RGB or Grayscale color modes. To check your document's color mode, select [File] - [Document Color Mode] from the menu bar. If you used a global process color in the selection, the Global color mode will be available. A global process color is linked to a swatch in the Swatches palette.

**B Color Sliders**: Drag the color sliders or enter values in the text boxes to adjust the values of the color components. The sliders that appear will change depending on the selected color mode.

**C Adjust Options**: Choose whether the filter will be applied to the selection's fill surface, stroke, or both.

## Blend Filters

The three blend filters in the Colors submenu–Blend Front to Back, Blend Horizontally, and Blend Vertically–only work on a group with three or more filled objects. The filters take two objects as starting and endings points, then color the remaining object(s) with intermediate colors.

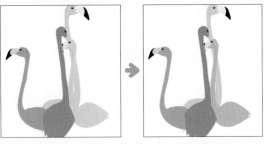

▲Blend Front to Back: This filter sets the frontmost and backmost objects as the start and end points, blending the objects in between.

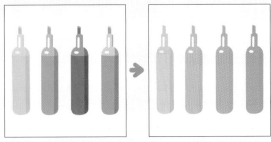

▲Blend Horizontally: This filter sets the leftmost and rightmost objects as the start and end points, blending the objects in between.

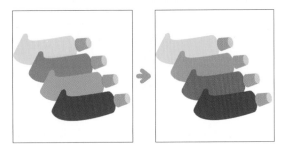

▲Blend Vertically: This filter sets the topmost and bottommost objects as the start and end points, blending the objects in between.

## Convert Filters

The convert filters are used for converting selection between Grayscale and the document's native color mode (CMYK or RGB). So if your document color mode is CMYK, the Convert to Grayscale and Convert to CMYK filters will be available in the Filter menu.

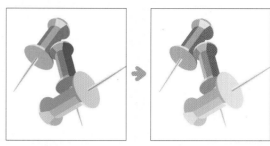

▲Convert to CMYK or Convert to RGB: These options change the color mode to CMYK or RGB, depending on your document's native color mode. If you apply this filter to grayscale objects, they will not be colorized automatically. The color has to be added using the [Filter] - [Colors] - [Adjust Colors] filter.

▲Convert to Grayscale: Changes the color mode to Grayscale.

## Invert Colors Filter

The Invert Colors filter turns the original selection into a negative image-like what you see on a roll of film negatives.

▲Select the multi-colored object.

▲In the Adjust Colors dialog box, use the slider to adjust the overall color.

## Overprint Black Filter

By default, when objects overlap, overlying colors knock out any colors used beneath them in the image. So if the top color is yellow and the bottom color is red, the image will print yellow. When an object is set to overprint, however, each overlapping color is printed. In the example above, both the yellow and red inks will print, producing an orange color.

The Overprint Black filter lets you trigger overprinting for any fill that contains black. The filter also lets you remove the Overprint Black command from any object. Before using this filter, you should select [View] - [Overprint Preview] to preview the filter's effect on screen.

### Overprint Black Dialog Box

Ⓐ **Add Black/Remove Black**: Choose Add Black or Remove Black to apply or remove the filter.
- *Percentage*: The percentage of black in an object will determine whether it will be affected by the filter. For example, if you set the Percentage value to 50%, only objects containing exactly 50% black will be set to overprint.
- *Apply to*: Choose whether the filter will be applied to the selection's fill surface, stroke, or both.

**Ⓑ Options**

- *Include Blacks with CMY*: Select this option to enable overprinting for objects containing cyan, magenta, or yellow.
- *Include Spot Blacks*: Select this option to enable overprinting for objects containing spot colors.

## Saturate Filter

Use this filter to saturate or desaturate the colors in an object.

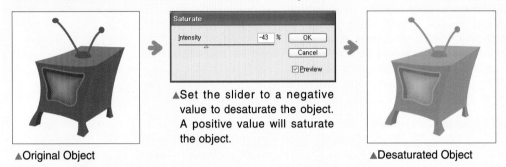

▲Original Object

▲Set the slider to a negative value to desaturate the object. A positive value will saturate the object.

▲Desaturated Object

# Create Submenu

The Create submenu contains only the Crop Marks and Object Mosaic filters. The only similarity between the two filters is that they both add new objects to the artboard.

## Crop Marks Filter

The Crop Marks filter is used to insert crop marks around the selected object. These crop marks will appear when you print your image, and can be moved or edited like any other group of paths.

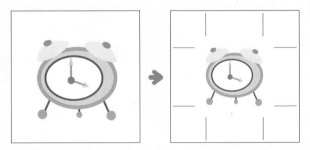

## Object Mosaic Filter

Unlike the other filters that have been covered, the Object Mosaic filter can only be used on bitmap images-not vector images. The Object Mosaic filter clumps the pixels in a bitmap image to create a mosaic version of the image. The resulting mosaic is a vector-based image comprising numerous colored tiles. It appears directly on top of the original bitmap image.

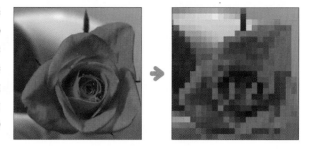

### Object Mosaic Dialog Box

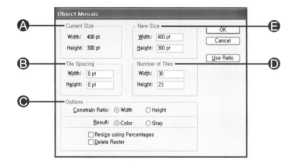

Ⓐ **Current Size**: Indicates the size of the selected bitmap image.

Ⓑ **Tile Spacing**: Determines the spacing between the tiles that make up the mosaic.

Ⓒ **Options**

- *Constrain Ratio*: If this option isn't selected, the settings you enter in New Size and Number of Tiles fields may give you a mosaic that is not proportional to the original bitmap. The resulting mosaic might also use rectangular, rather than square, tiles. To create a mosaic that is proportional to the bitmap image and uses only square tiles, you have to decide if you want to prioritize the tile-to-width or the tile-to-height ratio that is derived from the settings entered in the New Size and Number of Tiles fields. When you've selected Width or Height, click the [Use Ratio] button to reset the values that are not constrained in the dialog box.
- *Result*: Click to choose between a color or grayscale mosaic pattern.
- *Resize Using Percentages*: Changes the unit of measurement for the New Size field to percentage (%).
- *Delete Raster*: Deletes the bitmap image once the mosaic is complete.

Ⓓ **Number of Tiles**: Determines the number of tiles to be used to create the mosaic's width and height.

Ⓔ **New Size**: Sets the width and height of the mosaic graphic.

# Distort Submenu

The distort filters are used to change the shape of an object or group of objects.

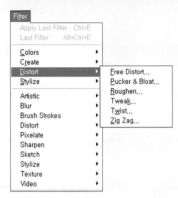

## Free Distort Filter

The Free Distort filter is similar to the Free Transform tool. After selecting the filter, the Free Distort dialog box will appear. You can then click and drag the four corner-handles of the object in the dialog box to change the object's shape.

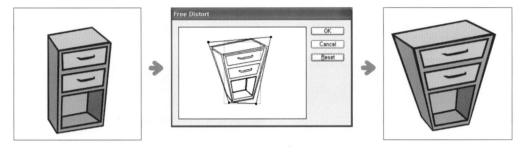

## Pucker & Bloat Filter

This filter is used to create the effect of the object being ballooned out (bloated) or sucked into (puckered) the object's center.

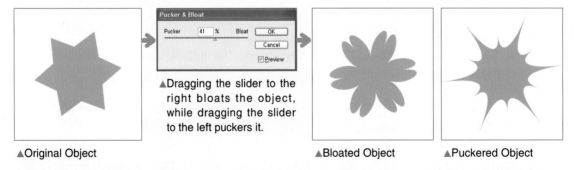

▲Original Object                    ▲Bloated Object        ▲Puckered Object

## Roughen Filter

The Roughen filter crumples the outline of an object by increasing the number of segments in its path. This creates irregular peaks and valleys in the object's path.

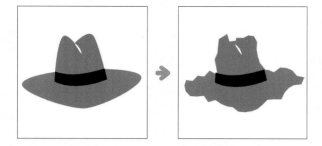

## Roughen Dialog Box

### Ⓐ Options
- *Size*: The Size slider sets the maximum length of each segment. Choose Relative to set the length as a percentage relative to the object's total path length, or Absolute to set the length to an absolute value.
- *Detail*: Sets the density of segments per inch. A high value creates more segments than a low value.

**Ⓑ Points**: Select Smooth to create a smooth outline or Corner to create a jagged outline.

## Tweak Filter

The Tweak filter randomly distorts an object outline.

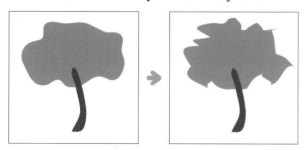

## Tweak Filter Dialog Box

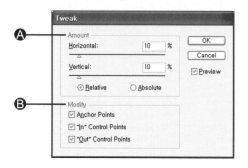

**Ⓐ Amount**: Sets the amount of horizontal and vertical distortion. Choose Relative to set the distortion as a percentage relative to the object's edge, or Absolute to set the distortion to an absolute value.

**Ⓑ Modify**: Choose whether the filter will modify the anchor points or the control points (i.e., direction lines) leading into or out of from anchor points.

## Twist Filter

The Twist filter twirls an object clockwise or counterclockwise with respect to the object's center point.

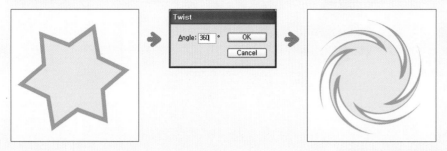

## Zig Zag Filter

The Zig Zag filter turns the outline of an object into uniformly jagged or wavy ridges.

### Zig Zag Dialog Box

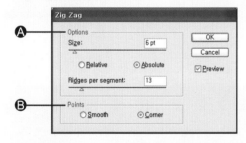

**Ⓐ Options**
- *Size*: Sets the height of the ridges. Choose Relative to set the height as a percentage relative to the object's edge, or Absolute to set the height to an absolute value.
- *Ridges per segment*: Sets the number of anchor points added to each segment.

**Ⓑ Points**: Select Smooth to create a smooth outline or Corner to create a jagged outline.

# Stylize Submenu

The Stylize submenu contains filters that make it easy to create commonly used design elements, such as arrowheads, drop shadows, and rounded corners.

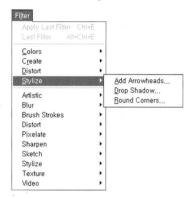

## Add Arrowheads Filter

The Add Arrowheads filter adds arrowheads to the ends of open paths.

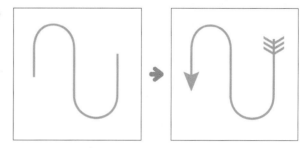

## Add Arrowheads Dialog Box

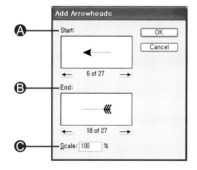

**Ⓐ Start**: Determines the arrowhead design to be used at the start end of the path. Click on the forward and back arrow buttons to select a design.

**Ⓑ End**: Determines the arrowhead design to be used at the end of the path. Click on the forward and back arrow buttons to select a design.

**Ⓒ Scale**: Scales the arrowhead as a percentage relative to the stoke weight of the path.

## Drop Shadow Filter

The Drop Shadow filter, which adds shadows to objects to create the illusion of depth, is one of the most useful filters in Illustrator.

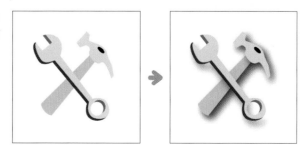

### Drop Shadow Dialog Box

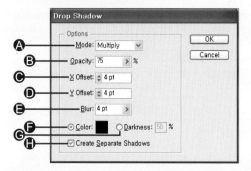

**A Mode**: Sets the blending mode of the shadow. This determines how the shadow will blend with any objects that appear underneath it.

**B Opacity**: Sets the shadow's opacity.

**C X Offset**: Determines how far the shadow will be offset from the object horizontally.

**D Y Offset**: Determines how far the shadow will be offset from the object vertically.

**E Blur**: A higher Blur value creates more blurring in the shadow and spreads the shadow out more.

**F Color**: Sets the shadow color.

**G Darkness**: Determines the amount of black in the shadow.

**H Create Separate Shadows**: If you check this option, you will create a shadow that is grouped with the object and is placed directly behind it. If you uncheck this option, you will create a shadow that is not grouped with the overlying object; the shadow will be placed below all of the objects in the layer containing the object.

## Round Corners Filter

The Round Corners filter turns the corners of an object into smooth curves. In the Round Corners dialog box, you can determine the degree of roundness by adjusting the Radius value. A higher radius will create rounder corners.

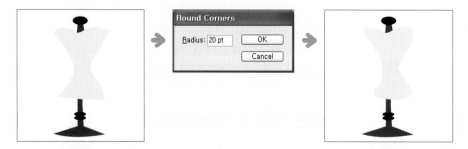

<< tip

### Locking an Object

To lock an object and prevent it from being changed by a filter or any other operation, select [Object] - [Lock] - [Selection] or press the keyboard shortcut, [Ctrl]-[2].

# 1

# Making a Christmas Card

In this exercise, you will edit an illustration to create a Christmas card. You will practice using the selection color mark to move objects to different layers. You'll also apply transformations using tools like the Scale tool, Reflect tool, and Rotate tool. In addition, you'll create crop marks and folding lines to help you crop and fold the card accurately once it's printed.

**Start File**
  \Sample\Chapter05\christmas.ai

**Final File**
  \Sample\Chapter05\christmas_fin.ai

Original Image

Final Image

1 Open the christmas.ai file. The file contains a Christmas card design.

2 Let's create crop marks for the card. Use the Selection tool ( ) from the toolbox to select the white background, then choose [Filter] - [Create] - [Crop Marks]. The crop marks are grouped automatically.

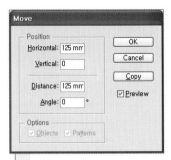

**3** Because the card will be folded in half, let's insert a fold line. Since the width of the card is 250 mm, the fold line should be created in the center—at the 125 mm mark. Selecting the Group Selection tool ( ) from the toolbox, click outside the artboard to deselect all. Then select the vertical crop mark in the top-left corner and—holding down the [Shift] key—select the vertical crop mark at the bottom left. Choose [Object] - [Transform] - [Move] to make a displaced copy. In the Move dialog box, type in 125 mm for the horizontal position and 0 mm for the vertical position, then click [Copy].

**4** The fold line will be created at the 125 mm mark, as shown. To differentiate the fold line from the crop marks, let's turn the fold line into a dotted line. With the fold line selected, go to the Stroke palette. Check the Dashed Line option and set the first dash to 3 pt and the first gap to 3 pt.

**5** As they are, the crop marks will crop exactly at the card's border, as shown here. In most cases, you will not be able to make such a clean cut by hand, and a white fringe may appear around the card if you are using white paper. (The color of the fringe depends on the color of the paper used, of course.) To avoid fringing, let's expand the background of the card on all sides so that it extends beyond the crop marks. This will allow you some room for error when you cut out the printed card.

**6** Selecting the white background of the card, hold down the [Shift] key and select the yellow background, as well.

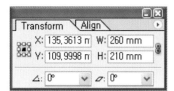

7 Go to the Transform palette and check that the Reference Point is set to the mid point ( ). Then set W to 260 mm and H to 210 mm.

8 The card's background now extends 5 mm beyond the crop marks.

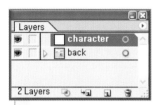

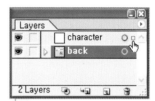

9 Let's move some of the objects to other layers. Go to the Layers palette and double-click on the Layer 1 layer to rename it **back**. Holding down the [Alt] key, press the Create New Layer icon ( ) to open the Layer Options dialog box. Type in **character** for the name and click [OK].

10 Select the Selection tool ( ) and then, holding down the [Shift] key, select the snow, the Merry Christmas text, and the Santa piggy. Click on the selection color mark ( ) of the back layer and drag it onto the character layer as shown.

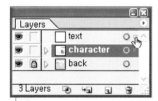

11 Lock the back layer by clicking on the Toggles Lock box ( ). Holding down the [Alt] key, click on the Create New Layer icon ( ) to open the Layer Options dialog box. Name the layer **text** and click [OK]. Holding down the [Shift] key, click on the Santa piggy to deselect it. Then click on selection color mark of the character layer and drag the text and snow objects onto the text layer, as shown above.

12 Holding down the [Alt] key, click on the Create New Layer icon ( ) and type in **snow** for the name, then click [OK]. Holding down the [Shift] key, click on the text object so that it is no longer selected.

13 Click on the selection color mark (▢) of the text layer and drag it onto the snow layer. Click on the Toggles Lock box (🔒) of the snow layer to lock it.

14 Select the Santa piggy using the Selection tool (▶) and then double-click on the Selection tool in the toolbox. When the Move dialog box appears, set Horizontal to 15 mm, Vertical to 75 mm, and click [Copy].

15 Let's make the Santa piggy copy smaller to create a sense of distance. Double-click on the Scale tool (⬚) in the toolbox. When the Scale dialog box appears, check the Uniform option and enter 30% to scale down the object. Click [OK].

16 Let's flip the Santa piggy copy. Double-click on the Reflect tool (⬚) in the toolbox and check the Vertical option in the Reflect dialog box.

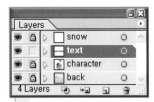

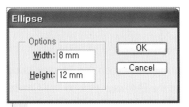

17 Let's embellish the text with holly leaves. Lock the character layer and select the text layer.

18 In the Color palette, check that the Fill color swatch is selected and enter C: 100%, M: 10%, Y: 60%. Then select the Ellipse tool (⬚) from the toolbox and click on the artboard. When the Ellipse dialog box appears, set the Width to 5 mm and the Height to 7 mm. Click [OK].

19 A very small ellipse will be created. Click on the Zoom tool (🔍) and click on the ellipse a few times to zoom in on it.

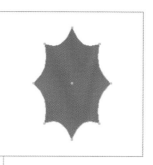

20 Select [Object] - [Path] - [Add Anchor Points] to add anchor points to the ellipse. Choose [Filter] - [Distort] - [Pucker & Bloat]. Check that you select the Distort submenu farther up in the Filter menu. (The Distort submenu farther down the Filter menu does not contain the Pucker & Bloat command.) In the Pucker & Bloat dialog box, set Pucker to -18%. This will turn the ellipse into the shape of a holly leaf.

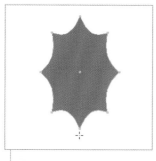

21 Let's copy the leaf and rotate the copy. Selecting the Rotate tool (🔄) from the toolbox, click on the bottom tip of the leaf. This will set a new reference point for the leaf. Release your mouse.

22 Click and drag the leaf counterclockwise. Then, holding down the [Alt] key, drag farther left to make a copy.

23 Repeat the previous step to create a total of four leaves.

24 With the fourth leaf selected, choose the Scale tool (🔲) from the toolbox. Click on the fourth leaf and drag towards the reference point. This will make the leaf smaller.

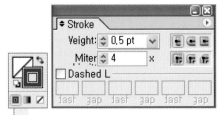

25 Holding down the [Ctrl] key to change the tool to a Selection tool (▨), select the third leaf. Click on the uppermost tip to reset the reference point. Click and drag towards the reference point to make the leaf smaller. Press [Shift]-[Ctrl]-[A] to deselect the leaf.

26 In the toolbox, check that the Fill color swatch is selected and click on the None icon to set no fill color. Activate the Stroke color swatch and set the stroke color to C: 100%, M: 30%, Y: 100%, K: 10%. Go to the Stroke palette and set the stroke weight to 0.5 pt.

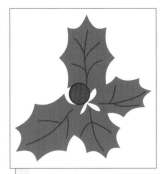

27 Use the Pencil tool (▨) to draw the leaf veins. Using the Selection tool (▨) with the [Shift] key pressed, select all four leaves (and their veins) and then press [Ctrl]-[G] to group them together.

28 Holding down the [Shift] key, drag the Ellipse tool (▨) over the center of the leaves to draw a circle. Set the stroke color (▨) to C: 30%, M: 85%, Y: 100%, K: 25% in the Color palette and check that the stroke weight is 0.5 pt in the Stroke palette. In the Color palette, set the fill color (▨) to C: 17%, M: 100%, Y: 100%. Press [Shift]-[Ctrl]-[A] to deselect.

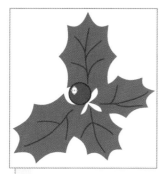

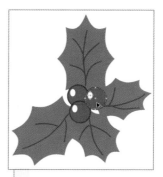

29 In the toolbox, click on the Default Fill and Stroke icon (▣) to set the fill color to white. Next, select the Stroke color swatch and set it to None (▱). Draw an oval inside the red circle to create a highlight. Select both the circle and oval and press [Ctrl]-[G] to group them together.

30 Holding down the [Alt] key, use the Selection tool (▶) to drag the red circle to make a copy. Create another copy. Selecting the holly leaves and the berries, press [Ctrl]-[G] to group them together.

31 Go to the Zoom pop-up menu at the bottom-left of the screen and select Fit on Screen to zoom out and view the entire image. Move the holly leaves and berries to the Merry Christmas text area as shown above. This completes the Christmas card.

*Exercise*

# 2 Completing a Fashion Illustration

In this section, you will complete a fashion illustration. You will be learning new commands such as the Collect in New Layer command. You'll also learn the keystrokes for transforming pattern fills without changing the shape of the fill. You will also practice using clipping masks and applying various transformations.

**Start File**
  \Sample\Chapter05\model.ai

**Final File**
  \Sample\Chapter05\model_fin.ai

Original Image

Final Image

1  Open the model.ai file. You can see from the Layers palette that this illustration contains a number of layers.

2  There are quite a few layers in this file, so let's combine a few to make things less complicated. Select the back layer in the Layers palette. Holding down the [Shift] key, select the stair-1 and stair-2 layers.

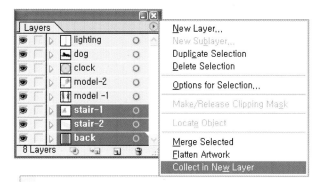

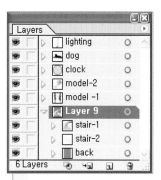

3 Clicking the triangle button (▸) in the Layers palette to open the pop-up menu, choose [Collect in New Layer] to move the staircase and background objects to a new layer.

4 Click on the triangle icon to the left of the new Layer 9 layer. You will see that the stair and back layers have been moved to Layer 9.

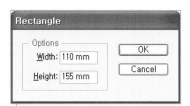

5 Double-click on the Layer 9 layer and change the layer name to **background**. Click [OK]. Let's create a layer mask to hide the jagged edges on the right of the staircase. With Layer 9 selected, choose the Rectangle tool (▭) from the toolbox and click on the illustration. When the Rectangle dialog box appears, set the Width to 110 mm and the Height to 155 mm and click [OK]. A rectangle with these dimensions will be drawn. Since this rectangle will be used as a mask, you do not need to worry about the rectangle's fill or stroke colors.

6 Go to the Zoom pop-up menu at the bottom-left of the screen and select Fit on Screen to zoom out and view the entire image. Using the Selection tool (▸), move the rectangle to the position as shown.

7 Click on the Make/Release Clipping Mask icon (⬛) at the bottom of the Layers palette. All of the objects outside the rectangle, except for the dog, are hidden by the rectangle clipping mask. The dog is unaffected because the dog layer is not in the background layer. In the Layers palette, the rectangle mask is represented by a <Clipping Path> sublayer located right at the top of the background layer.

8 Click on the triangle icon (▶) to the left of the background layer to close the layer. Next, click on the Toggles Lock box to lock the background layer. Let's edit the pattern on the left model's dress, as well as her bouquet. Select the Zoom tool (🔍) and click on the left model to zoom in. Selecting the Selection tool (▶) from the toolbox, click on her dress. To change the horizontal stripes on her dress to vertical stripes, double-click on the Rotate tool (↻). When the Rotate dialog box appears, set the Angle to 90°, uncheck the Objects option, and check the Patterns option. This will rotate the pattern 90° counterclockwise.

9 Let's edit the line pattern on the bouquet wrapper. Use the Selection tool (▶) and, holding down the [Shift] key, select the lines on the wrapper. Choose the Scale tool (🔲). Holding down the [~] and [Shift] keys, click and drag towards the reference point. The [~] key is used for transforming patterns while the [Shift] key constrains the movement of the tool while dragging.

10 Release the mouse first before releasing the keystrokes to snap the line objects' border back to its original size. There are now more lines on the bouquet wrapper.

11 Now, select the Rotate tool (⟳) from the toolbox and, holding down both the [Shift] and [~] keys, click and drag roughly 45° in the counterclockwise direction. This will rotate the lines and create diagonal line patterns.

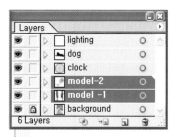

12 Let's merge the model-1 and model-2 layers in the Layers palette. When layers are merged, the new merged layer takes the name of last layer clicked. We want to keep the model-1 name, so select the model-2 layer and then, holding down the [Shift] key, select the model-1 layer.

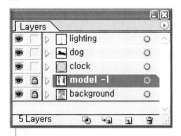

13 Click on the triangle button (▶) in the Layers palette to open the pop-up menu and apply [Merge Selected]. The two layers will be merged into the model-1 layer. Click on the Toggles Lock box to lock the layer.

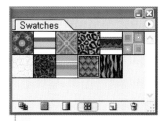

14 Let's create a clock. Use the Selection tool (▸) to select the orange circle at the top of the illustration. Check that the Fill color swatch is activated in the toolbox. Click on the Show Pattern Swatches icon (▦) in the Swatches palette. Click on the triangle icon (▶) and select [Large Thumbnail View] from the pop-up menu.

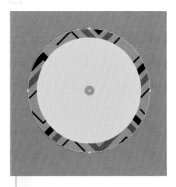

15 Choose the Zigzag Diamond pattern (▦) and then press [Ctrl]-[R] to show the rulers. Select the Zoom tool (🔍) and click on the clock to zoom in on it.

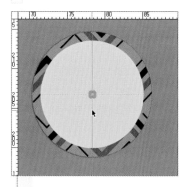

16 Select the small orange circle in the center of the clock. Click and drag a guideline from the horizontal ruler and position the guideline to cut through the clock's center point. Repeat this step using the vertical ruler to create a vertical guideline. Press [Shift]-[Ctrl]-[A] to deselect.

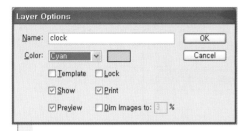

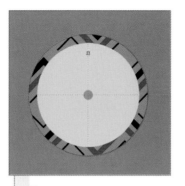

[17] Because both the clock face and the selection color mark for the clock layer are yellow, it will be hard to see the selection border for the objects on the clock face when they are selected. Let's change the color of the selection color mark for the clock layer before we start working on the clock face. Double-click on the Clock layer. In the Layer Options dialog box, set the color to Cyan or any other color that will stand out against a yellow background.

[18] In the Color palette, check that the CMYK mode is selected. If it is not, click on the CMYK icon to convert. Set the fill color (▦) to C: 20%, M: 100%, Y: 15%. Holding down the [Shift] key, use the Ellipse tool (◯) to draw a small circle at the 12 o'clock position.

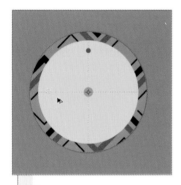

[19] Select the Rotate tool (◯) and click in the center of the clock to set a new reference point. To rotate and copy at the same time, hold down the [Alt]-[Shift] keys and rotate the object 90° counterclockwise. Press [Ctrl]-[D] twice to rotate and copy two more iterations.

[20] To make the hands of the clock, go to the toolbox and double-click on the Stroke color swatch (▣). In the Color Picker dialog box, enter C: 90%, Y: 100%. Select the Line tool (◻) and draw the clock hands as shown above. Selecting the center circle, press [Ctrl]-[Shift]-[]] to bring it to the front.

21 Select Fit on Screen in the Zoom pop-up menu to see the entire image. Look for the candle object and zoom in on it using the Zoom tool ( ). Let's complete the image by reflecting and copying the candle. Use the Group Selection tool ( ) to select only the flame. Next, select the Scale tool ( ).

22 Click at the base of the flame to set a new reference point. Then click and drag towards the reference point while holding down the [Alt]-[Shift] keys. This creates a scaled down copy of the flame.

23 In the toolbox, set the stroke color ( ) to None and the fill color ( ) to yellow.

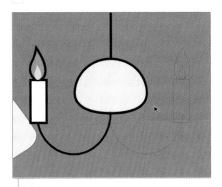

24 Select the Group Selection tool ( ) and double-click on the flame to select the entire group of objects. Choose the Reflect tool ( ) and click on the right anchor point of the candle holder to set a new reference point. Then, holding down [Alt]-[Shift], click and drag the group clockwise to create a mirror copy, as shown above.

25 The illustration is now completed.

**Chapter** | 6

# Creating and Editing Text

Illustrator CS comes with a variety of tools for entering and editing type. You can place text on a path, align text vertically, and even add text inside an object. Illustrator now supports OpenType fonts for increased cross-platform compatibillity, and you can now preview typefaces in the Font menu. The Text Wrap feature, which wraps text around objects, has been improved in this version of Illustrator. It is also now easier to set up and cancel text field threads. These improvements, coupled with Illustrator's ability to apply artistic special effects to text, provide ample creative inspiration for anyone with a taste for type.

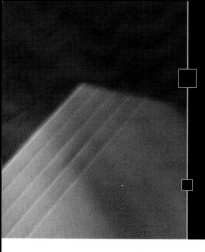

# Type Tool Features

I n this chapter, you will learn about the type tools that allow you to create and edit text. We'll also cover both the Character and Paragraph palettes, and review techniques for creatively combining text with paths and shapes. Finally, we'll introduce the Envelope Distort filter, which can be used to distort text for artistic effect.

## Type Tools

There are six different type tools in the toolbox. The Type tool and Vertical Type tool allow you to enter text horizontally or vertically. The Area Type tool and the Vertical Area Type tool confine text within the path of an object, while the Type on a Path tool and the Vertical Type on a Path tool place text along a path. Let's take a closer look at each of these tools.

### Type Tool (T) and Vertical Type Tool (T)

When you select the Type tool, the mouse pointer will change to an I-beam (I). This is also called a text cursor. Clicking the Type tool (T) on the work space will create a text insertion point using the bottom line of the text cursor (I) as the baseline for any entered text.

▲Click the Type tool on the image and enter some text. To move to the next line, hit the [Enter] key.

Along with scientifically sensible and green marketing activities, Household Goods Division applies the latest technology in developing environment-friendly products, thereby enriching the customers' lives.

▲With the Type tool selected, drag out a text field and enter some text. The text will be confined to the text field and there is no need to hit the [Enter] key to move to the next line.

The Vertical Type tool (T) is used in the same way as the Type tool, except that it enters text vertically.

▲Use the Vertical Type tool to enter vertical text.

## Area Type Tool (T) and Vertical Area Type Tool (T)

The Area Type and Vertical Area Type tools are used to insert text within the fill area of an object. (The Type tool and Vertical Type tool can also be used for this purpose.) Most objects with an enclosed path can be used as a text field for these tools. However, compound shapes and shapes to which a clipping mask has been applied cannot be used as text fields. In order to use these objects, you need to first Expand merged objects or undo any interfering clipping masks.

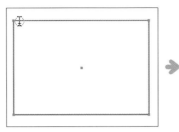

▲Create an enclosed path and click the Area Type tool on the path to change it into a text field. Notice that this will remove the fill and stroke attributes of the path. Enter some text.

▲The text will be confined within the object area. If the text exceeds the boundaries of the text field, a red square symbol with a cross inside (⊞) will appear at the bottom-right side of the text field.

The Vertical Area Type tool (T) is used in the same way as the Area Type tool, except that it enters text vertically.

<< note

### Using the Type Tool As the Area Type Tool

With the Type tool (T) selected, place the cursor over a closed path until the cursor changes to the Area Type cursor (I). Click to enter text just like the Area Type tool.

## Type on a Path Tool (⟋) and Vertical Type on a Path Tool (⟍)

The Type on a path and Vertical Type on a Path tools are used for entering text along an open path. (The Type tool and Vertical Type tool can also be used for this purpose.) Simply click either tool along an open path to begin entering text. The Vertical Type on a Path tool works similarly to the Type on a Path tool, except–as you might expect–it enters text vertically.

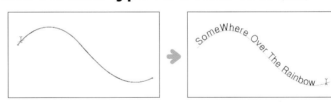

▲Create an open path and click on it with the Type on a Path tool. Notice that the path loses its line and fill attributes.

▲Enter some text. The text will follow the path.

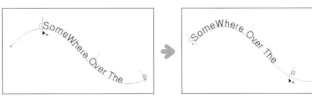

▲When the Selection tool is used to select the path, square symbols will appear on both ends and a bracket will appear in the middle. Dragging the square symbols (ports) will adjust the position of the text on the path.

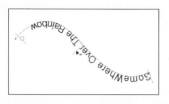

◄With the path selected, click and drag the middle bracket to flip the text. You can hold down the [Ctrl] key while dragging the bracket to adjust the position of the text without flipping it over.

&lt;&lt; note

## Using the Type Tool As the Type on a Path Tool

With the Type tool (⊤) selected, place the cursor over a path until the cursor changes to the Type on a Path tool cursor (ɪ̺). Click to enter text just like the Type on a Path tool.

&lt;&lt; note

## Importing or Exporting Text Files

Using one of the type tools, click on the work space or a text field and select [File] - [Place] to import an external text file. To export text, select the text and choose [File] - [Export].

&lt;&lt; note

## Updating Text in Files from Previous Versions of Illustrator

When you use Illustrator CS to open a file from a previous version of the program, you will see a message asking you to update the file. Select [Update] to automatically update text properties, line spacing, row spacing, and hyphenation. If you click [OK] without updating, you will not be able to edit the text.

▲The pre-existing text is updated for use in Illustrator CS.

Another warning will display once you attempt to edit any updated text. Click [Update] to replace the old text with updated text. Click [Copy Text Object] to update the text while preserving the original text layout for reference. If you select this button, you will see the original text field in grey below the new, updated text field.

When you are done editing, and have no further use for the original text field, press [Ctrl]-[2] to unlock it so that it can be deleted.

▲By clicking [Copy Text Object], the original text field is preserved (in grey) for reference.

## Editing Text

Text can be edited in many ways. You can change text properties such as font type, color, and size, or change paragraph properties such as text alignment and spacing. The first step in editing text is, of course, selecting it. We'll start by reviewing this process.

## Selecting Text

Selecting text in Illustrator is similar to selecting text in most word processors. With one of the type tools selected, click and drag to select the desired text. Alternatively, hold down the [Shift] key and use the arrow keys to make partial selections within a text block. Double-clicking a word selects the entire word, while triple-clicking selects the entire line or text block. You can also use the [Ctrl]-[A] shortcut to select all of the text within a block.

## Editing Text Properties

Text properties such as the font type or character spacing can be changed using the Type menu. The Character, Swatches, and Color palettes also provide options for editing text properties. Right-clicking selected text will produce a shortcut menu that can also be used to modify type settings.

### Changing Text Color

By default, the text color is black. To change the text color, highlight the desired text and choose a new color from the Swatches or Color palettes.

▲Selecting a New Text Color in the Swatches Palette

### Changing Font Type and Size

To change the font type, select the desired text and choose [Type] - [Font] from the menu bar. To change the font size, go to [Type] - [Size]. A faster approach is to right-click on the highlighted text and select a font or font size from the shortcut menu.

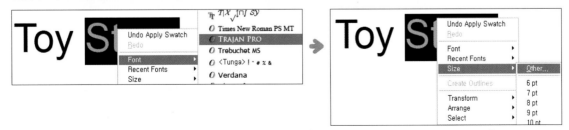

▲Using the Shortcut Menu to Select a New Font Type and Size

**215**

When very small font sizes are used, the screen resolution will not be high enough to display the text accurately. Instead of the actual letters, you will see a grayed out area representing the text on the screen. By default, the Greeking value is set to 6 points so that text smaller than 6 points will be grayed out on screen. You can adjust the Greeking value by selecting [Edit] - [Preferences] - [Type & Auto Tracing]. If you have a lengthy document and the Greeking value is set too low, it can increase the time required to preview your document.

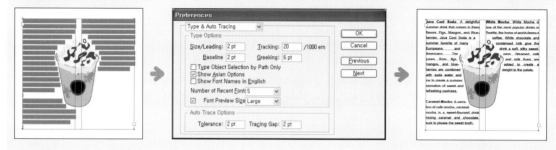

You can adjust the size of the typefaces displayed in the Font submenu by selecting [Edit] - [Preferences] - [Type & Auto Tracing] - [Font Preview Size].

## Character Palette

The Character palette allows you to change text attributes such as font face, font size, line spacing, and row spacing. If the palette is not displayed, choose [Window] - [Type] - [Character Palette] to bring it up.

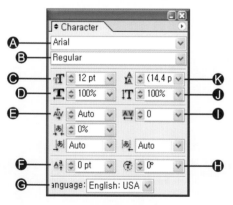

**Ⓐ Font**: Selects the font.

**Ⓑ Font Style**: Selects the font style for the selected font. The selections can include Regular, Italic, Bold, and numerous other possibilities that depend on the selected font.

**Ⓒ Font Size**: Selects the font size. This is the same as using the [Type] - [Size] method.

**Ⓓ Horizontal Scale**: Shows the width of the text as a percentage.

216

**ⓔ Kerning**: Kerning refers to the space between specific pairs of letters. The spacing between certain character pairs, such as LA, P., To, Tr, Ta, Tu, Te, Ty, Wa, WA, We, Wo, Ya, and Yo, needs to be set differently because the shapes of these letters create spacing problems when paired together. In Illustrator CS, such character pairs have built-in kerning values to automatically prevent improper spacing. If you need to change the default kerning, adjust the kerning options as needed. If multiple typefaces or font sizes are adjacent to each other, be sure to select the Optical option to kern the character pairs based on their shapes and not by their pre-defined spacing values.

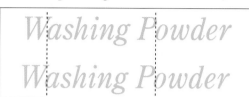

▲Auto Kerning (Above) and Optical Kerning (Below)

**ⓕ Baseline Shift**: A negative value will enter text below the baseline, and a positive value will enter text above the baseline.

▲A negative Baseline Shift value moves "4" below the baseline while a positive value moves "5" above the baseline.

**ⓖ Language**: Select the language dictionary used for spell checking and hyphenation. You can set the language either in the Character palette or by choosing [Edit] - [Preferences] - [Hyphenation].

**ⓗ Character Rotation**: You can rotate either the entire text field or a specific selection. This option is useful when using special symbols and numbers in vertical Asian lettering.

**ⓘ Tracking**: Tracking refers to the spacing between characters. A negative value reduces the spacing and a positive value increases the spacing.

**ⓙ Vertical Scale**: Shows the height of the text as a percentage.

**ⓚ Leading**: Leading refers to the spacing between the baselines of each line of text. The default setting is Auto. To set a leading value equal to the font size, double-click on the Leading icon (🄰).

<< tip

## Font Size and Character Spacing Shortcut Keys

The character spacing and font size shortcut keys are great for making incremental adjustments to text. Here are the shortcut keys that you can use to repeat font-related tasks that you often use.

- *Leading*: [Alt]-[ ↑ ] or [Alt]-[ ↓ ]
- *Kerning*: [Ctrl]-[Alt]-[→] or [Ctrl]-[Alt]-[←]
- *Baseline Shift*: [Alt]-[Shift]-[ ↑ ] or [Alt]-[Shift]-[ ↓ ]
- *Font Size*: To increase the font size by 2 points, highlight the text and press [Ctrl]-[Shift]-[>]. Conversely, pressing [Ctrl]-[Shift]-[<] decreases the font size by two points.

## Duplicating Text Properties

You can use the Eyedropper tool (![eyedropper icon]) and the Paint Bucket tool (![paint bucket icon]) to duplicate text properties such as font type, size, and color easily. With text selected, clicking on another text object with the Eyedropper tool samples and applies the text's properties to the original selection. With your source text still selected, select the Paint Bucket tool (![paint bucket icon]) and click on another piece of text to transfer your source text's properties. Be careful not to use the Eyedropper tool when transferring properties in this direction, as this will copy the properties from the clicked text to your selected text.

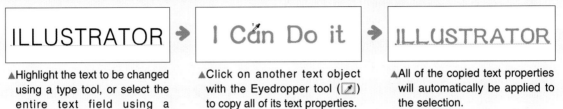

▲Highlight the text to be changed using a type tool, or select the entire text field using a selection tool.

▲Click on another text object with the Eyedropper tool (![eyedropper icon]) to copy all of its text properties.

▲All of the copied text properties will automatically be applied to the selection.

To continue applying the copied text properties to other text in your artwork, you can use the Paint Bucket tool in three ways.

a. With your source text still selected, select the Paint Bucket tool (![paint bucket icon]) and click on another piece of text to transfer your source text's properties. Be careful not to use the Eyedropper tool (![eyedropper icon]), as this will copy the properties from the clicked text to your selected text.

b. To apply text properties from one object to another without altering the clicked object's fill or stroke properties, first select the text to be changed. This will change the color of the Fill and Stroke boxes in the toolbox to the fill and stroke colors of the text. Now select the Paint Bucket tool (![paint bucket icon]) and click on the text to be changed.

c. To apply a modified set of text properties, select the Selection tool (![selection tool icon]) in the toolbox and click on an empty space in the artboard to deselect all. Change the text property settings to your liking, then click on the text to which you'd like these settings applied.

# OpenType Palette

The OpenType palette is used for modifying OpenType fonts. OpenType fonts are compatible across Windows and Macintosh operating systems and they support a wide range of glyphs and characters. In addition, some OpenType fonts contain ligatures that can be activated in Illustrator to replace certain characters.

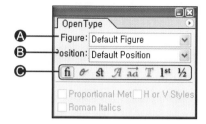

**Ⓐ Figure**: Selects the character shape setting.

**Ⓑ Position**: Selects the character position setting.

**Ⓒ Ligatures**: Ligatures are character combinations that are designed as a single unit. Selecting one of the ligature options replaces specific character combinations with their ligature counterparts.

[fi]: Most OpenType fonts include the Standard Ligatures option, which replaces character combinations such as fi, fl, ff, ffi, and ffl.

Original (Above) and Standard (Below) Ligatures ▶

[∂]: The Contextual Alternates setting creates connections between characters so that the text looks more like handwriting.

[st]: Some fonts contain optional ligatures (in addition to the standard ligatures) for letter pairs such as ct, ft, and st. Selecting the Discretionary Ligatures option will replace these letter pairs with their ligature counterparts.

Original (Above) and Discretionary (Below) Ligatures ▶

[𝒜]: The Swash option creates characters with exaggerated flourishes.

Original (Above) and Swash (Below) ▶

[aa]: The Stylistic Alternates option creates stylish-looking characters.

[T]: Select the Titling Alternates option when using large characters; for example, when designing titles.

[1st]: The Ordinals option sets the letters found in ordinal numbers—such as 1st, 2nd, and 3rd—to superscript.

Original (Above) and Ordinals (Below) ▶

[½]: Select the Fractions option to turn numbers separated by a slash into the fractions format. For example, "1/4" will be turned into "$\frac{1}{4}$".

# Editing Paragraph Properties

The Paragraph palette is used to edit paragraph properties such as alignment, indentation, and spacing. To edit a single paragraph, place the cursor in the desired paragraph and select options from the Paragraph palette. You can apply the options to more than one paragraph by selecting multiple paragraphs or entire text fields.

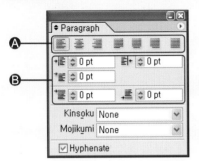

**<< note**

**Aligning and Justifying Text**

You can choose to align text along the sides or center of a paragraph field using the Alignment options. If you want to align your text along both sides of a paragraph field, choose from one of the Justify options.

**Ⓐ Alignment**

≣: Left-align.

≣: Center-align.

≣: Right-align.

≣: Justify Left. Text is justified and the final line of text is left-aligned.

≣: Justify Center. Text is justified and the final line of text is centered.

≣: Justify Right. Text is justified and the final line of text is right-aligned.

≣: Justify All. Text is justified, including the final line of text.

▲Left-Align

▲Center-Align

▲Right-Align

▲Justify Left

▲Justify Center

▲Justify Right

▲Justify All

**Ⓑ Indent**

≣: Left Indent. Moves the paragraph in from the left.

≣: Right Indent. Moves the paragraph in from the right.

≣: First Line Left Indent (units = pt). Moves the first line of the paragraph inwards from the left.

≣: Space Before Paragraph. Adds space before the start of the paragraph.

≣: Space After Paragraph. Adds space after the paragraph ends.

Hyphenate: Activates hyphenation of text when a Justify option is used.

<< tip
## Paragraph Shortcut Keys

The paragraph shortcut keys let you align text in a paragraph quickly.
- *Paragraph Alignment (left, center, right)*: [Ctrl]-[Shift]-[L], [Ctrl]-[Shift]-[R], [Ctrl]-[Shift]-[C]
- *Justify All*: [Ctrl]-[Shift]-[J]

## Every-line and Single Line Composers

The Every-line Composer is found in the Paragraph palette's pop-up menu. When the command is selected, it automatically evens out the spacing between words and letters, and it controls line breaks to minimize hyphenation while maintaining consistent line lengths.

The Single-line Composer command, which is also found in the pop-up menu, performs the same function, but does it line-by-line. When the Single-line Composer is used, only the text in the selected line is adjusted. Both of these commands work with the area type tools and the type on a path tools.

◀Using the Every-line Composer (Left) and the Single-line Composer (Right)

## Wrap Text

When creating advanced layouts, you might need to arrange text so that it flows around an object or image. This technique is called text wrapping. Place the object on top of the text and, with the object selected, select [Object] - [Text Wrap] - [Make Text Wrap]. For this technique to work, you have to make sure that the object is on top of the text. If the object is behind the text, select the object, right-click, and select Bring to Front. Adjusting the Offset value will determine the spacing between the image and the surrounding text. You can remove the text wrap with [Object] - [Text Wrap] - [Release Text Wrap].

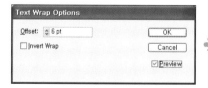

◀Place the image on top of the text and select [Object] - [Text Wrap] - [Make Text Wrap].

**221**

## Area Type Options

If text is entered using one of the area type tools, you can change text and paragraph properties by selecting [Type] - [Area Type Options]. You can use this option to divide the text into rows or columns and to add spacing. 'Number' refers to the number of type areas, 'Span' refers to the overall length of the field, and 'Gutter' refers to the space between areas.

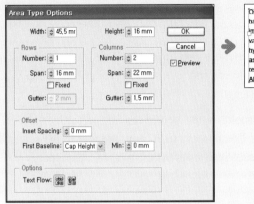

▲Select the text field and choose [Type] - [Area Type Options]. The settings shown create two columns.

To create spacing around the text field, increase the Inset Spacing value in the Offset area of the dialog box. There are five First Baseline styles available.

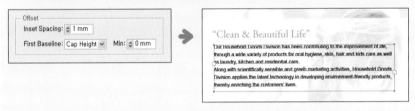

## Editing Text Fields

After text has been entered, clicking on one of the selection tools or pressing the [Ctrl]-[Enter] shortcut will exit the text editing mode. The text field will then be selected, making it possible to edit the text field's position and shape. To return to text editing mode, double-click on the text with one of the selection tools, or click once on the text with one of the type tools.

◄Click on the Selection tool (🔲) in the toolbox to leave text editing mode and select the text field. When a text field is selected, the text field's bounding box will appear.

## Showing or Hiding a Bounding Box

The bounding box is necessary for manipulating the shape of the text field. If the bounding box does not appear, select the text field with the Selection tool (🔲) and select [View] - [Show Bounding Box] to display the bounding box. To hide a bounding box, select [View] - [Hide Bounding Box].

As with other shapes created in Illustrator, you can use the Selection tool, Direct Selection tool (⬛), or Group Selection tool (⬛) to move a text field. You can also use the Direct Selection tool, Rotate tool (⬛), Shear tool (⬛), or Scale tool (⬛) to change the shape or position of the text field.

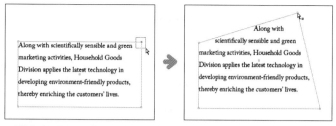

▲With the Direct Selection tool selected, click and drag a handle on the bounding box. This changes the shape of the text field and the text inside the field will be re-distributed to fit the new dimensions.

## Threading Text Between Objects

If you enter more text than can fit inside a text field, you can change the size of the field using the Direct Selection tool (⬛). You can also make the additional text flow into another text field; this is called threading text. To thread or unthread overflowing text, you need to work with the in and out ports of a text field. These ports are only found in text fields created using the area type or type on a path tools. When the ports are empty (□), it means that all the text is shown and the text field is not threaded. If the out port shows a red cross (⊞), the text field contains overflow text that is not shown. If the out port shows an arrow sign (⬛), the text is threaded to another text field.

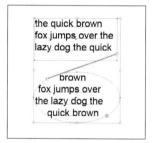

▲Threaded Text Fields

## Threading Text

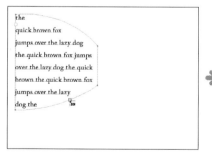

▲To thread overflowing text, select the text field and click on the out port (⬛) with a selection tool. In this case, the out port is clicked.

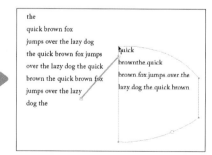

▲When the cursor changes to the loaded text icon (⬛), click on a point on the artboard where you want the overflow text to start. Notice that the new text field is in the same shape and size of the original text field.

## Breaking Text Threads

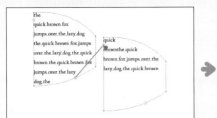

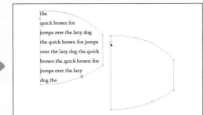

▲There are two ways to break a thread between text fields. The easiest way is to double-click on the port where you want to break the link. The second method, as shown here, is to click on a port once and mouse over the port on the other side of the thread. When your cursor turns into the unthread icon (), click on the port to break the link.

▲After the thread is broken, the red cross in the out port of the first text field indicates that there is overflow text.

&lt;&lt; tip

### Show/Hide Text Threads

To show or hide text threads in the work space, select [View] - [Show Text Threads].

## Threading Text to an Existing Object

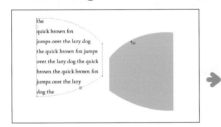

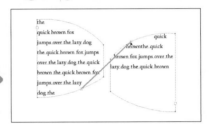

▲To thread text to a text field of a different shape or size, create the objects first and then enter the text in one of the objects. When the text overflows, click on the out port (▤). You should see your cursor turn into the loaded text icon.

▲Click on the other object to thread the text. Click on the path of the second object to thread the contents together.

## Reversing the Thread Flow

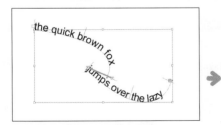

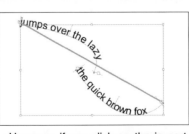

▲In most cases, you will click on the out port when threading text to a new text field. As shown here, the text will start in the original text field and flow to the new text field.

▲However, if you click on the in port when threading text to a new text field, the text will flow differently. The text will start in the new text field and flow back to the original text field.

## Text Effects

If you want to apply gradients, blends, distortions, or other effects to your text, you'll need to use the Create Outlines feature. Use the Selection tool ( ) to select the text. When the baseline appears, choose [Type] - [Create Outlines]. The text will be converted into an object.

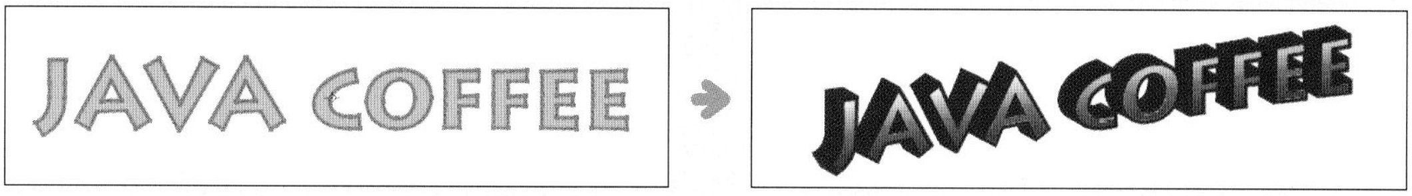


▲Select [Create Outlines], then apply gradients and other effects.

If the text is entered using the Type on a Path tool ( ), you can apply five preset effects from the [Type] - [Type on a Path] submenu. Selecting the Type on a Path Options command opens up a dialog box where you can select the effects, as well as choose options for Align to Path, Spacing, and Flip.

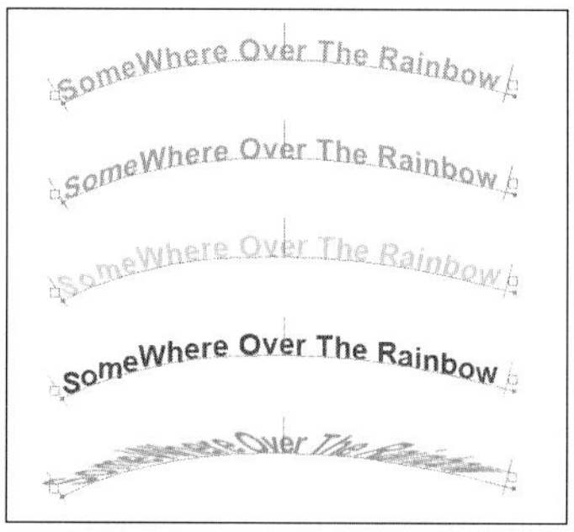


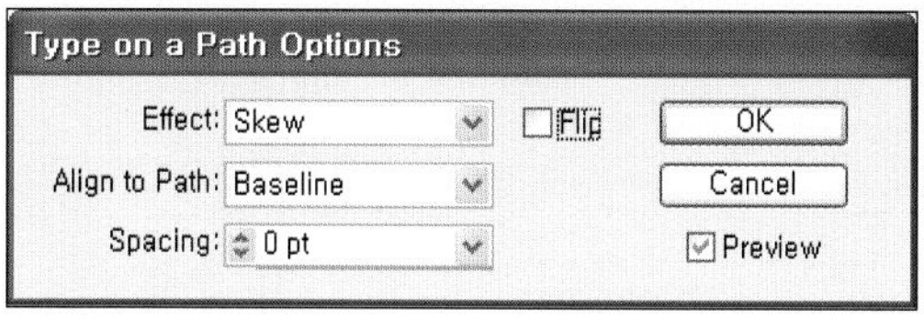


▲Type Effects (from Top to Bottom): Rainbow, Skew, 3D Ribbon, Stair Step, and Gravity

## Envelope Distort

The Envelope Distort command is used to distort an object by resizing it to fit into a different shape or size. This command can be applied to text, bitmap images, brushes, symbols, and other objects. In edit mode, you can edit both the object and the Envelope effect.

To get started, select the object that you want to distort and choose [Object] - [Envelope Distort] - [Make with Warp]. You can choose from fifteen Style options. Once you've applied an envelope, choose [Object] - [Envelope Distort] - [Edit Contents] to edit the object and use [Object] - [Envelope Distort] - [Edit Envelope] to edit the envelope effect.

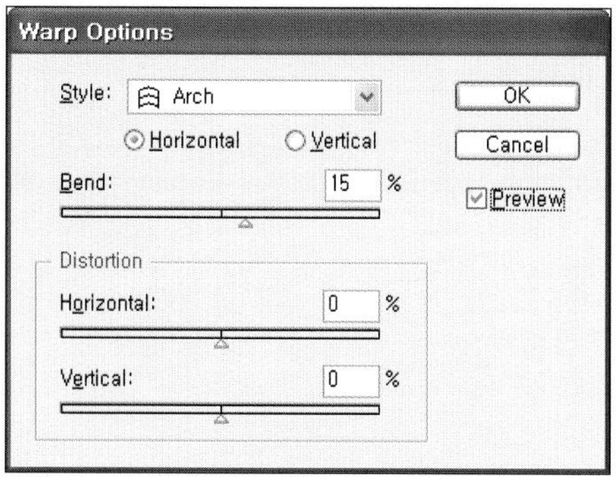


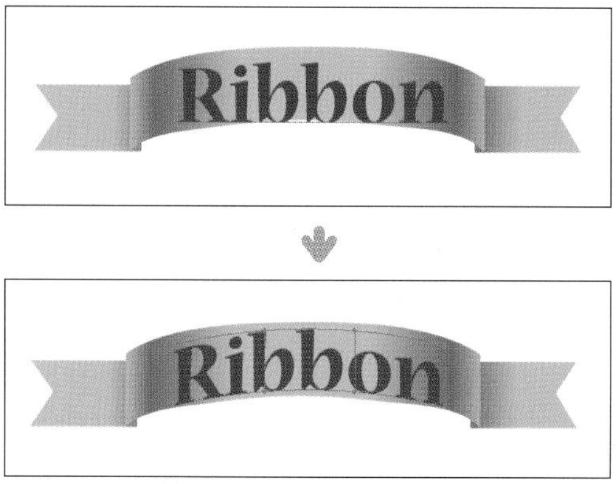


▲Select the text. In the Make with Warp dialog box, choose [Arch] and set the Bend to 15% horizontal.

## Envelope Distort Using a Mesh

You can distort an object with a mesh by choosing [Object] - [Envelope Distort] - [Make with Mesh]. This option creates a grid that allows you to create detailed or dynamic distortions. You can simply apply a mesh distortion, or apply a warp distortion and then apply a mesh distortion.

Meshed objects can be edited using the Direct Selection tool ([icon]). [Object] - [Envelope Distort] - [Release] is used to separate the original object from the mesh object. The Mesh Selection tool ([icon]) can also be used to edit mesh points and mesh handles.

  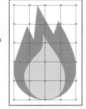 

▲Select the object to be distorted. Select [Make with Mesh] and create a 5x4 (5 rows and 4 columns) mesh.

▲Use the Direct Selection tool to adjust the mesh points and handles, thus warping the original object.

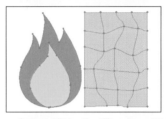

▲Select [Object] - [Envelope Distort] - [Release] to undo the envelope effect.

## Envelope Distort Using a 'Top Object' Path

The [Object] - [Envelope Distort] - [Make with Top Object] feature uses a second object as an envelope to distort another object. This feature is edited in the same way as the other envelope effects. Similar to the mesh envelope, choose [Object] - [Envelope Distort] - [Expand] to remove the envelope selection frame so that the object can be used as a normal object again.

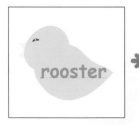   

▲We'll apply a top object mesh to the 'rooster' text.

▲Create a target object on top of the object to be enveloped.

▲Select both the object to be enveloped and the object that will be used as the envelope. Choose [Make with Top Object].

▲Use [Expand] to turn the object's selection frame back from the envelope to the object's shape.

# Creating a Page Layout

In this exercise, you will lay out a document using both text and images. You will be applying a filter to the background, then format the document to improve its appearance. You will also use text wrapping so that the text flows around the images.

**Start Files**

\Sample\Chapter06\compilation.ai
\Sample\Chapter06\files\text.doc

**Final File**

\Sample\Chapter06\compilation_fin.ai

Original Image

Final Image

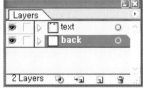

1. Open compilation.ai from the sample folder. The file has two layers—back and text.

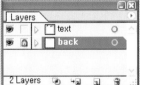

2. To add a filter to the background, use the Selection tool (⬚) to select the rectangular background object. Choose [Effect] - [SVG Filters] - [AI_Alpha_4] and click [OK]. Lock the back layer by clicking the Toggles Lock box (□) in the Layers palette. The document should look like the image shown here.

3 Let's use the Type tool (T) to add text. Use the tool to click at the top of the document, then type **Managing Time**. Press [Ctrl]-[Enter] to leave text edit mode. Make sure that the text is selected, then use the Character palette to set the Font to Adobe Caslon Pro, the Style to Semibold Italic, and the font size to 40 pt.

4 Lighten the color by setting black (K) to 75% in the Color palette.

5 Use the Area Type tool (T) to click the path of the rectangular text object. You should see a blinking text cursor indicating that the box is now a text field.

6 Choose [File] - [Place] and select the text.doc file. Click [OK] when the Microsoft Word Options dialog box appears.

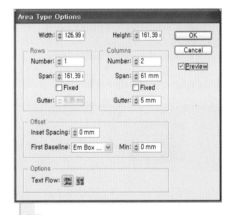

7 Press [Ctrl]-[Enter] to leave edit mode. Choose [Type] - [Area Type Options] and under Columns, enter Number: 2 and Gutter: 5. Click [OK].

<< tip

## [File] – [Place]

The Place feature is typically used to import external images into Illustrator. When the text cursor is blinking, however, you can use Place to import text from external files.

8  To add a text wrap, select the left image with the Selection tool (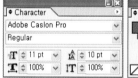). Hold down the [Shift] key and click the image on the right. Both images should be selected. Choose [Object] - [Text Wrap] - [Make Text Wrap] and set Offset to 8 pt.

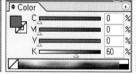

9  Select the text field with the Selection tool (▶) and, in the Character palette, set the Font to Adobe Caslon Pro, the Font Size to 11 pt, and the Leading to 10 pt.

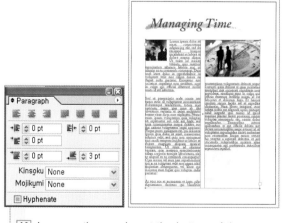

10  Increase the spacing at the bottom of the paragraph by setting the Space After Paragraph (▤) to 3 pt.

11  The exercise is now completed.

# Composing a Poster

In this exercise, you will create another document with text wrapping. You will also learn how to use character and paragraph styles.

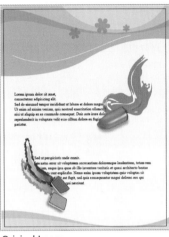

Original Image

Final Image

**Start File**

\Sample\Chapter06\compilation-2.ai

**Final File**

\Sample\Chapter06\compilation-2_fin.ai

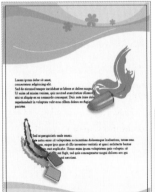

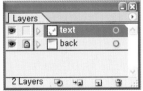

1 Open compilation-2.ai from the sample folder. The file contains a text and background layer.

2 Select the Type on a Path tool (⟋) and click the I-beam (Ⅰ) cursor on the start of the path at the top of the document. You will be entering a title along this path.

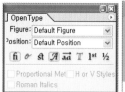

3 | Type **Spring Colors Here and Now!** and press [Ctrl]-[Enter] to leave edit mode. In the Character palette, set the Font to Minion Pro, the Style to Semibold Italic, the Font Size (T) to 27 pt, and the Leading (A) to Auto.

4 | Click the Swash icon (A) in the OpenType palette to embellish the text.

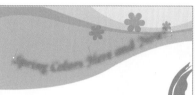

5 | Change the text color to white. Copy the text using [Ctrl]-[C] and fill it using the settings C: 17%, M: 100%, and K: 0% in the Color palette. Choose [Effect] - [Blur] - [Gaussian Blur] and set the Radius to 3. Press [Ctrl]-[F] to paste the copied text on top of the edited text.

6 | Make sure that the text is no longer selected. To enhance the flower patterns, select them by holding down the [Shift] key as you click each with the Selection tool (▶). Choose [Effect] - [Stylize] - [Outer Glow] and change the settings to Mode: Screen, Opacity: 100, Blur: 1.4, Color: White. Click [OK].

7 | To create the text wrap around the images, select both images, choose [Object] - [Text Wrap] - [Make Text Wrap] and set the Offset to 10 pt.

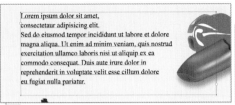

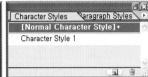

8 | Select the text field beside the lipstick image. In the Character palette, set the Font to Adobe Garamond Pro, the Style to Regular, the Font Size (🔠) to 10 pt and the Leading (🔠) to 12 pt. Save these settings by clicking the Create New Style icon (🔲) in the Character Styles palette.

9 | Double-click the top text field and select the first two rows. This is the text title.

10 | Use the Color palette to fill the text using M: 45%, Y: 80% in the Color palette. In the Character palette, set the Font to Minion Pro, the Style to Bold Italic, the Font Size (🔠) to 14 pt, and the Leading (🔠) to Auto.

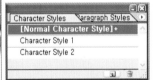

11 | Click the Create New Style icon (🔲) in the Character Styles palette to save these settings.

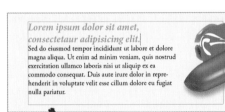

12 | Click at the end of the second row of text and, when the cursor starts blinking, set Space After Paragraph (🔳) to 3 pt in the Paragraph palette.

13 | Click the Create New Style icon (🔲) in the Paragraph Styles palette to save this paragraph style.

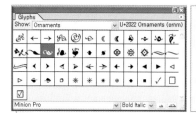

14 Place the cursor at the front of the first line and set [Type] - [Glyphs] - [Show] to Ornaments. Double-click on the glyph shown above to insert it into the poster.

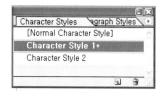

15 Press [Ctrl]-[Enter] to leave edit mode. Click the Right-Align icon (▤) in the Paragraph palette.

16 Select the text field at the bottom. The Character Styles palette shows [Normal Character Style]+. Click Character Style 1. It changes to read Character Style 1+.

<< tip

## Style Override

The + sign beside a style in the Character Style or Paragraph Style palettes indicates that there are overrides to the style. A style override is any formatting that differs from the attributes defined by the style. By default, characters automatically assume the Normal character style, while paragraphs are assigned the Normal paragraph style. Therefore, when you change the settings in the Character, OpenType, or Paragraph palettes, you create an override to the current character or paragraph style. There are several ways to remove style overrides. To clear overrides and return text to the appearance defined by the style, you can reapply the same style as you did in step 16 or use the [Clear Overrides] command.

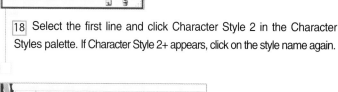

17 In order to add the same style, click on Character 1+ in the Character Styles palette.

18 Select the first line and click Character Style 2 in the Character Styles palette. If Character Style 2+ appears, click on the style name again.

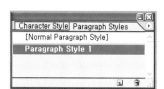

19 In the Paragraph Styles palette, click Paragraph Style 1. You may need to click the style again if Paragraph Style 1+ appears.

20 As shown, enter the same glyph you used in step 14. The image is now complete.

**233**

# 3 Emblem Design

In this exercise, you will create an emblem using the Blend feature. You will also use the Path tool to apply distortion styles.

Original Image

Final Image

**Start File**
\Sample\Chapter06\worldfair.ai

**Final File**
\Sample\Chapter06\worldfair_fin.ai

1. Open worldfair.ai from the sample folder. The file contains the text 1, earth, text 2, and character layers.

2. First, let's create the globe with the Blend tool. In the Layers palette, hold down the [Alt] key and click the eye icon (👁) next to the earth layer. Only the earth layer is visible now. Select the circle with the Selection tool (➤) and copy it with the [Ctrl]-[C] shortcut. Press [Ctrl]-[3] to hide the selected object, then paste the new object in place with [Ctrl]-[F].

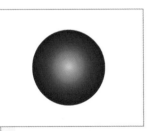

3. In the Color palette, select None for the fill color (▱) and set the stroke color (◼) to black. In the Stroke palette, set the edge thickness to 7 pt.

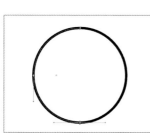

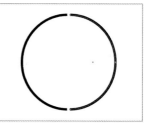

4 Select the Scissors tool (✄) and click the top and bottom of the circle to cut it in half. Select the right semicircle with the Selection tool (▶) and double-click the Selection tool in the toolbox. In the Move dialog box, set Horizontal to 3 mm. This will spread out the semicircles slightly.

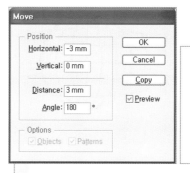

5 Double-click the Blend tool (🔧) and select a Spacing setting of Specified Steps, 5. Click [OK]. Click on the ends of each semicircle to create the blend.

6 Double-click the Group Selection tool (▶). In the Move dialog box, enter a Horizontal value of to -3 mm to move the semicircle on the right to join the other semicircle.

7 Choose [Object] - [Blend] - [Expand] to break apart the blend, then select [Object] - [Path] - [Outline Stroke]. This will change the stroke to a fill.

8 To create latitude lines, select the Line tool (◥). In the Color palette, Set the stroke color (■) to black. In the Stroke palette, set the edge thickness to 7 pt. Hold down the [Shift] key and draw two straight lines—one at the top and one at the bottom of the globe.

9　Select both lines and double-click the Blend tool (). Choose Specified Steps, 3 for the Spacing setting. Press [Ctrl]-[Alt]-[B] to apply the blend.

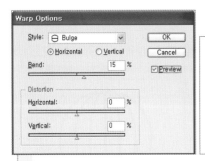  

10　Let's use the Envelope Distort command to change the shape of the horizontal lines so they look three-dimensional. Choose [Object] - [Envelope Distort] - [Make with Warp]. Select Style: Bulge, Bend: 15%. You can check the preview box to see the effect. Click [OK].

11　Choose [Object] - [Envelope Distort] - [Expand] to break apart the blend. Select [Object] - [Path] - [Outline Stroke] to change the stroke to a fill.

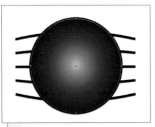 

12　Press [Ctrl]-[F] to paste in place the circle that was copied earlier. Select [Object] - [Path] - [Divide Objects Below] to use the circle to remove the lines around the edges. The object at the top will disappear and the objects at the bottom will be divided based on the top object's path.

13　Use the Group Selection tool () to select the lines on the left and right one by one and delete them. Press [Ctrl]-[A] to select all.

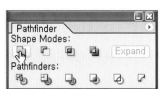

14 Display the Pathfinder palette ([Window] - [Pathfinder]). Hold down the [Alt] key and click the [Add to shape area] icon ( ).

15 Select New Gradient Swatch 2 ( ) from the Swatches palette. Select the Gradient tool ( ) and drag the tool from the top left of the globe to the bottom right, as shown here.

16 Press [Ctrl]-[Alt]-[3] to unhide the circle that was hidden earlier. Show all layers in the Layers palette. Lock ( ) all layers except text 2.

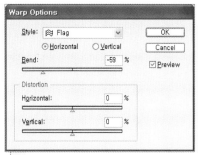

17 Let's bend the text and banner. Select the rectangular object in the center and choose [Object] - [Envelope Distort] - [Make with Warp]. Select the Flag Style with a Bend setting of -59%. Click [OK].

18 You can change the angle of the text so that it looks more natural. Select the text and choose [Type] - [Type on a Path] - [Type on a Path Options]. Set the Effect to Skew and click [OK]. The image is now complete.

Chapter 7

# Using Symbols

The concept of symbols holds unique meaning in the Illustrator environment. In Illustrator, symbols allow you to reuse objects in a document without increasing the overall file size. You can either use the symbols that come with Illustrator CS or create your own symbols. Illustrator includes several different symbol libraries, including 3D Symbols, Arrows, Charts, Logos, Maps, and People. You can add your own symbols by creating objects and then registering them in the Symbols palette.

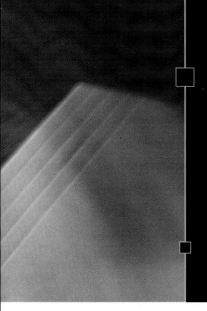

# An Introduction to Symbols

With the exception of graphs, most objects can be registered in the Symbols palette so that they can be reused infinitely in your document. Registering objects as symbols has several advantages. First, symbol instances do not increase the file size of your document. Also, all instances of a symbol are linked to the stored symbol in the Symbols palette; as a result, every occurance of a symbol can be edited simultaneously simply by changing the original symbol. The following chapter covers symbols extensively, and will provide you with a solid foundation for using them in Illustrator CS.

## Symbols Palette

The Symbols palette is where you will insert, replace, manage, and delete symbols. If you can't see the Symbols palette in your work space, select [Window] from the menu bar and check [Symbols]. In the Symbols palette, you will see some symbols that are included with the Illustrator program. You can use these symbols or create symbols of your own. First, let's have a look at the options in the Symbols palette.

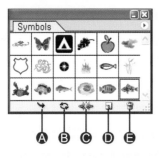

**Ⓐ Place Symbol Instance**: Inserts an instance of the selected symbol into the work area.

**Ⓑ Replace Symbol**: Replaces the selected symbol instance with one chosen from the palette.

**Ⓒ Break Link to Symbol**: Unlinks the selected symbol instance from its registered symbol in the palette.

**Ⓓ New Symbol**: Registers the selected object as a symbol.

**Ⓔ Delete Symbol**: Deletes the highlighted symbol.

<< tip

### What Is a Symbol Instance?

When you add a symbol to the work area, you are creating an instance of that symbol. Rather than being an object in its own right, an instance is more like a marker that tells Illustrator where a symbol should be displayed.

## Registering and Using Symbols

Registering an object that is used repeatedly in your work will reduce your document's file size and save time on repetitive tasks. You can register an object as a symbol using the Symbols palette.

After you have drawn an object, you can register it by either dragging it to the Symbols palette or clicking the New Symbol icon ( ▣ ) at the bottom of the palette. If the palette is not opened, go to [Window] - [Symbols] on the main menu. You can also click the triangle button ( ▸ ) at the top-right corner of the Symbols palette and choose [New Symbol] from the menu.

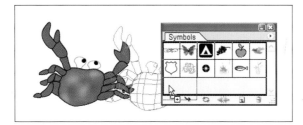

◄Click and drag an object to the Symbols palette to register it as a symbol.

After registering an object in the Symbols palette, the original object on the artboard will remain, but you can now use the object's symbol to create additional instances. You should note that the original object on the artboard is still an object and not a symbol, so duplicating it will increase the file size. An instance has to be inserted using the object's symbol in the Symbols palette. You can drag a symbol from the Symbols palette to the work area to place it in a document. You can also click the Place Symbol Instance icon ( ) at the bottom of the palette or use the Symbol Sprayer tool ( ) to place a symbol instance in your document. The symbols inserted using the Symbol Sprayer tool will be grouped by default.

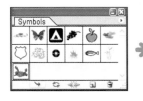

▲Option 1: Click the Place Symbol Instance icon ( ) in the Symbols palette.

▲Option 2: Drag the symbol onto the work area.

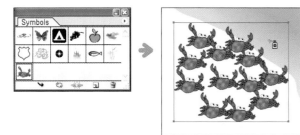

▲Option 3: Select a symbol from the Symbols palette and use the Symbol Sprayer tool ( ) to place one or more instances of the symbol.

<< tip

When registering a symbol or using a registered symbol, you cannot use the copy-and-paste method. Either drag the symbol from the Symbols palette to the document window or click on Place Symbol Instance and copy-and-paste the symbol instance that appears.

## Replacing and Editing Symbols

You can replace a symbol instance in your document with an instance of another symbol from the Symbols palette. To do so, select the symbol instance in the work area, then select the desired symbol in the Symbols palette. Click the Replace Symbol icon ( ) to replace the selected symbol with the symbol from the palette.

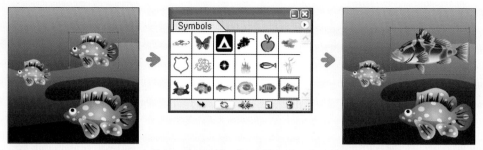

▲Select a symbol instance in the work area and a replacement symbol in the Symbols palette. Click the Replace Symbol icon ( ⟳ ) to replace the selected symbol instance with the symbol from the palette.

To edit a symbol instance (but not the registered symbol in the palette), you need to select it in the work area and click the Break Link to Symbol icon ( ⇌ ). The object will no longer be a symbol instance, and you will be able to edit it as a normal shape. If you wish to use the edited object as a basis for redefining the original registered symbol, click the triangle button ( ▸ ) at the top-right corner of the Symbols palette and select [Redefine Symbol]. This will update the symbol in the Symbols palette.

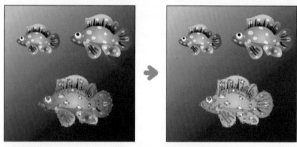

◀Make changes as you would for any other object.

▲Select a symbol instance and click the Break Link to Symbol icon ( ⇌ ) to change the symbol into an object.

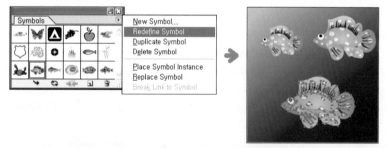

▲Select the edited object and click the triangle button ( ▸ ) in the Symbols palette. Choose [Redefine Symbol] to update the original symbol and all its instances in the work space.

<< tip

## Registering a Symbol and Adding an Instance at the Same Time

To turn an object into a symbol instance while registering it as a symbol in the Symbols palette, drag it to the Symbols palette while holding down the [Shift] key.

## Symbol Tools

You can work with the Symbols palette options, but it is often quicker to use the symbol tools in the toolbox. Double-clicking on a tool displays the options for that tool. If you hold down the [Alt] key as you use a symbol tool, the effect of the tool is reversed. We'll begin by covering the options available for customizing the symbol tools, then move on to cover each of the symbol tools individually.

## Symbolism Tools Options Dialog Box

The Symbolism Tools Options dialog box lets you adjust the settings for all the symbol tools. To open the dialog box, double-click on any of the symbol tools in the toolbox. The Symbolism Tools Options dialog box contains two sets of options. The options at the top–Diameter, Intensity, and Symbol Set Density–are common to all the symbol tools. When you change these options within one tool, the change will apply to all the symbol tools. The options at the bottom apply only to the selected tool; click on a tool icon in the middle of the window to change the individual options for that tool.

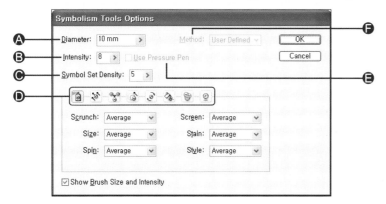

**A** **Diameter**: Sets the brush size.

**B** **Intensity**: Determines the intensity of the symbol tool's effect. For example, a Symbol Sprayer tool sprays more symbols when set to high intensity.

**C** **Symbol Set Density**: Determines spray density as the tool is dragged over the document. The higher the number, the smaller the distance between instances.

**D** **Symbol Tool Icons**: Click an icon to display the options for that tool. If you select the Symbol Sprayer tool, the Scrunch, Size, Spin, Screen, Stain, and Style options can be set to either Average or User Defined. Average applies the average value of the symbol instance to the area inside the brush, and User Defined allows you to change the option manually.

**E** **Use Pressure Pen**: This option is availabe only when using a tablet pen. The pressure of the pen determines the intensity of the spray.

**F** **Method**: Determines how the symbol tool will be used. Choose User Defined to manually control the effect, Random to create a random effect, or Average to smooth out the effect. The Method option is not available for the Symbol Sprayer and Symbol Shifter tools.

# Symbol Sprayer Tool (🖼️)

As previously mentioned, the Symbol Sprayer tool adds one or more instances of the symbol to the work area. Select a symbol in the Symbols palette and place the Symbol Sprayer tool (🖼️) on the document. You will see a circle showing the brush size. Click on the work area to add an instance. If you hold down the mouse and drag the tool, many instances will be created.

Sprayed symbol instances, by default, are tied together to form a symbol set. To create symbol instances in another set, deselect the current set and use the Symbol Sprayer tool to create another set of instances. You can hold down the [Alt] key to remove instances or reduce the number of symbol instances in the symbol set.

  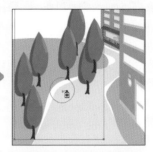

▲Add an instance with the Symbol Sprayer tool. Press [Ctrl]-[Shift]-[A] to deselect the instance. When you click the tool again, you will create another instance that is not grouped with the first.

▲Use the mouse to drag the Symbol Sprayer tool over the document. Symbol instances are created in the direction that the tool is dragged. These symbols are tied together to form a symbol set.

▲Hold down the [Alt] key with the Symbol Sprayer tool to reduce the number of symbol instances created, or to remove instances.

<< note

## Place Symbol Instance Button vs. Symbol Sprayer Tool

Symbol instances inserted into an image using the Place Symbol Instance button ( ↘ ) in the Symbols palette are not grouped; this lets you edit one symbol instance on the artboard at a time. Symbol instances inserted using the Symbol Sprayer tool (🖼️), however, are grouped, and these instances will remain grouped even after breaking the link to the symbol. When all of the symbol instances are grouped or selected, edits will apply to all the instances as a group. For example, selecting a new color in the toolbox will alter the color for all the instances simultaneously.

<< tip

## Adjusting the Brush Size

Use the ] and [ keys to increase or decrease the brush size.

# Symbol Shifter Tool (🖼️)

The Symbol Shifter tool moves an instance created with the Symbol Sprayer tool. The tool is used on a selected symbol instance to move an instance within a symbol set.

▲Drag the Symbol Sprayer tool over the document to spray the symbols.

▲Click on an instance inside the symbol set and drag to move it in the desired direction.

# Symbol Scruncher Tool (⬚)

The Symbol Scruncher tool changes the distribution of instances inside a symbol set. You can either gather the instances together, or spread them apart by holding down the [Alt] key. Drag to apply the effect.

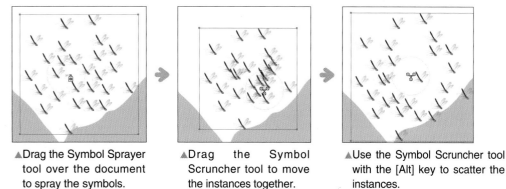

▲Drag the Symbol Sprayer tool over the document to spray the symbols.

▲Drag the Symbol Scruncher tool to move the instances together.

▲Use the Symbol Scruncher tool with the [Alt] key to scatter the instances.

# Symbol Sizer Tool (⬚)

The Symbol Sizer tool changes the size of symbol instances. Hold down the mouse to increase the size of the symbol instances. When the Method option is set to User Defined in the Symbolism Tool Options dialog box, holding down the [Alt] key makes the instances smaller.

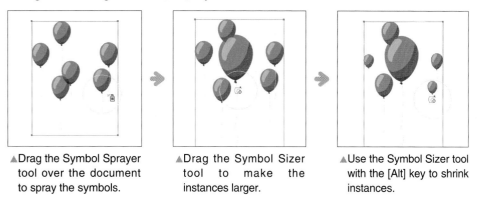

▲Drag the Symbol Sprayer tool over the document to spray the symbols.

▲Drag the Symbol Sizer tool to make the instances larger.

▲Use the Symbol Sizer tool with the [Alt] key to shrink instances.

### Symbol Sizer Tool Options

When using the Symbol Sizer tool, the Method, Diameter, and Density options can be used to create many different effects.

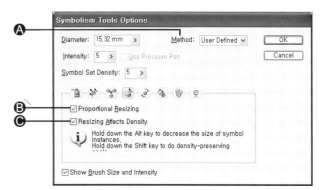

**Ⓐ Method**: Three options are available.

-*User Defined*: Makes gradual changes to the instance size.

-*Random*: Randomly changes instance size.

-*Average*: Calculates and applies the average of the instance size.

Created Using the Random Method Setting ▶

**Ⓑ Proportional Resizing**: The size is adjusted while maintaining horizontal and vertical proportions.

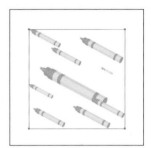

Created Using the Proportional Resizing Setting ▶

**Ⓒ Resizing Affects Density**: With this option selected, adjusting the size has an effect on the density of the instances. As symbol sizes are increased, they are spread apart (and vice versa). You can use this option to maintain some sense of spatial balance between the instances as you resize them.

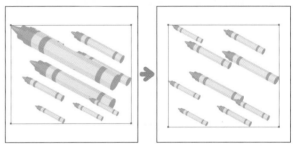

▲The images shown demonstrate the effects of the Resizing Affects Density option.

## Symbol Spinner Tool (⟳)

The Symbol Spinner tool adjusts the direction of a symbol instance. When you click an instance, a perpendicular rotating arrow will appear. Move the arrow to the left or right to rotate the symbol. Setting the Method option to Random rotates the instances randomly. Changing the brush size allows you to better isolate which instances will be rotated.

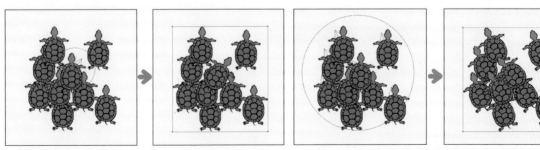

▲Click the Symbol Spinner tool on the instance to see the perpendicular rotating arrow. Drag the tool to rotate the instance.

▲A larger brush size allows you to rotate all symbol instances in the same direction.

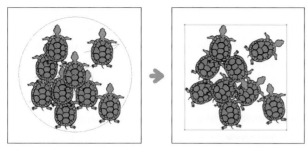

▲Set the Method option to Random to randomize the rotation of the instances.

## Symbol Stainer Tool (🖌)

The Symbol Stainer tool changes the color of symbol instances. Specify the fill color and either click or drag the Symbol Stainer tool to change the color of an instance. The color will build up gradually. When the Method option is set to User Defined, holding down the [Alt] key removes the new color and reverts the instance to its original color.

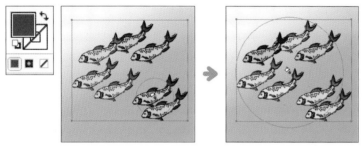

▲Choose the fill color and click or drag the Symbol Stainer tool. The instance color will be changed.

▲Set the Method option to Random to randomize the color change.

## Symbol Screener Tool (🖱)

The Symbol Screener tool adjusts the opacity of an instance. You can either click or drag over the instance to apply the effect gradually. When the Method option is set to User Defined, hold down the [Alt] key to change the opacity to its original state.

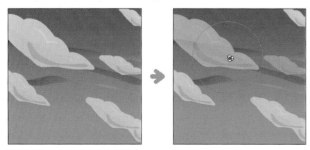

▲Click or drag the tool on the symbol instance to apply transparency.

# Symbol Styler Tool ( ⚙ )

The Symbol Styler tool applies the effects selected in the Graphic Styles palette. Click or drag the Symbol Styler tool over the symbol instance to apply the selected style. You can use the tool to apply styles to a symbol set or to a single symbol instance. When the Method option is set to User Defined, hold down the [Alt] key to return the symbol instance to its original state.

▲Create a symbol set with the Symbol Sprayer tool. Select the Symbol Styler tool and select a style from the Graphic Styles palette.

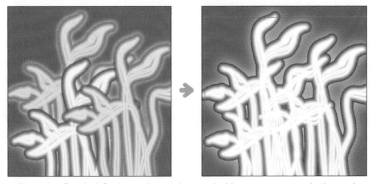

▲Drag the Symbol Styler tool over the symbol instances to apply the style. Drag or click again to intensify the style.

◀If you don't use the Symbol Styler tool, selecting a style from the Graphic Styles palette will apply the style uniformly to all instances.

248

# Creating a Nature Poster with Symbols

*Exercise* **1**

In this exercise, you will use basic symbol functions to create a nature poster. Through this example, you will learn how to add symbols to the Symbols palette, how to use the Symbol Spray tool to spray symbols, how to use the Symbol Scruncher tool to adjust how closely the symbols are packed together, how to use the Symbol Shifter tool to move symbols, and how to use the Symbol Spinner tool to rotate symbols.

**Start File**
\Sample\Chapter07\nature.ai

**Final File**
\Sample\Chapter07\nature_fin.ai

Original Image

Final Image

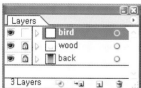

1 Open nature.ai from the sample folder. The bird layer contains three birds in flight. Let's use symbols to add more birds and make them appear to take flight.

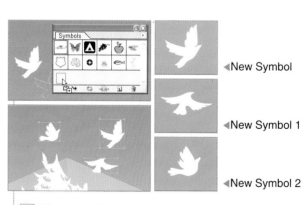

◀New Symbol

◀New Symbol 1

◀New Symbol 2

2 First, we will register each of the three birds as symbols. Use the Selection tool ( ) to select first the bird. Drag the bird to the Symbols palette and hold down the [Shift] key before you release the mouse. This registers the symbol and creates an instance at the same time. Do the same for the other two birds.

3 Click the Selection tool (⬉) on the bird to the far right and select the Symbol Sprayer tool (▣). Double-click the tool and adjust the brush size, intensity, and density as shown above. Drag the tool inside the selected instance.

4 Select the Symbol Scruncher tool (▣) and press ] on the keyboard three times to increase the brush size. Click or drag the mouse on the bottom-left corner to bring the birds closer together. Hold down the [Alt] key and drag the tool over the top-right corner to spread the birds out. Press [Ctrl]-[3] to hide the symbol set.

<< tip

## Adjusting Intensity

If you have created too many instances, reduce the Intensity to a value between 2 and 4.

5 Use the Selection tool (⬉) to click the bird in the center. Use the ] or [ key to increase or decrease brush size. Click the Symbol Sprayer tool (▣) twice to create four birds. You can remove extra birds by holding down the [Alt] key and clicking.

6 Select the Symbol Shifter tool (▣) and change the brush size so that it is large enough to include one bird. Drag the instance at the bottom downward and the instance at the top upward to spread out the birds.

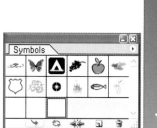

7  Select New symbol 2 in the Symbols palette. Click the Place Symbol Instance icon ( ) and use the Selection tool ( ) to adjust the position of the instance. Use the Symbol Spinner tool ( ) to click the instance and drag it to the left.

8  Press [Ctrl]-[Alt]-[3] to unhide the hidden symbol set. Use the Symbol Scruncher tool ( ) to gather the birds towards the bottom. You should be aiming for a greater concentration of birds near the box. When the image matches the one shown above, the exercise is complete.

# Using Symbols and Transition Effects

In this exercise, you will learn how to set up the Symbol Spray tool options and how to edit symbols to meet specific needs and purposes. You will also learn how to use the Symbol Sizer tool to adjust the size of the symbols, how to use the Symbol Stainer tool to change the color of the symbols, and how to update existing symbols.

**Start File**
 \Sample\Chapter07\summer.ai

**Final File**
 \Sample\Chapter07\summer_fin.ai

Original Image

Final Image

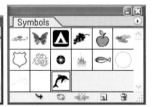

1 Open summer.ai from the sample folder. The file has one layer, back, and four symbols are registered in the Symbols palette.

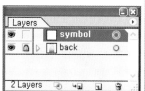 

2 | Lock the back layer. Hold down the [Alt] key and click the New Layer icon (⬛) in the Layers palette. Enter the name **symbol** and click [OK]. Select the Symbol Sprayer tool (🖌) and set the following options by double-clicking the tool–Diameter: 40, Intensity: 1, and Symbol Set Density: 7. Click [OK].

 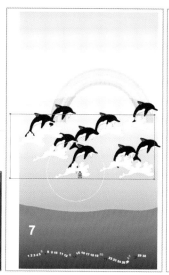 

3 | Select the dolphin from the Symbols palette and drag the Symbol Sprayer tool (🖌) to position dolphins on the work area as shown. Press [Ctrl]-[Shift]-[A] to deselect the symbol set. Select foam from the Symbols palette and drag over the dolphins' tails. Deselect the foam symbol. Add cloud symbols in the sky and deselect that symbol set.

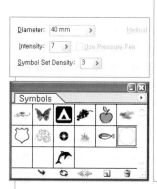 

<< tip

## Applying Symbols

If you have a symbol set selected when you use the Symbol Sprayer tool, any symbols you create will be added to that symbol set. You won't be able to make changes to the options of the new symbols. It is best to create separate symbol sets by deselecting the previous symbol set first.

4 | You can now add the bubbles. The bubbles will be scattered far apart, so you must change the Symbol Sprayer tool options. Double-click the Symbol Sprayer tool (🖌) and set the Intensity to 7 and the Symbol Set Density to 3. Click [OK]. Select the bubble symbol, then click and drag the tool to draw bubbles. Leave this symbol set selected.

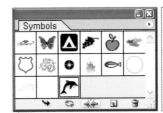

**5** Select the Symbol Sizer tool (🖐), hold down the [Alt] key, and drag it over the bubble instances to make them smaller. Create another symbol set containing bubbles and resize them. Deselect this symbol set.

**6** Let's change the dolphin color and update the dolphin symbol definition. Select the dolphin symbol in the Symbols palette and click the Place Symbol Instance icon (🡒) to position the symbol on the work area. Click the Break Link to Symbol icon (🡒) so that the dolphin becomes an object.

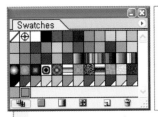
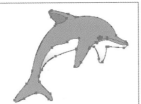
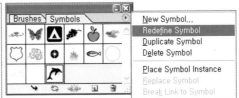

**7** Use the Direct Selection tool (🡒) to shade the body and fins of the dolphin with the last color saved at the bottom of the Swatches palette. Select the edited dolphin and click the triangle button (▶) at the top-right of the Symbols palette. Choose [Redefine Symbol] from the menu.

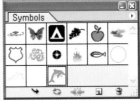

**8** The dolphin in the Symbols palette will be updated, as will the dolphin instances in the work area.

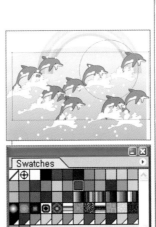

**9** Select the dolphin symbol set with the Selection tool (🡒). Choose the Symbol Stainer tool (🖐) and fill the dolphins at the top with the Night Blue swatch (■) from the Swatches palette. Fill the dolphins at the bottom using the Plum swatch (■). The image has been completed.

# 3

# Using Symbol Tools to Make a Poster

In this example, you will be making an advertisement poster for a certain brand of cosmetics. You will be using the Object and Effect menus to make the label and the reflection on the container, and you'll use symbols and layer masks to make the background for the poster. This example will help you get a better handle on using the symbol tools, such as the Symbol Sizer tool, Symbol Shifter tool, Symbol Screener tool, and the Symbol Spinner tool.

**Start File**
\Sample\Chapter07\cosmetic.ai

**Final File**
\Sample\Chapter07\cosmetic_fin.ai

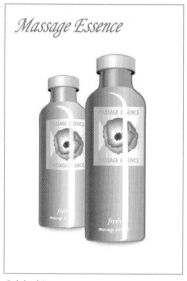

Original Image

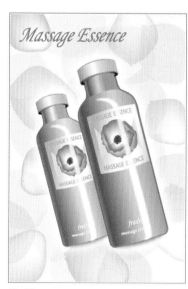

Final Image

1 Open cosmetic.ai from the sample folder. The file contains an image of a product, a logo, and a background layer. You will use these to create the poster.

2 Let's make the label reflect the curve of the bottle. Use the Selection tool ( ) to select the label on the right container. Select [Object] - [Envelop Distort] - [Make With Warp]. Select the Bulge Style and set the Bend to 10%. Click [OK] to apply the distortion.

3 The reflection on the left container has a softened edge, and you'll need to create the same effect for the reflection on the right container. Click the Selection tool () on the right reflection and choose [Effect] - [Blur] - [Gaussian Blur]. Change the Radius to 1.5. You will need to soften the reflection so that you can read the label. Use [Ctrl]-[C] to copy the selection. In the Transparency palette ([Window] - [Transparency]), reduce the Opacity to 75%. Select the label and press [Ctrl]-[B] to paste the copied reflection behind the label.

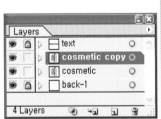
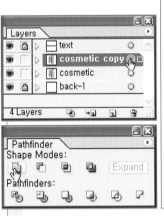

4 To create a luminous halo effect around the containers, you need to merge them. Drag the cosmetic layer to the New Layer icon (🗐). The cosmetic copy layer will be created. The Merge command will not apply to underlying objects that are covered, so you can select the labels and delete them.

5 Click the target icon (◎) of the cosmetic copy layer to select the containers. In the Pathfinder palette, hold down the [Alt] key and click the [Add to shape area] icon (🗐).

6 Select [Object] - [Path] - [Offset Path] and set the Offset value to 3 mm. Choose [Effect] - [Blur] - [Gaussian Blur] with a setting of 10.

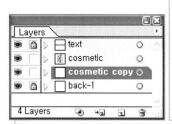

7 Move the cosmetic copy layer below the cosmetic layer in the Layers palette. Select all objects with the [Ctrl]-[A] shortcut. Double-click the Rotate tool (⟳) and set the Angle to 15°. Rotate the cosmetic and cosmetic copy layers.

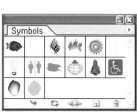

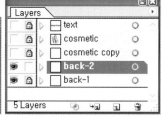

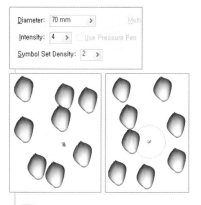

8 Let's use the rose and leaf symbols in the Symbols palette to create the background image. Lock both the cosmetic copy and cosmetic layers and hide all layers except back-1. Select the back-1 layer, hold down the [Alt] key, and click the New Layer button (🔲). Enter the name **back-2** and click [OK].

9 Select the petal symbol from the Symbols palette. Double-click the Symbol Sprayer tool (🖌) and set the Diameter to 70, the Intensity to 4, and the Symbol Set Density to 2. Drag the tool twice over the work area to create petals on the background. If you've added too many petals, hold down the [Alt] key and use the tool to reduce the number of instances. Double-click the Symbol Shifter tool (🖌) and set the Intensity to 8. Use the tool to move the petals to the edges of the work area.

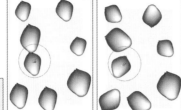

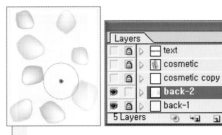

10 Randomize the size of the petals with the Symbol Sizer tool (🖳). Double-click the tool, uncheck the Proportional Resizing option, and click [OK]. Use the tool to make some petals larger, then hold down the [Alt] key to make others smaller. Use the Symbol Spinner tool (🖳) to randomize the rotation of the petals.

11 Use the Symbol Screener tool (🖳) to make the petals semi-transparent.

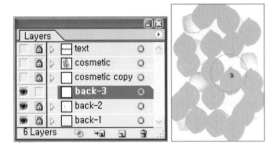

12 Lock the back-2 layer. Hold down the [Alt] key and click the New Layer icon (🖳). Name the new layer **back-3** and click [OK]. Select the leaf symbol and use the Symbol Sprayer tool (🖳) to draw many leaves.

13 Adjust the size of the leaves with the Symbol Sizer tool (🖳). Double-click the tool and check the Proportional Resizing option. Use the [Alt] key to make some instances smaller. Use the Symbol Spinner tool (🖳) to randomize the rotation of the leaves.

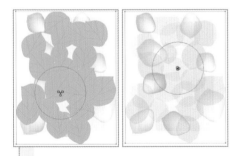

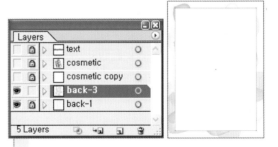

14 Use the Symbol Scruncher tool (🖳) to move the instances closer together. Use the Symbol Screener tool (🖳) to make the leaves semi-transparent.

15 Click the back-3 layer, hold down the [Shift] key, and click the back-2 layer to select both layers. Click on the triangle button (🖳) at the top right of the Layers palette and choose [Merge Selected] from the menu. Use the Rectangle tool (🖳) to create a rectangle to cover the entire background. The background color isn't important, as this shape will be used as a mask.

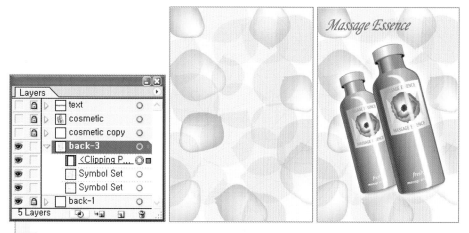

16 Click the Layer Mask icon ( ) at the bottom of the Layers palette. Show all hidden layers to reveal the final image.

**Chapter** | 8

# Using the Mesh and Liquify Tools

In this chapter, you will learn to use the mesh and liquify tools to create complicated color transitions and shapes. These techniques, along with the Create Gradient Mesh command, are essential for creating realistic images such as portraits and landscapes. Chapter 8 will introduce you to these tools and the numerous ways in which you can use them to improve your artwork.

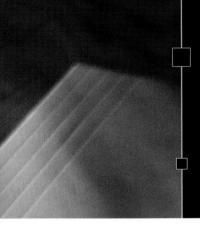

# Advanced Techniques

The Create Gradient Mesh command and the Mesh tool make it possible to paint an object's fill with more than one gradient, blending the gradients to create a smooth color transition. The liquify tools, on the other hand, are used to change the shape of an object for creative effect. These advanced techniques and more will be covered in the following sections.

## Meshes

Before we can get started, you'll need to understand the general concept of meshes. A mesh is made up of vertical and horizontal lines that are superimposed on an object to create a sort of map. These mesh lines can be moved or manipulated like paths, but they appear only on screen (they do not print). At the intersections of these lines are mesh points, to which you can add color selections. Color selections radiate out from their mesh points, blending with the colors inserted at other mesh points. By coloring and moving mesh points or mesh patches enclosed by mesh points, you can color an object realistically, creating smooth color transitions.

The Create Gradient Mesh command and the Mesh tool are used to insert a mesh onto a selected object. With a mesh created, you can then color an object or modify its shape using the mesh to achieve great control and flexibility. Because the best way to understand meshes is to see one for yourself, let's have a look at the following example of a mesh object:

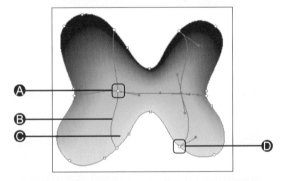

**ⓐ Mesh Point** (▨): Mesh points can be added, edited, moved, or deleted like anchor points. However, unlike anchor points, mesh points can add a patch of color to the object.

**ⓑ Mesh Line**: Mesh lines define the surface "map" of the mesh. Mesh points are created wherever they intersect.

**ⓒ Mesh Patch**: A mesh patch is an area enclosed by four mesh points.

**ⓓ Anchor Point** (▨): An anchor point in a mesh object is just like any other anchor point. Note that an anchor point is represented by a square icon, while a mesh point is shown as a diamond icon.

# Mesh Tool

To add mesh points to an object one at a time, you can click on an object with the Mesh tool (⊞). A horizontal mesh line and a vertical mesh line, intersecting at a mesh point, will automatically be created. At the same time, adding a mesh point adds a patch of radiating color to the object. The color used is the selected fill color. If you hold down the [Shift] key as you click, you will add a mesh point without adding color. The color of a mesh point can be changed in the Color palette.

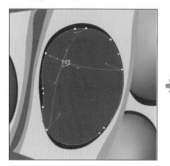

▲Select an object with a fill surface and click to add a mesh point.

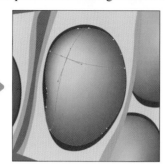

▲The fill color will be applied to the mesh point. You can use the Color palette to change the color.

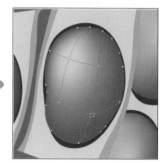

▲Holding down the [Shift] key while clicking adds a mesh point without adding a color.

To delete a mesh point and its mesh lines, hold down the [Alt] key while clicking with the Mesh tool.

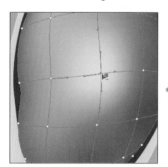

▲Delete a mesh point by clicking with the [Alt] key.

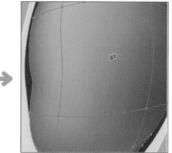

▲This also removes any color added to the mesh point.

# Editing Meshes

Both the Mesh tool (⊞) and the Direct Selection tool (▷) can be used to move mesh points or their direction lines. Moving a mesh point or a direction line changes the distribution of the color determined by the mesh point.

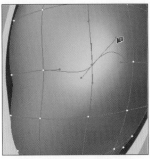

▲Click on a mesh point to select the mesh point, the point's four direction lines, and a direction line from each of the four adjacent mesh points. Click and drag the point to adjust its color distribution.

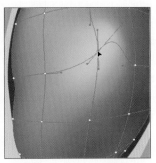

▲You can also click and drag a mesh point to adjust the color spread.

When the Mesh tool is selected, holding down the [Shift] key when you move a direction line will move all four direction lines of the mesh point at the same time. Using the [Shift] key while moving a mesh point constrains the movement of the point to its horizontal or vertical mesh line.

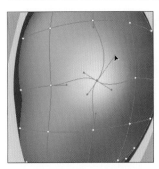

▲Hold down the [Shift] key while moving a direction line to move all the direction lines.

▲Hold down the [Shift] key while moving a mesh point to move it along its horizontal or vertical mesh lines.

A mesh can also be edited using the usual path tools. The Add Anchor Point tool (⬚) and the Delete Anchor Point tool (⬚) add and delete mesh points, while the Convert Anchor Point tool (⬚) is used to adjust a direction line. The use of these tools is covered in Chapter 3.

<< tip

## Adding and Deleting Mesh Points

A mesh point added with the Add Anchor Point tool (⬚) can only be deleted using the Delete Anchor Point tool (⬚). Similarly, a mesh point added with the Mesh tool (⬚) can only be deleted with the Mesh tool.

# A Quick Exercise: Making a Mesh

Because the best way to master the Mesh tool is through practice, you will learn to create realistic color transitions in a leaf object in the following exercise. This simple exercise will also prepare you for the more advanced tutorials at the end of this chapter.

**Start File**
\Sample\Chapter08\mesh.ai

**Final File**
\Sample\Chapter08\mesh_fin.ai

1. With the Mesh tool (⊞) selected, click inside the leaf object to insert a mesh point.

2. To color the leaf realistically, you should first adjust the mesh so that it follows the shape of the leaf. Hold down the [Shift] key and use the Mesh tool (⊞) to drag the bottom mesh point to the leaf's outer corner. Holding down the [Shift] key moves the mesh point along the leaf's edge without altering the leaf's shape.

3. Hold down the [Shift] key and use the Mesh tool (⊞) to drag the top mesh point to the leaf's tip.

4. Move the mesh points on the horizontal mesh line while holding down the [Shift] key, as shown.

5. Add mesh points to the horizontal mesh line by clicking with the Mesh tool (⊞).

6. Add color to each of the mesh points to create a natural, airbrushed effect.

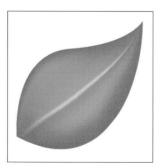

## Applying Mesh Color Using the Paint Bucket Tool

You can also use the Paint Bucket tool (🄰) to apply color to a mesh. Choose a fill color and apply it by clicking the Paint Bucket tool on a mesh point, a mesh line, or a mesh patch.

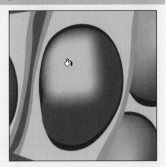

Click on the object with a selection tool to display the mesh. Select the ▶ Paint Bucket tool (🄰) and click on the mesh to add color.

## Limits of Mesh Usage

A mesh cannot be applied to compound paths, text objects, linked EPS files, or an object's stroke. Features such as the Pathfinder commands, Scissors tool, Blend command, Brush tool, and some filters cannot be used on mesh objects. If you need to use these features, you will have to convert the mesh object into a normal object. You can do this by selecting [Object] - [Path] - [Offset Path] and entering zero for the offset value when the Offset Path dialog box appears.

# Using the Create Gradient Mesh Command

You can choose [Object] - [Create Gradient Mesh] to create a mesh for an object automatically. Meshes created this way have mesh lines that follow the shape of the object's curves. This feature is ideal for creating meshes for detailed objects. The command also has an option for adding a highlight to the object.

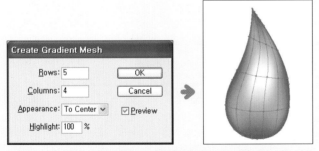

▲Select the object and choose [Object] - [Create Gradient Mesh].

## Create Gradient Mesh Dialog Box

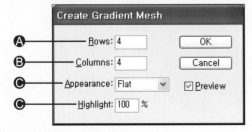

Ⓐ **Rows**: The number of horizontal mesh lines.

Ⓑ **Columns**: The number of vertical mesh lines.

Ⓒ **Appearance**: Choose Flat to have no highlight, From Center to highlight the object from the center, or From Edge to create a highlight emanating from the object's perimeter.

Ⓓ **Highlight**: The intensity of the highlight as a percentage. The highlight appears in shades of gray. At 100%, the highlight is white.

<< tip

## Converting Objects with Gradients into Meshes

You can convert objects containing a gradient to a mesh object by choosing [Object] - [Expand] and checking the Gradient Mesh option. This feature is useful when you want to color a gradient differently. For example, instead of using the standard linear or radial gradient, you can color the points of the star in the example shown here in five different colors.

 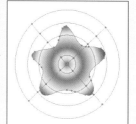

## Liquify Tools

The liquify tools in the toolbox are used to distort an object's shape. Liquify tools can be used on any objects, with the exceptions of text, graphs, and symbols. You don't need to select an object before choosing a liquify tool from the toolbox; the tools work in 'spray can' fashion. If you want to apply a liquify effect to a section of an object, you need to select the anchor points in the section with the Direct Selection tool ( ) first. The effect of a liquify tool is applied as long as the mouse button is held down.

## Warp Tool ( )

The Warp tool allows you to create fluid transformations on any part of an object. Dragging the Warp tool over an object pushes or pulls the paths in the object. It is a little like molding a piece of clay.

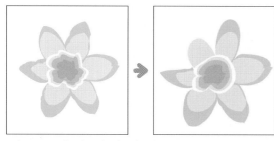  

▲Increase the brush size for the Warp tool to warp the overall shape of the object.

▲Decrease the brush size to warp more detailed shapes, such as the strands of hair.

## Warp Tool Options Dialog Box

Double-click the Warp tool in the toolbox to open the Warp Tool Options dialog box.

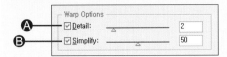

**Ⓐ Detail**: Set the spacing of points outside the object. The larger the value, the closer the points will be to each other.

**Ⓑ Simplify**: Removes unnecessary points to simplify the object. Choose a value between 0.2 and 100; the higher the value, the simpler the object becomes.

# Twirl Tool (⟲)

The Twirl tool creates a waved or spiral effect on an object and can be used to create shapes such as curly hair or waves. Twirled objects can also be blended or combined to make backgrounds.

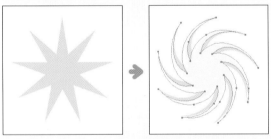

▲Increase the brush size and click the middle of the object to create an object that spirals from the center.

▲Move the center point to twirl a straight line.

◀Use [Create Gradient Mesh] to apply a mesh to a bitmap image. Click with the Twirl tool (⟲) to create a distortion.

## Twirl Tool Options Dialog Box

Double-click the Twirl tool in the toolbox to open the Twirl Tool Options dialog box.

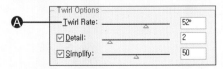

**Ⓐ Twirl Rate**: Determines the angle of the twirl. Choose a value between -180 and 180. A higher value creates a stronger effect. A negative value creates a clockwise twirl, while a positive value creates a counterclockwise twirl.

# Pucker Tool ()

Click or drag the Pucker tool on an object to gather the vertices together and create a pinched effect.

▲Puckering a Rounded Rectangle

▲Puckering a Star to Create a Flower

# Bloat Tool ()

The Bloat tool is used to expand or bloat the vertices of an object. This tool is useful for creating protruding shapes.

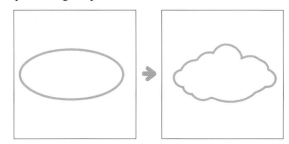

▲Use the Bloat tool on an elongated oval to create a cloud.

▲The Bloat tool can also be applied to a section within an image.

# Scallop Tool ()

The Scallop tool creates wrinkle or scallop shapes along the inside or outside of a path. Double-click the tool to adjust the size and spacing of the wrinkles.

▲Original Image

▲Set the Scallop tool options to Complexity: 0 and Detail: 1. Drag the tool on the outside of the path to create the arc shapes for the flower petals.

▲Set the Scallop tool options to Complexity: 1 and Detail: 1. Drag the tool on the inside of the path to create spikes.

### Scallop Tool Options Dialog Box

Double-click the Scallop tool in the toolbox to open the Scallop Tool Options dialog box.

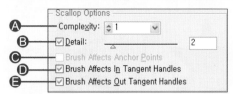

Ⓐ **Complexity**: Set the complexity of the object using values between 0 and 15. The larger the value, the more detailed the wrinkles.

Ⓑ **Detail**: Set the spacing of the points in the object. The larger the value, the closer the points will be to each other.

Ⓒ **Brush Affects Anchor Points**: Check this option to gather wrinkles at one anchor point.

Ⓓ **Brush Affects In Tangent Handles**: The brush affects the inside of a tangent handle to create the wrinkles.

Ⓔ **Brush Affects Out Tangent Handles**: The brush affects the outside of a tangent handle to create the wrinkles.

# Crystallize Tool (⬚)

The Crystallize tool creates crystalline formations on the edge of an object. Increase the brush size to create larger crystals. The Crystallize tool options are the same as those for the Scallop tool.

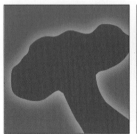

▲Original Image ▲Drag the Crystallize tool from the outside of the object inward. ▲Drag the Crystallize tool from inside of the object outward.

# Wrinkle Tool (⬚)

The Wrinkle tool creates sharp vertical wrinkles to roughen the edge of an object. Create deeper wrinkles by using a larger sized brush.

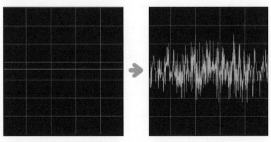
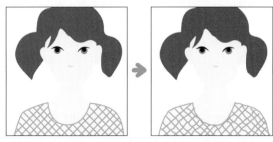

▲Set the Wrinkle tool options to the default values and drag it repeatedly. ▲Using the Wrinkle tool on the girl's blouse with the settings: Vertical: 20%, Complexity: 1, Detail: 2.

### Wrinkle Tool Options Dialog Box

Double-click the Wrinkle tool in the toolbox to open the Wrinkle Tool Options dialog box.

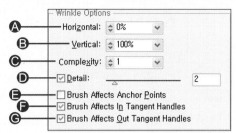

**Ⓐ Horizontal**: Set the horizontal distance of the wrinkles from an anchor point. The larger the value, the greater the horizontal distance.

**Ⓑ Vertical**: Set the Vertical distance of the wrinkles from an anchor point. The larger the value, the greater the vertical distance.

**Ⓒ Complexity**: Larger values create more complex wrinkle shapes. The default value is 1.

**Ⓓ Detail**: Set the spacing of points outside the object. The larger the value, the closer the points will be to each other.

**Ⓔ Brush Affects Anchor Points**: Check this option to create wrinkles by moving the anchor points.

**Ⓕ Brush Affects In Tangent Handles**: The brush affects the inside of a tangent handle to create the wrinkles.

**Ⓖ Brush Affects Out Tangent Handles**: The brush affects the outside of a tangent handle to create the wrinkles.

# Changing Brush Size

You can change the brush size of a liquify tool by double-clicking the tool and entering the brush dimensions in the options dialog box. Alternatively, you can change the brush size by holding down the [Alt] key and clicking-and-dragging with the tool. Dragging vertically or horizontally changes the height and width of the brush shape, while dragging diagonally alters the overall size. Holding down the [Shift] key as you drag with the tool adjusts the size of the brush in proportion to the current brush shape.

**Ⓐ Global Brush Dimensions**: Specifies the dimensions of the brush. The options in the Global Brush Dimensions are found in the options dialog boxes of all the liquify tools, and the dimensions entered in any of the tools' dialog boxes will apply to all the liquify tools. Click [ Reset ] to revert to the default values.

**Ⓑ Width**: Brush width.

**Ⓒ Height**: Brush height.

**Ⓓ Angle**: Angle of the brush shape.

**Ⓔ Intensity**: Intensity of the effect.

**271**

# 1

# Using the Liquify Tools

In this example, you will practise using the liquify tools to modify the shape of some objects in a poster. You'll be using the liquify tools to add spikes to a cactus, wrinkle the grid design on the salad bowl, make the salad greens and flower look more leafy, and add some sparkle to the stars in the sky.

**Start File**
   \Sample\Chapter08\table.ai

**Final File**
   \Sample\Chapter08\table_fin.ai

Original Image

Final Image

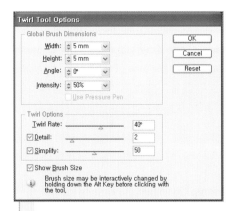

1 Open table.ai from the sample folder. Let's use the liquify tools to enhance parts of the drawing.

2 Let's start by working on the flowers in the vase. Select the Twirl tool (⟲) and double-click to open the Twirl Tool Options dialog box. Set the Global Brush Dimensions to Width 5 and Height 5. Click [OK].

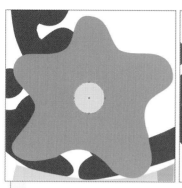 

3 Hold down the [Ctrl] key and click on the circle in the middle of the flower. Position the Twirl tool ( ) on the bottom-left edge of the circle and drag it diagonally slightly towards the top-right edge. Hold down the mouse button and release it when you have created an effect similar to the one shown here.

4 Let's use the Warp tool on the flower. Press [Ctrl]-[Shift] to choose the Selection tool ( ), then click the flower. Choose the Warp tool ( ) from the toolbox.

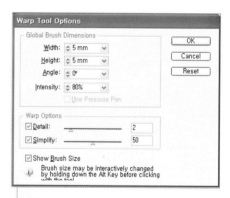

5 Hold down the [Alt]-[Shift] keys and drag the tool diagonally towards the bottom-right corner to increase the brush size. Click the top-right edge beyond the flower and drag the tool diagonally towards the bottom left to warp the flower.

6 Let's use the Warp tool on the leaves. Double-click the Warp tool ( ) to open the options dialog box. Set both the Width and Height to 5 mm and the Intensity to 80%. Click [OK].

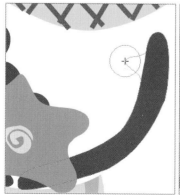 

7 Hold down the [Ctrl] key to change to the Selection tool ( ), then select the purple leaf on the right. Click the Warp tool ( ) in the center of the stem and drag to the left to create the protrusions shown here.

273

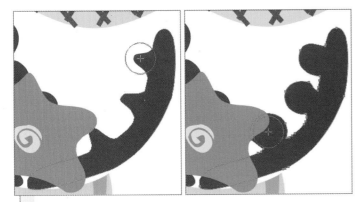

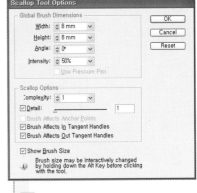

8 Select the Bloat tool (⊕) and click inside the protrusions to round the shapes.

9 Let's use the Scallop tool on the cactus and salad greens. Select and double-click the Scallop tool (▨). Set both the Width and Height to 8 mm, the Intensity to 50%, and the Complexity to 1. Click [OK].

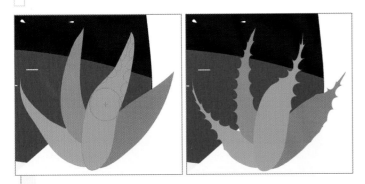

10 Hold down the [Ctrl] key to activate the Selection tool (▸), then select one of the cactus leaves. Drag the mouse from the inside edge to the bottom. This will create spikes on the cactus leaves. Repeat for the remaining leaves.

11 Activate the Selection tool (▸) with the [Ctrl] key and select the salad greens. Drag the mouse over the outside edge of the greens.

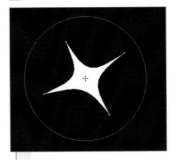

12 Select the grid pattern on the salad bowl. Choose the Wrinkle tool (▨) and drag it over the grid pattern.

13 Let's make some of the stars sparkle. Hold down the [Ctrl] key and select the middle star. Choose the Crystallize tool (▨) and click the center of the star to form crystalline edges. Repeat for the stars on the left and right to complete the exercise.

# Exercise 2

# Using the Mesh Tool

To create images with soft, airbrushed effects, you need to know how to edit using the Mesh tool. In this illustration, you will use the Mesh tool to make a leaf look more three-dimensional and realistic.

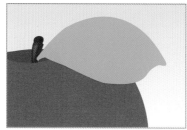
Original Image

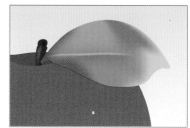
Final Image

**Start File**
\Sample\Chapter08\label_1.ai

**Final File**
\Sample\Chapter08\label_1_fin.ai

1 Open label_1.ai from the sample folder. Let's use the Mesh tool () to color the leaves.

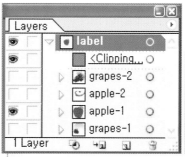

2 In the Layers palette, hide the grapes-1, grapes-2, and apple-2 sublayers of the label layer. Select the apple, the top of the apple, and the apple stem and press [Ctrl]-[2] to lock these objects.

275

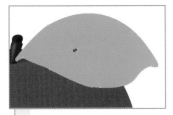

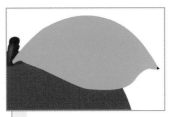

3 Use the [Ctrl]-[+] shortcut to zoom to 400%. Let's work on the leaf. Select the Mesh tool (⌧) and click the center of the leaf towards the left side, as shown here.

4 To create a more natural mesh, you will move the anchor point. Hold down the [Shift] key and drag the left point towards the left edge. Repeat with the right anchor point.

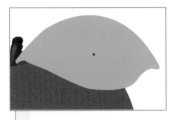

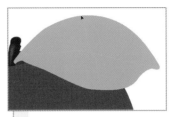

5 Hold down the [Shift] key and move the center mesh point so that the bottom vertical mesh line is perpendicular to it, as shown here.

6 Click the top anchor point, hold down the [Shift] key, and drag it to the right as shown here.

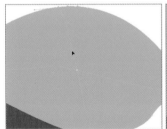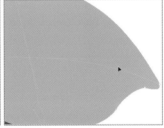

7 Click the center mesh point and drag the top tangent handle to the right to flatten the curve. Drag the right tangent handle towards the top right to create a curve that bends downward. Drag the tangent handle of the right anchor point to modify the mesh line as shown here.

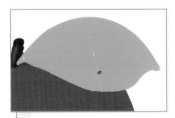

8 Click to add new horizontal mesh lines above and below the center horizontal mesh line and above and below the top and the bottom points. See the image for reference.

<< tip
### Modifying the Mesh

When modifying the mesh curves, the Convert Anchor Point tool (⌧) can be used to adjust the mesh tangent handles. You can also select a mesh point and drag it or move it with the arrow keys on the keyboard.

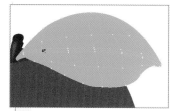

9 Click to the right of any of the horizontal mesh lines to add a vertical mesh line. Add more vertical mesh lines as shown above.

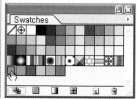

10 Select the leaf with the Selection tool ( ) and click New Color Swatch 1 at the bottom of the Swatches palette.

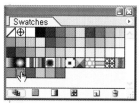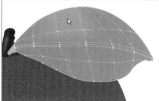

11 Use the Direct Selection tool ( ) to click the top mesh patch as shown. Click New Color Swatch 2 in the Swatches palette. The color will be applied to the four mesh points surrounding the mesh patch.

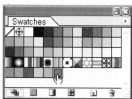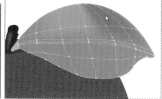

12 Click the top-right area of the mesh patch and select New Color Swatch 6.

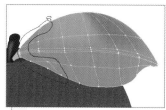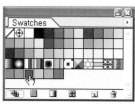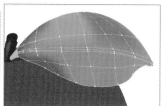

13 Select the Lasso tool ( ) and drag it over the mesh points shown above. Select New Color Swatch 3 from the Swatches palette.

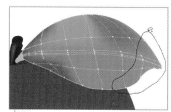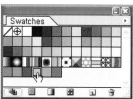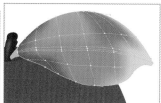

14 Select the mesh points on the right edge, as shown, and apply New Color Swatch 4.

277

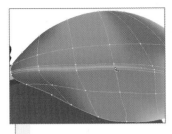

15  Hold down the [Shift] key and use the Direct Selection tool (⬀) to select the mesh points where the third horizontal mesh line from the top and the second, third, and fourth vertical mesh lines from the left intersect. Apply New Color Swatch 5.

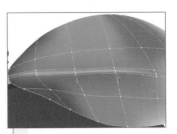

16  Hold down the [Shift] key and select the mesh points where the fourth horizontal mesh line from the top and the third and fourth vertical mesh lines from the left intersect. Apply New Color Swatch 6.

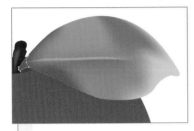

17  Press [Ctrl]-[Alt]-[2] to unlock the locked objects. Select the stalk of the leaf and apply New Color Swatch 3. The completed image is shown here.

# 3 Using and Editing Meshes

For objects with a more regular shape, it is not necessary to use the Mesh tool to manually create mesh lines. It will be faster and easier to use the Create Gradient Mesh command. In this exercise, you will learn to use the Create Gradient Mesh command to make a flat-looking apple appear three-dimensional.

**Start File**
\Sample\Chapter08\label_2.ai

**Final File**
\Sample\Chapter08\label_2_fin.ai

Original Image

Final Image

1 Open label_2.ai from the sample folder. This file contains an apple image with a leaf similar to the one created in the previous exercise.

2 Hold down the [Shift] key and use the Selection tool (🔍) to select both the leaf and the stalk. Press [Ctrl]-[3] to hide these objects.

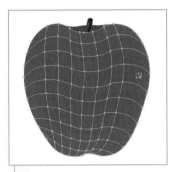

3 Let's create a mesh for the apple with the Mesh menu. Select the apple and choose [Object] - [Create Gradient Mesh]. Enter the following values: Rows 10, Columns 10, and Appearance Flat. Click [OK].

4 Select the Mesh tool (), hold down the [Alt] key, and click to delete vertical mesh lines 1 and 9 (the first one on the left and last one on the right).

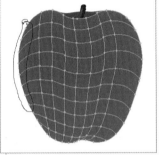

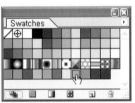

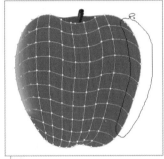

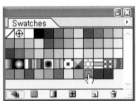

5 Use the Lasso tool to select the anchor points on the left edge as shown here. In the Swatches palette, click New Color Swatch 8.

6 Use the Lasso tool to select the anchor points on the right edge as shown here. In the Swatches palette, click New Color Swatch 9.

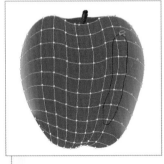

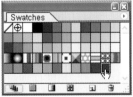

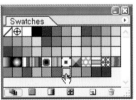

7 To create shadows, select the points in the last vertical mesh line as shown. Click New Color Swatch 11 in the Swatches palette.

8 Drag the Lasso tool over the points shown above and click New Color Swatch 7 in the Swatches palette to add a highlight.

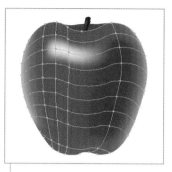

9 To blend the colors naturally, use the Mesh tool ( ) with the [Alt] key to delete the fifth and sixth vertical mesh lines from the left and the second horizontal mesh line from the bottom. You should have three vertical lines remaining on the left and one on the right.

10 Hold down the [Shift] key and use the Direct Selection tool ( ) to select the anchor points at the top edge of the apple below the stem, as shown above. Click New Color Swatch 10 in the Swatches palette.

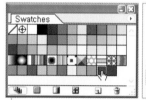
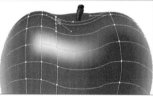

11 Use the Selection tool ( ) to click the first horizontal line and hide the mesh tangent handles. Select the Mesh tool ( ) and click the vertical mesh line near the top edge to add a horizontal mesh line.

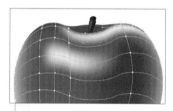

12 Click New Color Swatch 8 in the Swatches palette. Apply New Color Swatch 7 to the mesh point on the right end of the first horizontal mesh line.

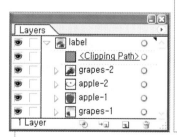

13 Press [Ctrl]-[Alt]-[3] to unhide the leaf and the stalk. Show all the layers in the Layers palette to view the finished image.

Chapter | 9

# Using Brushes

Earlier versions of Illustrator were used mainly to create sharp-edged designs, shapes, and symbols. In more recent versions, the Paintbrush tool has been enhanced so that the program is now a powerful painting tool capable of creating realistic brushstrokes. For non-painters, the Paintbrush tool can be used to apply images, patterns, textures, or a variety of different brush effects to achieve creative, artistic results. Regardless of how you use them, learning to use the brush tools is crucial if you want to get the most from Illustrator CS.

# Getting Acquainted with the Paintbrush Tool

The Paintbrush tool is a freeform drawing tool for drawing paths using brush strokes. It can also be used to apply brush strokes to existing paths. The Brushes palette contains numerous preset brush styles, as well as tools for building your own custom brushes. Learning the ins and outs of the brush features in Illustrator will open whole new worlds in your artwork.

## Paintbrush Tool ( ), [B]

To use the Paintbrush tool, click on the Paintbrush tool in the toolbox and select a brush style from the Brushes palette. Check that the Fill color box is set to None in the toolbox. Then double-click on the Stroke color box to choose a stroke color from the Color Picker. You can then drag the tool to draw a picture in the work area. When you complete your picture, you can deselect the image and use the Direct Selection tool ( ) to make changes where necessary. If you hold down the [Alt] key, this tool changes to the Smooth tool ( ), which can be used to smooth out existing lines.

▲Image Painted with the Paintbrush Tool

▲Dragging the Paintbrush Tool over a Brush Path to Edit the Shape of the Path

▲The Amended Path

# Paintbrush Tool Preferences Dialog Box

Double-click the Paintbrush tool (✎) to access the Paintbrush tool (✎) to Preferences dialog box and make changes to the tool options. Increase the Fidelity value to create smoother, less detailed lines.

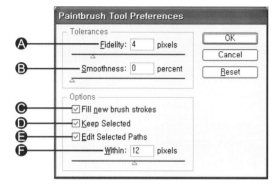

**A Fidelity**: Fidelity refers to how accurately the brush stroke follows your input. The higher the Fidelity value, the lower the accuracy of the stroke. The number of anchor points on the stroke also reduces as the Fidelity value increases. Increase the Fidelity value to create smoother, less detailed lines.

**B Smoothness**: The higher the Smoothness value, the smoother the stroke.

**C Fill new brush strokes**: Check this option to enable brush strokes to take on a fill color. When this option is unchecked, the fill color will be set to None.

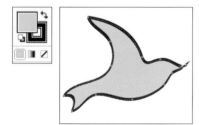

◀An Image Drawn with the Fill New Brush Stroke Option Checked

**D Keep Selected**: When checked, the brush stroke remains selected after you release the mouse.

**E Edit Selected Paths**: Determines whether or not the Paintbrush tool can be used to edit an existing path.

**F Within __ pixels**: This option, which is only available when the Edit Selected Paths option is checked, determines the how close an existing path must be to the user's cursor before the path can be edited with the Paintbrush tool.

The Brushes palette contains different brush shapes and includes both preset and custom brushes. There are four brush styles—Calligraphic, Scatter, Art, and Pattern. To see all of the brushes that come with Illustrator, click on the arrow icon (▶) in the Brushes palette and choose [Open Brush Library] from the palette menu. When the Open Brush Library submenu appears, click on a brush library to open the selected brush library in a separate palette in your work window.

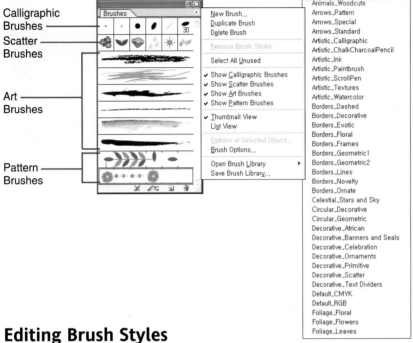

## Editing Brush Styles

There are a few ways to edit brush styles. To edit all the instances of a given brush style in your document, you can double-click on the brush style in the Brushes palette, then make changes in the brush options dialog box. To edit only the selected brush stroke, click the [Options of Selected Object] icon (◢═) at the bottom of the palette or double-click on the Stroke attribute in the Appearance palette.

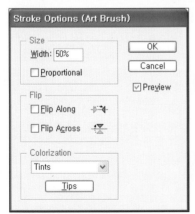

▲Click the [Options of Selected Object] icon (◢═) at the bottom of the Brushes palette to edit only the selected path.

▲To change the style of a stroke in the work area, select the object and double-click the brush used to draw it in the Brushes palette. Click [OK].

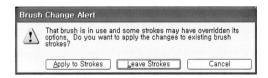

▲When the Brush Change Alert dialog box appears, click [Apply to Strokes] to change the brush strokes immediately. If you select [Leave Strokes], the brush style will be updated in the Brushes palette but all of the objects drawn with the brush style will remain unchanged.

<< tip
## Applying Brush Styles to Existing Objects

The brush styles in the Brushes palette can be applied to any path in your artwork, regardless of whether the path is drawn using the Paintbrush tool. For example, after drawing a rectangle with the Rectangle tool, you can select a brush style in the Brushes palette to apply it to the rectangle's outline.

▲Select a brush style, then draw an object using the Paintbrush tool.

▲Click the Remove Brush Stroke icon ( ✕ ) in the Brushes palette to remove the brush stroke from the path.

# Creating Brushes

You can create and save customized brushes in a number of ways.

1. First, select the object you wish to save as a brush. This step is not necessary for creating Calligraphic brushes and is optional when creating pattern brushes.

2. Next, you can click the New Brush icon (   ) or select the [New Brush] option from the Brushes palette pop-up menu. Alternatively, you can drag and drop an object onto the New Brush icon (   ) or into the brush styles preview area to turn it into a brush style.

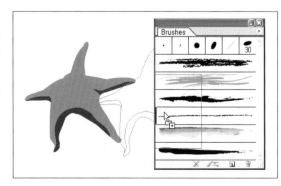

Select an object and drag it to the Brushes ▶ palette to create a brush.

3. Choose a brush type from the New Brush dialog box. Click [OK].

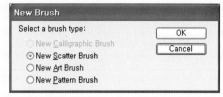

4. The options dialog box for the selected brush type will then appear. Enter the desired settings and click [OK]. (The options dialog boxes for each of the brush types will be covered in detail in the next section.)

5. The object will be added as a brush style to the Brushes palette.

<< tip

**Restrictions to Brush Creation**

Objects with effects such as gradients cannot be registered as brushes.

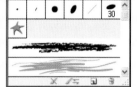

## Calligraphic Brushes

Calligraphic brushes simulate the use of a calligraphic pen tip. The roundness and angle of the brush tip can be changed to create natural-looking lines.

◄ The image to the left was drawn using a calligraphic style. This drawing uses the following settings: Angle = 40°, Roundness = 50%, Diameter = 2 pt.

## Calligraphic Brush Options Dialog Box

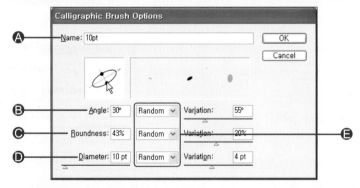

**A** **Name**: Enter the name of the brush.

**B** **Angle**: Set the brush angle.

**C** **Roundness**: Roundness refers to the brush shape. The lower the value, the more elongated the shape. A value of 100% creates a brush tip with a perfect circle.

**D** **Diameter**: Set the brush thickness.

**E** **Fixed, Random, Pressure**: These options control the Angle, Roundness, and Diameter values in real-time as you draw using the brush style.
- *Fixed*: Uses the value entered with no room for variation.
- *Random*: Uses a random value between the range specified by the Variation slider. For example, a 4 pt Variation setting on a diameter of 10 pt tells the program to choose a value from 6 pt to 14 pt.
- *Pressure*: Ties the value used to the pressure exerted while using a pen tablet peripheral.

## Scatter Brushes

Scatter brushes scatter an object repeatedly along a path.

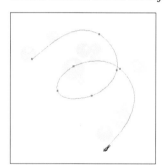

◀Drag the Paintbrush tool (✎) to apply the scatter brush.

## Scatter Brush Options Dialog Box

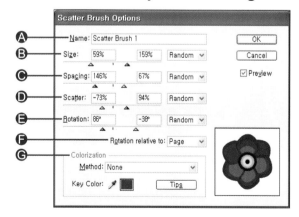

**A** **Name**: Enter the name of the brush.

**B** **Size**: Sets the size of the template object.

**C** **Spacing**: Adjusts the spacing between each object.

**D** **Scatter**: Determines how closely the objects follow the path. A higher amount moves objects away from the path.

**E** **Rotation**: Sets the range of rotation of the objects.

**F** **Rotation relative to**: Choose from Page or Path. Page rotates the object relative to the document and Path rotates the object relative to the path.

**G** **Colorization**: (See the Colorization section that follows.)

## Colorization

The Colorization option, which is found in the Scatter, Art, and Pattern options dialog boxes, lets you change the color of the brush design. Let's have a look:

ⓐ **Method**: Click on the drop-down menu to choose one of the following methods to color the brush.

- *None*: Choose None to keep the brush color as it is shown in the Brushes palette.

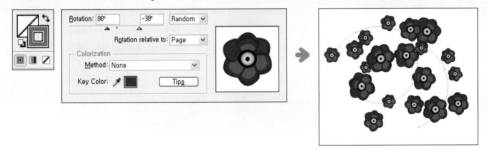

- *Tints*: Uses various tints of the selected stroke color to color the brush strokes. The black areas in the original design are colored with the stroke color, while the grey areas are colored in various tints of the stroke color. White areas remain white. The Tints method works best on black-and-white brush designs.

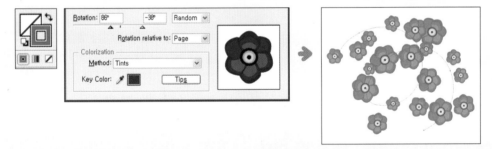

- *Tints and Shades*: Uses black, white, and the selected stroke color to color the brush strokes. The grey areas in the original design are colored in tints and shades of the stroke color, while the black and white areas remain unchanged.

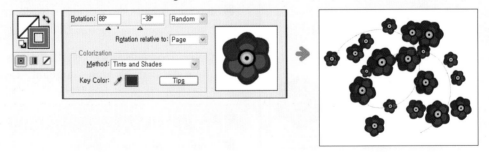

- *Hue Shift*: Replaces a color in the original brush design with the selected stroke color. The color to be replaced is known as the key color. You can select the key color by clicking in the brush preview window with the Key Color eyedropper () found in the Key Color area of the dialog box. The other colors in the brush are replaced by the stroke color's complementary colors. While all of the colors in the original brush design will be changed, the brush's tonal range will remain unchanged.

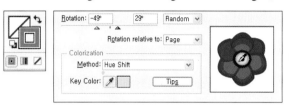

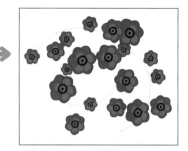

▲Set the stroke color to red in the toolbox. In the Scatter Brush Options dialog box, click on the Key Color Eyedropper icon and click on the yellow area in the brush preview window. The yellow color selected will appear in the color box beside the Key Color Eyedropper icon.

▲The yellow color will change to red, and the other colors will change to red's complementary color: blue.

**Ⓑ Tips**: Clicking this button displays examples of the different colorization methods.

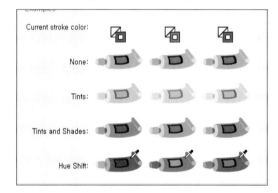

<< tip

## Expand Appearance Command and Deleting Brushes

After drawing an object with a brush, you can edit the brush strokes like any other object by selecting one or more brush strokes and selecting [Object] - [Expand Appearance]. This command turns a brush stroke into paths and fills that can be edited like normal objects. Unlike the Brushes palette, this command lets you change a brush stroke without affecting all of the strokes applied using the brush.

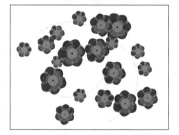

If you select a brush in the Brushes palette and click the Delete Brush icon (), the Delete Brush Alert dialog box will appear if there are instances of the brush on the artboard. To delete the brush, you will need to expand or remove the existing instances from the artboard. Just like the Expand Appearance command, clicking the Expand Instances button will turn the instances into paths and fills that can be edited. After the brush instances are expanded or deleted, the brush will be deleted from the Brush palette.

Art brushes, like scatter brushes, use an object for the brush design. The difference between the two types of brushes is that art brushes stretch the template object along the entire path, while scatter brushes "spray" copies of the brush along the path.

◀With an art brush selected, click and drag the Paintbrush tool ([✎]) to determine the shape and length of the brush stroke.

## Art Brush Options Dialog Box

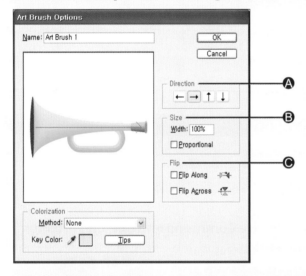

Ⓐ **Direction**: The arrow icons set the direction of the object with respect to your stroke. The arrowhead represents the end of the stroke. For example, based on the preview window above, the trumpet will be drawn from left to right. The blue arrowhead indicates the end of the stroke.

Ⓑ **Size**: Determines the width of the object. Width adjusts the object size using a percentage. Checking Proportional adjusts the object size proportionately to the stroke length.

Ⓒ **Flip**: Flips the object horizontally or vertically.

Pattern brushes repeat a pattern along a path. A pattern brush is made up of many tiles and each of these tiles has its own artwork. Together, these tiles form a pattern that is distributed along the brush stroke.

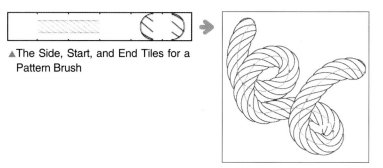

▲The Side, Start, and End Tiles for a Pattern Brush

▲Using the Paintbrush tool (✎) to Draw the Pattern

# Pattern Brush Options Dialog Box

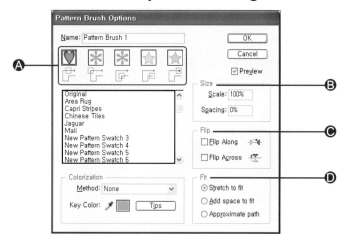

Ⓐ **Tile**: Each of the thumbnails represents a type of tile. To select a design for each of these tiles, click on a tile thumbnail and choose a pattern from the list.

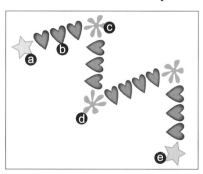

a. *Start Tile* (▣): The tile that appears at the start of the stroke.
b. *Side Tile* (▣): The tile that appears at a straight segment of the stroke.
c. *Outer Corner Tile* (▣): Pattern for a path that bends outward.
d. *Inner Corner Tile* (▣): Pattern for a path that bends inward.
e. *End Tile* (▣): The tile that appears at the end of the stroke.

Ⓑ **Size**: Enter a percentage in the Scale field to magnify or reduce the object. Spacing determines the pattern spacing. When set to 100%, the pattern is continuous, with no empty spaces.

Ⓒ **Flip**: Flips the pattern along the path. Flip Along flips the pattern from side to side with respect to the path, and Flip Across flips the pattern from top to bottom with respect to the path.

Ⓓ **Fit**: Fits the pattern to the length of the path. [Stretch to fit] lengthens or shortens the pattern to fit the path. [Add space to fit] creates empty spaces between patterns along the path. [Approximate path] optimizes the pattern to fit the path length.

The artwork available for the tiles in the Pattern Brush Options dialog box are actually pattern swatches. To make your own tile design, create an object to be used as a tile design in the artboard and then drag it to the Swatches palette. The artwork will then be included in the list of tile designs in the Pattern Brush Options dialog box.

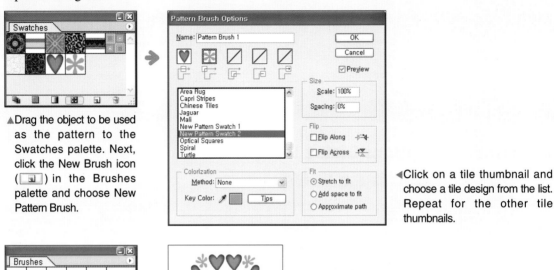

▲Drag the object to be used as the pattern to the Swatches palette. Next, click the New Brush icon (⬚) in the Brushes palette and choose New Pattern Brush.

◄Click on a tile thumbnail and choose a tile design from the list. Repeat for the other tile thumbnails.

◄This image was drawn with the Polygon tool. The pattern brush was applied from the Brushes palette.

## Making Pattern Swatches

A major consideration when designing pattern swatches is to make sure that the pattern does not have obvious seams when repeated. Pattern swatches can be applied to objects directly from the Swatches palette or used as a tile to form a pattern brush. Patterns are often used to make a background or to add texture to an object. Illustrator CS allows you to register gradients, brush meshes, and other effects as patterns.

To use an object as a pattern, it must be registered in the Swatches palette. Select the object and drag it to the Swatches palette or click the New Swatch icon (⬚). For more complex patterns, you must calculate the points at the top, bottom, and sides where each pattern tile will connect. Otherwise, your brush strokes will look haphazard when painting with your custom pattern brush.

### Making Basic Patterns

The easiest way to make a pattern is to create the object that will be used as the pattern and then register it in the Swatches palette. A repeating pattern will be created automatically when you fill an object with the pattern.

▲Drag the object to the Swatches palette.

▲The object is repeated automatically. Note that the edges of the object touch.

# Registering Pattern Areas

For more complicated patterns, you must register a pattern area. The area must be rectangular and must not have any fill or stroke attributes. The also must be placed behind the objects to be used as the pattern.

1. Use the Rectangle tool (▢) to create the pattern area (i.e., the box that defines the area of your pattern) and use [Ctrl]-[Shift]-[[] to place it at the back. Remove all fill and stroke attributes.

2. Use the Selection tool (▶) to select everything and drag it to the Swatches palette.

3. Apply the pattern to an object. You will notice that empty spaces exist between the repeating apple images. These are created by the rectangle you drew in step 1.

# Making Uniform Patterns

To create uniform patterns, you will have to consider how the pattern connects at the top, bottom, and sides when the pattern is tiled for repetition. The best way to achieve this is to draw a rectangular pattern area with which you can visualize the edges of your pattern.

1. Draw the pattern area with a fill color to help it stand out.

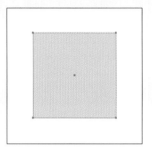

2. Line up the center of the Ellipse tool ( ) to one corner to add a circle.

3. Repeat for the remaining corners.

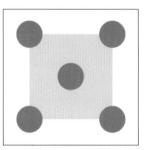

4. Set the view to Outline. It should be fairly easy to see that this pattern will be seamless when tiled.

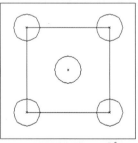

<< tip

## Revealing an Object's Center Point

If you are using objects drawn with the Pen tool or Pencil tool that do not have center points, click the Show Center icon ( ) in the Attributes palette. There will be times you will need to know the object's center in order to create a border for the pattern. Showing the object's center will be helpful in these instances.

5. Select the rectangle and press [Ctrl]-[C] to copy. Use [Ctrl]-[B] to paste at the back. You will use this duplicate rectangle to define your pattern area.

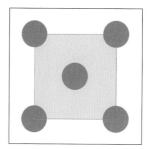

6. In the toolbox, set the fill and stroke colors to None, then drag everything to the Swatches palette.

7. Apply the pattern to an object. Notice that the pattern is seamless.

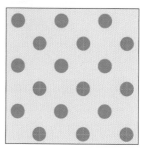

## Expanding Patterns

Some programs are unable to interpret Illustrator patterns. To view files containing patterns in these programs, the patterns must be expanded, or "broken apart." This process converts patterns into normal vector shapes.

Another reason to expand patterns in Illustrator is if you wish to edit an individual pattern instance without altering other instances of the pattern or the original pattern/tile template found in the Swatches palette. Without expanding the pattern instance you wish to edit, only global changes are possible.

To break apart patterns, select the object containing the pattern instance and choose [Object] - [Expand]. The object will revert to a normal fill, and the pattern will be converted into a mask.

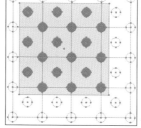

▲Apply [Object] - [Expand] to the pattern object to remove the pattern. The shapes and colors in the pattern area can now be edited.

# 1 Basic Brush Use and Pattern Registration

In this example, we'll concentrate on patterns and brushes. We'll cover making, registering, and editing patterns, as well as importing, registering, and sizing brushes.

**Start File**
\Sample\Chapter09\showwindow.ai

**Final File**
\Sample\Chapter09\showwindow_fin.ai

Original Image

Final Image

1  Open showwindow.ai from the sample folder. Let's apply a background to the show window in the picture and use brushes to create a necklace for the woman. We'll also add a pattern to her dress.

2  The document contains a woman and a back layer.

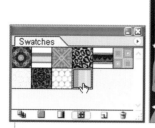 

**<< tip**

## Viewing the Patterns in the Swatches Palette

If you want to see only the pattern thumbnails in the Swatches palette, click the Show Pattern Swatches icon ( ) at the bottom of the palette. You can choose [Large Thumbnail View] from the pop-up menu to make the thumbnails larger.

**3** To apply a striped pattern in the show window, select the pink object on the far left of the window display with the Selection tool ( ). Click Stripes 1 in the Swatches palette.

 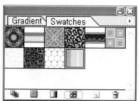

**4** To edit the pattern, click and drag Stripes 1 from the Swatches palette to the work area.

 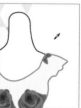 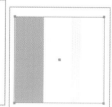

**5** Select the pink object with the Direct Selection tool ( ). Click the eyedropper ( ) onto the yellow background behind the mannequin to change the background color.

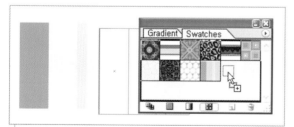

**6** Click the edited pattern with the Selection tool ( ) and drag it back to the Swatches palette. This creates a new pattern.

**7** Press [Delete] to remove the pattern sample from the work area. Select the background behind the mannequin, then click New Pattern in the Swatches palette. Click the Toggles Lock icon ( ) next to the back layer in the Layers palette.

**<< tip**

## Editing Brush Libraries

Brush libraries cannot be edited. However, brushes selected from these libraries can be edited if you register them in the Brushes palette. To do so, click on the desired brush's thumbnail in a brush library palette (for example, the Borders_Floral palette). The brush will automatically be registered in the Brushes palette. You can now use the edit features in the Brushes palette to edit the brush.

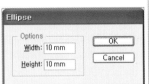
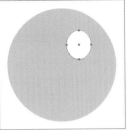

8  Let's register the necklace as a pattern brush. Set the stroke color to None and the fill color to K: 30%. Click the Ellipse tool () on the work space and draw a circle with the Width and Height set to 10 mm. Draw a small ellipse on top and set the fill color to white to create a highlight. You may need to zoom in to the objects.

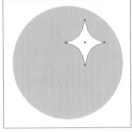

9  Choose [Filter] - [Distort] - [Pucker & Bloat] and set the Pucker to -53% to create a sparkle.

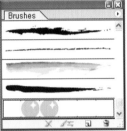

10  Select the bead and sparkle with the Selection tool () and click the New Brush icon () in the Brushes palette. Choose New Pattern Brush and click [OK] twice. Press [Delete] to delete the pattern sample from the work area.

11  Apply the pattern brush by selecting the two necklace strands around the woman's neck. In the Brushes palette, click New Pattern Brush 1. You will notice that the beads are too large.

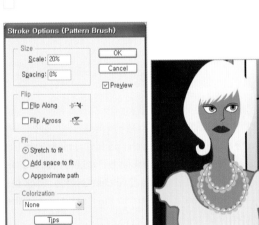

12  Click the Edit Brush icon () at the bottom of the Brushes palette and reduce the size by setting the Scale to 20%. Click [OK] and deselect the necklace strands.

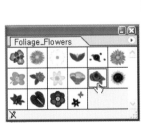

13  To create the dress pattern, choose [Open Brush Library] - [Foliage_Flowers] from the pop-up menu in the Brushes palette. Click Red Rose to automatically register the scatter brush in the Brushes palette.

14 Draw a zig-zag with the Paintbrush tool ( ) over the woman's dress to draw the roses.

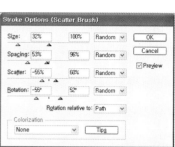

15 Click the Edit Brush icon ( ) in the Brushes palette. Set the Size to a minimum of 32 and a maximum of 100, the Spacing to a minimum of 53 and a maximum of 96, the Scatter to a minimum of -55 and a maximum of 60, and the Rotation to a minimum of -55 and a maximum of 52. Set the [Rotation relative to] to Path to rotate objects with respect to the path.

16 Let's now use the dress to mask the roses. Select the dress with the Selection tool ( ) and press [Shift]-[Ctrl]-[]] to place the object in front.

17 Click on the roses with the [Shift] key to add to the selection. Press [Ctrl]-[7] to create a clipping mask. The color information for the masked dress will disappear.

18 Press [Ctrl]-[Shift]-[A] to undo the selection. Use the Group Selection tool ( ) to select the edges of the dress. In the Swatches palette, apply New Color Swatch 1 to the fill surface and New Color Swatch 2 to the stroke.

19 Select the necklace and press [Ctrl]-[Shift]-[]] to bring it to the front. The exercise is completed.

# Using the Art Brush and Patterns

In this exercise, you will learn how to draw a line that looks like it was drawn by hand. We'll also cover using pattern areas to create patterns with transparent backgrounds. You will then use the rounded art brush to change the color of the poster and make a pattern, and then apply the pointed art brush to the edges.

**Start File**
\Sample\Chapter09\room.ai

**Final File**
\Sample\Chapter09\room_fin.ai

Original Image

Final Image

1  Open room.ai from the sample folder.

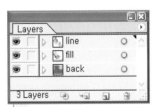

2  There are three layers—line, fill, and back.

3  Firstly, let's create the background pattern. Click the back layer in the Layers palette and draw a square with Width and Height 20 mm using the Rectangle tool (▭). Set the fill color to C: 38%, M: 47%.

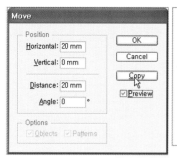

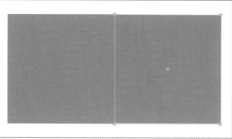

4 Double-click the Selection tool
(►). Set Horizontal to 20 mm and
press [Copy].

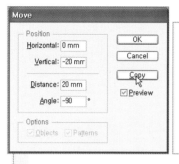

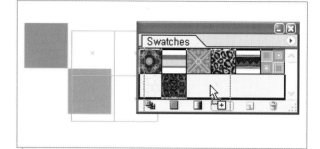

5 Select both squares and double-click the Selection tool
(►). Set Horizontal to -20 mm and press [Copy]. Line up
the four squares as shown. Set the fill color of the bottom-
right square to C: 20%, M: 47% and the remaining
surfaces to white.

6 Select all the boxes and drag them to the Swatches
palette. Delete the boxes from the work area. As the
pattern you created is already a square, you don't need to
draw out the pattern area. The edges of the object will line
up to create the repeating pattern.

<< tip

## Placing Objects with Precision

The Move command moves objects with respect to their center. As the Height of the square in step 5 is 20 mm, entering
20 mm in the Move dialog box copies the square to precisely the right location.

7 Select the floor of the background and click New
Pattern in the Swatches palette. Lock the back layer.

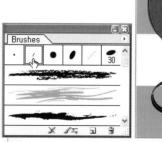

8 Use the Selection tool (►) to select the chair legs. In
the Brushes palette, select the 6 pt Flat Calligraphic
brush. This creates a line with flattened edges. Deselect
the chair legs.

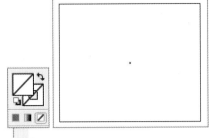

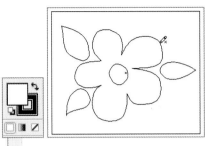

9 Let's now apply a flower pattern to the woman's skirt. Set the fill and stroke to None. Click the Rectangle tool (▣) and draw a rectangle with Width 56 mm and Height 45 mm. Press [Ctrl]-[Y] to change to Outline view.

10 Click the default icon (▣) in the color toolbox to change the fill color to white and the stroke color to black. Use the Pencil tool (✎) to draw a flower and leaves as shown here.

11 Press [Ctrl]-[Y] to change the view to Preview. Hold down the [Shift] key and use the Selection tool (▶) to select the leaves. Set the fill color to C: 43%, Y: 74%. Select the flower and set the fill color to M: 98%, Y: 4% for the petals and Y: 100% for the center.

12 To apply a roughened line to the edges, select all the petals and the leaves. In the Brushes palette click the Thick Pencil Art brush and set the stroke color to black.

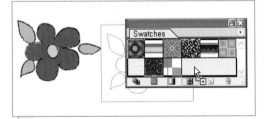

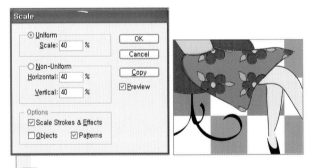

13 Select everything, including the square pattern area, and drag it to the Swatches palette. Delete the pattern sample from the work area.

14 Select the skirt with the Selection tool (▶). Press [Ctrl]-[C] and then [Ctrl]-[F] to copy and paste the skirt in front. Apply the pattern by clicking on it in the Swatches palette. Double-click the Scale tool (▶), check Patterns, and set the Scale to 40%.

 << tip

## Transparent Background Patterns

Place an object with an editable background color behind a pattern with a transparent background and the background color will show through.

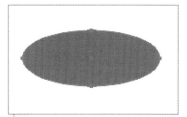

15 Let's add patterns to the woman's blouse. Click the Ellipse tool (⬭) to draw a circle with Width 5 mm and Height 2 mm. In the Color palette set the fill color to C: 5%, M: 78%, Y: 10%.

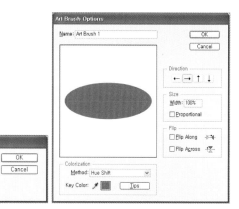

16 Click the New Brush icon (⬛) in the Brushes palette and choose New Art Brush. Set Method to Hue Shift.

&lt;&lt; tip

**Hue Shift Method Setting**

Hue Shift changes the brush color based on the stroke color.

17 Drag the Paintbrush tool (🖌) in short strokes over the woman's blouse to create the effect shown above.

18 Use the Selection tool (▶) to select some dots, then change the stroke color as shown. Lock the fill layer.

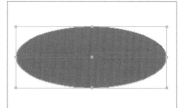

19 Drag Art Brush 1 from the Brushes palette onto the work space. Select the pattern sample and you will see a transparent rectangle as the pattern area for the art brush.

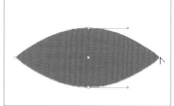 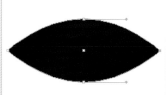

20 Choose the Convert Anchor Point tool (⬞) and click the anchor points on the left and on the right. Set the fill color to black.

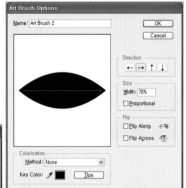

21 Select the brush sample with the Selection tool (⟰) and click the New Brush icon (▱). Choose New Art Brush and click [OK]. Set the Width to 70%.

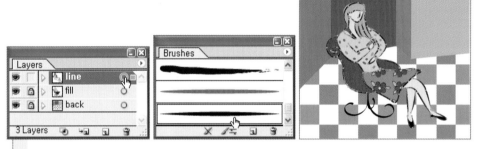

22 Click the target icon of the line layer to select all objects. Click Art Brush 2 in the Brushes palette.

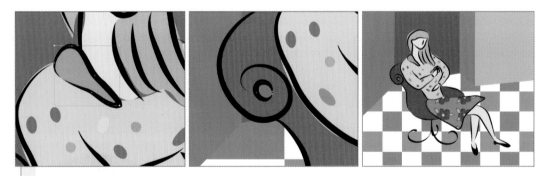

23 Color the collar of the woman's blouse orange and the adornments on the chair green. The finished image should look like the example here.

# 3 Using the Art Brush and the Paintbrush

In this example, let's create the illustration shown here using art and pattern brushes. You will register a leaf-shaped art brush to draw leaves of different lengths in the illustration. You will also create a pattern brush for the vine-and-leaf border around the image.

**Start File**
\Sample\Chapter09\jungle.ai

**Final File**
\Sample\Chapter09\jungle_fin.ai

Original Image

Final Image

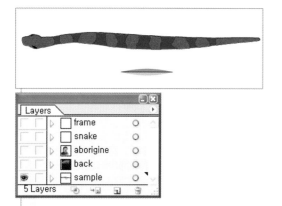

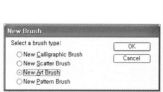

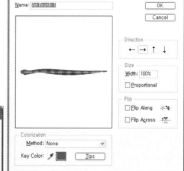

1  Open jungle.ai from the sample folder. You will see a snake and leaf image. The Layers palette will contain the layers shown in the image above.

2  Both the snake and leaf objects will be registered as art brushes. Use the Selection tool (▶) to select the snake object. In the Brushes palette, click the New Brush icon ( ▣ ), choose New Art Brush and click [OK]. Accept the default settings in the Art Brush Options dialog box and click [OK].

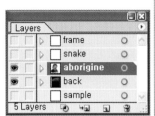

3 Register the leaf object as an art brush in the same way.

4 Click the eye icon (👁) next to the sample layer in the Layers palette to hide it from view. Show the back and aborigine layers. Guidelines will appear on the forehead and at the bottom of the screen.

&lt;&lt; tip

## Registering Art Brushes

The sample file included two objects to be registered as art brushes. The objects were placed horizontally to make the brush easier to use. When the art brush is applied, the starting point will correspond to the left side of the object and the finishing point to the right side.

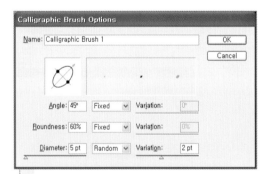

5 Let's use the calligraphic brush to make the patterns on the forehead. Click the New Brush icon (🔲) in the Brushes palette and choose New Calligraphic Brush. Click [OK] and enter Angle: 45, Roundness: 60, Diameter: 5 in the Calligraphic Brush Options dialog box. Set the Diameter to Random and the Variation to 2. Click [OK].

6 Set the stroke color to C: 70%, M: 86% and select the aborigine layer. Make sure that you do not have a fill color selected and drag the Paintbrush tool (✏) along the guidelines on the forehead.

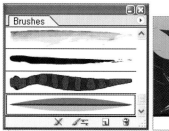

7 Use the Selection tool ( ) to select the line objects at the bottom-right side of the screen. Click Art Brush 2 in the Brushes palette to apply the brush to the selected lines.

8 Click the Edit Brush icon ( ) in the Brushes palette and set Colorization to Hue Shift. Click [OK] and, in the Color palette, set the stroke color to C: 85%.

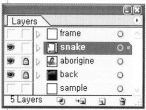

9 To draw the leaves on the selection lines at the bottom left of the image, place the brush at the end of each line and drag inwards. You will notice that the original brush is applied instead of the edited brush we created in the previous step. If the leaves are not smooth, you can either drag the brush over the line again or edit the path with the Selection tool ( ).

10 In the Layers palette, lock the back and aborigine layers and show the snake layer. Choose the snake layer and select the white line that is around the face. Let's use the snake art brush to draw along this line. Choose Art Brush 1 and apply it to the line, starting at the left side of the face. This will place the head of the snake on the left side of the screen, as shown here.

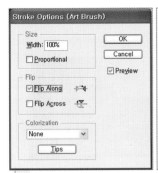 

11　You can change the direction of the snake by editing the brush. Click the Edit Brush icon () in the Brushes palette and set Flip to Flip Along. Click [OK] and the snake will flip along the path so that the head is at the bottom of the screen. Choose the lines at the bottom-right area of the screen and apply the leaf brush from the Brushes palette.

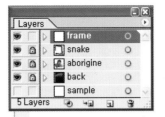

12　Lock the snake layer and show the frame layer in the Layers palette. Select the frame layer.

13　Drag the vine pattern from the Swatches palette onto the work space.

14　Let's make the Outer Corner Tile pattern for the pattern brush by duplicating and rotating the vine pattern as shown. Select the vine pattern, double-click the Rotate tool, enter 90°, and click [Copy].

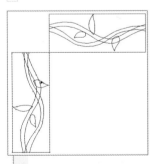

15　Press [Ctrl]-[Y] to change to Outline view, then use the Selection tool () to arrange the vine patterns as shown. Click the work space to deselect the pattern.

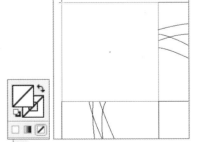

16　Choose the Rectangle tool () from the toolbox. Set both the fill and stroke colors to None. Click the mouse at the point where the two corners of the vine pattern meet, hold down the [Shift] key, and draw a square as shown here.

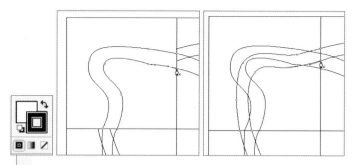

17 Click the default color icon (⬛) in the toolbox and select the Pen tool (✒). Use the Pen tool to connect the vine patterns and create a corner.

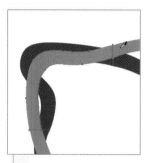

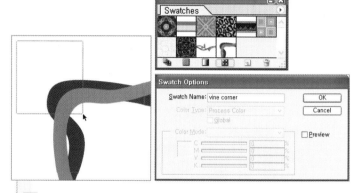

18 Press [Ctrl]-[Y] to change to Preview view. Use the Eyedropper tool (✐) to sample the colors from the connecting vines, then apply the color to the corners.

19 To register the pattern brush, use the Selection tool (▶) to select and drag the object to the Swatches palette. Click the work space so that the object is no longer selected. Double-click the swatch and name it **vine corner**. Select the vine patterns and delete them from the work space.

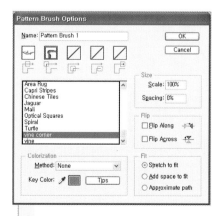

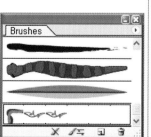

20 Create a pattern brush by clicking the New Brush icon (▱) and selecting New Pattern Brush. Click [OK] and set Side Tile to vine and Outer Corner Tile to vine corner. Click [OK].

21 Select the border shape on the frame layer and click the pattern brush to apply the vine pattern. Press [Ctrl]-[;] to hide the guides and review your work. The exercise is now complete.

Chapter | 10

# Effects, Appearance, and Transparency

Effects, like filters, change an object to create unique visual details. But unlike filters, effects can be edited. This chapter covers how effects and other object attributes such as stoke color and thickness can be edited using the Appearance palette. In addition, this chapter covers the use of the Transparency and Flattener Preview palettes. The Transparency palette is used for setting the opacity of objects and determining how objects overlap, while the Flattener Preview palette is useful for exporting or printing transparencies accurately.

# Advanced Illustrator Effects

We'll start by explaining the primary differences between filters and effects, then move on to introduce the interesting new effects available in Illustrator CS. We'll also discuss the Transparency, Appearance, and Flattener Preview palettes; these tools can be used in countless ways to improve your work in Illustrator.

## Differences Between Filters and Effects

Filters and effects are similar in that both features change the overall appearance of an object. One of the differences between filters and effects is that filters cannot be edited while effects can be changed in the Appearance palette. Another difference is that filters alter the paths of the object to which they are applied, while effects do not. In this way, effects are less permanent than filters.

◀Applying the [Filter] - [Distort] - [Pucker & Bloat] command and setting the filter to bloat turns a hexagon path into a flower path. Note that the object path now outlines the flower. To modify the effect of the filter, you must use the Undo command to restore the image to its original state, then apply the filter again using different settings. This makes fine-tuning the filter a difficult and time-consuming task.

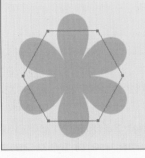

◀Applying the [Effect] - [Distort & Transform] - [Pucker & Bloat] command creates the same flower shape. However, the paths remain unchanged and continue to form the outline of the original hexagonal shape. To modify the effect of the command, you can double-click on the effect in the Appearance palette and open the Pucker & Bloat dialog box.

<< tip

### Document Color Mode

The filters and effects in the Artistic, Brush Strokes, Distort, Sketch, Stylize, Texture, and Video submenus are not available to documents in the CMYK color mode. To use these filters and effects, you must work in the RGB mode. You can set this mode by choosing [File] - [Document Color Mode] - [RGB Color].

## New Effects

In the latest version of Illustrator, a few exciting new effects have been added. These are the 3D Extrude & Bevel, 3D Revolve, 3D Rotate, and Scribble effects. The 3D Extrude & Bevel, 3D Revolve, and 3D Rotate effects are all found in the [Effect] - [3D] submenu, while the Scribble effect is found in the [Effect] - [Stylize] submenu.

You can use the 3D Extrude & Bevel and 3D Revolve commands to convert 2D objects into 3D shapes. The 3D Rotate effect rotates objects in three-dimensional space. The Scribble effect, on the other hand, makes an object look like it was drawn using scribbles. Let's have a look at these effects.

<< **note**

### Legacy Illustrator Effects

Because it is not within the scope of this book to cover all of the features found in Illustrator, only those effects that have been added with the release of Illustrator CS are covered here. Note that the principles associated with using effects in Illustrator apply to all the effects, so this chapter should provide a solid foundation for experimenting with Illustrator's full suite of effects.

## 3D Rotate

We'll start with the 3D Rotate effect. All of the options found in its options dialog box are applicable to the other 3D effects, so it makes a good starting point for exploring Illustrator's 3D features. To rotate an object in 3D space, you need to understand global and object axes. When you work in 3D, there are global axes (x, y, and z) and object axes (x, y, and z). Global axes are the typical axes that you are probably familiar with; they define the 3D space around an object and they are fixed (they do not move). Object axes, on the other hand, are fixed in relation to the object. The positions of the object axes change as you rotate or move the object in 3D space.

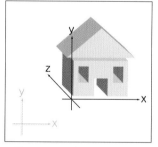

▲The axes in gray are the global axes and the axes in blue are the object axes.

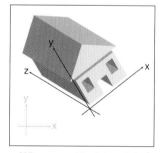

▲When an object is rotated, the object axes moves with the object while the global axes remain unchanged.

### 3D Rotate Options Dialog Box

The 3D Rotate Options dialog box will appear once you select [Effect] - [3D] - [Rotate] to apply the Rotate effect. Inside the dialog box, you can set the rotation of an object using the Position drop-down menu, the track cube, or the axis text boxes. See the image below for a full breakdown of the options available.

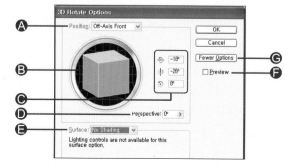

**Ⓐ Position**: Select a preset object position from the drop-down list. This will determine how your object looks when it's converted to 3D.

**Ⓑ Track Cube**: Click and drag the track cube to rotate the object. The track cube represents the selected object even though it does not take on the shape of the selected object.

To constrain the rotation along a global x or y axis, hold down the [Shift] key while dragging the track cube horizontally or vertically. To constrain the rotation to the global z axis, move the mouse to the blue circle surrounding the track cube and start dragging when you see the circular cursor (🔄).

To rotate the object around an object axis, mouse over the track cube's edges until you see the edges light up in fluorescent blue, red, or green. When the cursor turns into a double-headed pointer (↗), click and drag the track cube to rotate it around its own axis.

**Ⓒ Axis Text Boxes**: The values in the X (⊕), Y (⊕), and Z (🔄) axis text boxes show how much the object has been rotated around these axes in relation to the object's original position.

**Ⓓ Perspective**: Perspective distorts an object to affect the sense of depth. A small Perspective value creates a telephoto camera lens effect, while a large value creates a wide-angle camera lens effect.

**Ⓔ Surface**: Because there are very few Surface options in the 3D Rotate Options dialog box, we'll cover these in the section devoted to the 3D Extrude & Bevel effect, with which Surface options play a much greater role.

**Ⓕ Preview**: Checking this option shows the effects of your settings on the image (in the work area) as you enter them. If you click Cancel, the effect will not be applied to the image.

**Ⓖ More/Fewer Options**: Clicking this button reveals or hides the Surface options.

# 3D Extrude & Bevel

You can choose [Effect] - [3D] - [Extrude & Bevel] to extrude a 2D shape into a 3D object while creating bevel designs on the object's surface. A practical use for the 3D Extrude & Bevel command is creating 3D text and buttons.

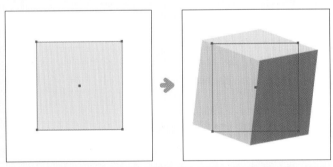

▲After drawing a square, use [Effects] - [3D] - [Extrude & Bevel] to turn the square into a cube.

### 3D Extrude & Bevel Options Dialog Box

When you extrude a 2D shape, you can fill the 3D object or leave it hollow. Clicking the [More Options] button in the 3D Extrude & Bevel Options dialog box reveals options for changing the texture and lighting of the object surface, should you wish to increase the 3D nature of the effect.

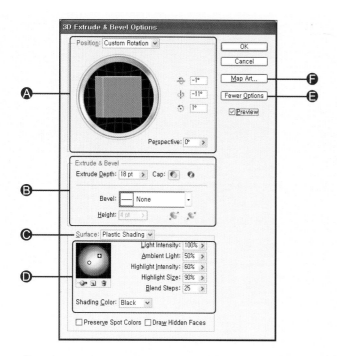

**Ⓐ Position**: All the options under Position are covered in the preceding section on the 3D Rotate effect.

**Ⓑ Extrude & Bevel**: Sets options for extruding and beveling the shape.

- *Extrude Depth*: Sets the depth of the extrusion.
- *Cap*: Determines whether the object will be capped to create a solid object (📦), or uncapped to create a hollow object (📦).

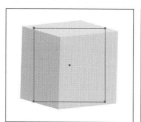
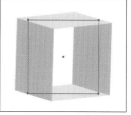

▲Turn Cap on for a solid appearance (📦).  ▲Turn Cap off for a hollow appearance (📦).

- *Bevel*: Choose from a list of bevel designs for the 3D object's surface.
- *Height*: Sets the height of the bevel design.
- *Bevel Extend Out/In*: Click the Bevel Extend Out icon (📦) to extend the bevel design beyond the shape, or click the Bevel Extend In icon (📦) to carve the design into the shape.

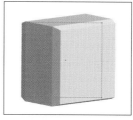
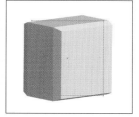

▲Bevel Extend Out (📦)  ▲Bevel Extend In (📦)

**Ⓒ Surface**: Choose the type of surface to be used. Options include Wireframe, No Shading, Diffuse Shading, or Plastic Shading.

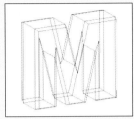 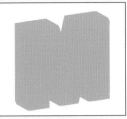 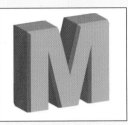 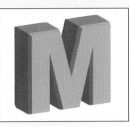

▲From Left to Right: Wireframe, No Shading, Diffuse Shading, Plastic Shading

**Ⓓ Lighting Controls**: When using Diffuse Shading or Plastic Shading with the [More Options] button selected, the options for setting lighting will appear.

**a. Lighting Sphere**: The lighting sphere shows how the object is lit.

- *Light Source* (⊙): This icon shows the position of the light source. You can click and drag the icon to move the light source. If the light source icon appears inside a square, the light source is selected. If the circle in the icon is colored white, the light source is in front of the object. If it is colored black, the light source is behind the object.
- *Move selected light to back/front of object* (⟲): Clicking this icon moves the selected light source to the back or front of the object.
- *New Light* (▣): Clicking this icon adds a new light source.
- *Delete Light* (🗑): Deletes the selected light source.

**b. Shading Color**: Choose None to have no shading color, which will turn the object translucent. Choose Black to shade normally or Custom to color the shadows using other colors.

**c. Light Intensity**: Sets the brightness of the light source.

**d. Ambient Light**: Sets the brightness of the surrounding light.

**e. Highlight Intensity**: Determines the brightness of the highlights on the object.

**f. Highlight Size**: Determines the spread of the highlights on the object.

**g. Blend Steps**: Determines how smoothly the shading on the object blends. The higher the number of blend steps, the smoother the blending.

**Ⓔ More/Fewer Options**: Click the [More/Fewer Options] button to show or hide the lighting controls available when a Diffuse Shading or Plastic Shading surface is selected.

**Ⓕ Map Art**: This button is used for mapping an image onto the surface of the 3D shape. The image to be mapped must be registered in the Symbols palette before it can be used.

An Object with an Image Mapped to One of Its Surfaces ▶

## Map Art Dialog Box

Clicking on the [Map Art] button opens the Map Art dialog box. The Map Art option is also available with the 3D Revolve effect, which is covered in the next section.

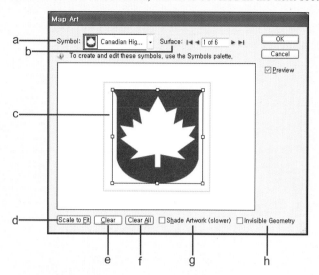

**a. Symbol**: Selects an image from the Symbols palette to be mapped to the object. Click the down-arrow button to the right to review the list of available symbols.

**b. Surface**: Choose the surface on the object to which the selected symbol will be mapped. Click First Surface (⏮), Previous Surface (◀), Next Surface (▶), or Last Surface (⏭) to choose an object surface.

The surface selected will be shown in the dialog box's preview window. If the surface appears in dark grey in the preview window, the surface is not visible in the document window because of the object's position. If the surface is shown in light grey, the surface is visible in the document window. When a surface is selected in the Map Art dialog box, the surface will appear with a red border in the document window.

**c. Bounding box**: Click and drag on the symbol's bounding box to adjust its size and position on the object surface.

**d. Scale to Fit**: Click this button to fit the symbol to the entire surface.

**e. Clear**: Removes the symbol from the selected surface.

**f. Clear All**: Removes the symbol from all of the object surfaces.

**g. Shade Artwork**: Applies the lighting conditions set in the 3D Extrude & Bevel dialog box to any symbols that were mapped to the object.

**h. Invisible Geometry**: Makes the object invisible except for the symbols that were mapped onto the object. These graphics will still appear with the 3D perspective given them by the object.

## Using the Map Art Function

In this section, let's go through all the steps for mapping a symbol on an object.

1. Click the [Map Art] button. When the Map Art dialog box appears, choose a symbol from the Symbols drop-down menu. Click and drag on the symbol bounding box to adjust its size and position on the object surface.

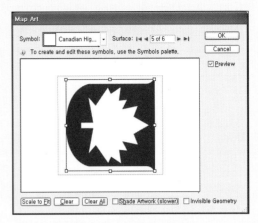

2. Click Previous (◀) and Next (▶) to apply the symbol to other surfaces. Check the Preview option to see the effect on the object in the document window.

3. Click Shade Artwork at the bottom of the Map Art dialog box to apply the lighting conditions set in the 3D Extrude & Bevel or 3D Revolve dialog boxes. Note that the sides of the object appear darker now.

4. If the mapped symbol is later changed in the Symbols palette, the changes will automatically be applied to the object.

<< tip

### Mapped Images Are Hidden When a Stroke Is Applied

When an object has a stroke color, the sides of the object will appear in the stroke color, and any artwork that is mapped to the sides will be hidden. To show the artwork on the sides, set the stroke color to None in the toolbox.

# 3D Revolve

The 3D Revolve effect rotates a shape around the global y axis to create a 3D object. This effect is similar to using a lathe in carpentry. The effect can be accessed by choosing [Effect] - [3D] - [Revolve]. The 3D Revolve effect is useful for making 3D shapes such as bottles, spheres, and cups.

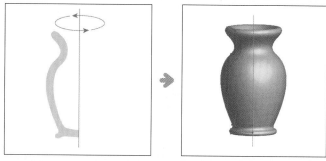

▲A path is revolved 360° to create a vase. Note that the revolve axis is set to the right edge of the shape in this case.

## 3D Revolve Options Dialog Box

The 3D Revolve Options dialog box contains many of the same options found in the 3D Rotate and 3D Extrude & Bevel Options dialog boxes. To find out about the Position options, look up the 3D Rotate Options dialog box section found earlier in this chapter. For the Surface and Map Art options, look up the sections devoted to the 3D Extrude & Bevel and Map Art dialog boxes. In this section, let's just look at the the unique options found in the 3D Revolve Options dialog box.

Ⓐ **Angle**: Determines the amount of rotation around the y axis. At 360°, the shape is "spun" completely around the axis.

Ⓑ **Offset**: Determines the distance to which the shape is offset from the axis. Any value more than zero creates an empty space in the center of the object, making the object hollow.

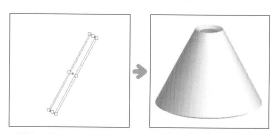

▲This shape was created using the following settings: 360° rotation, Offset: 25 pt, Surface: Diffuse Shading.

Ⓒ **(Offset) From**: Specifies whether the lathe axis is on the left or right edge of the shape.

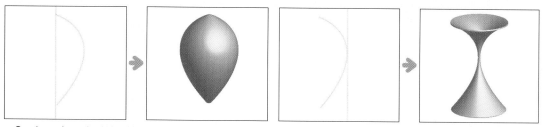

▲Set the axis to the left edge of the shape.　　　▲Set the axis to the right edge of the shape.

**① Cap**: Determines whether to create a filled (⊙) or hollow (⊙) 3D object.

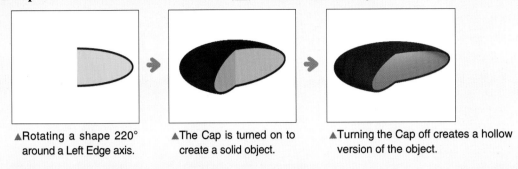

▲Rotating a shape 220° around a Left Edge axis.

▲The Cap is turned on to create a solid object.

▲Turning the Cap off creates a hollow version of the object.

<< tip

**Using 3D Objects**

You can save 3D shapes in the Graphic Styles palette and apply them to other objects. If you need to use a 3D shape in another program, you will need to apply [Object] - [Expand Appearance]. This will remove any Illustrator-specific effects to ensure compatibility.

# Scribble

The Scribble effect is used to make an object appear as if it was drawn using scribble strokes. You can access the effect by selecting [Effect] - [Stylize] - [Scribble]. After applying a Scribble effect to an object, you can save the effect in the Graphic Styles palette so that it can be applied to other objects using the same settings.

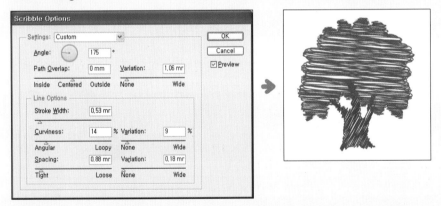

## Scribble Options Dialog Box

The Scribble Options dialog box, which appears once you select the Scribble effect from the Effect menu, lets you adjust many aspects of the scribbles used to redraw your object. For example, you can set the angle, stroke width, curviness, spacing, and variation of the scribbles.

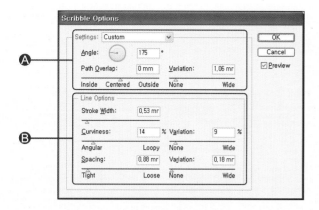

**Ⓐ Settings**: Choose from preset scribble effects or select Custom to enter your own settings.
- *Angle*: Sets the angle of the scribbles.
- *Path Overlap*: Sets the degree to which the scribbles diverge from the selected object's path.
- *Variation*: Sets the variation in the length of the scribbles.

**Ⓑ Line Options**: These are options for adjusting the line properties of the scribbles.
- *Stroke Width*: Sets the width of the scribble lines.
- *Curviness*: Determines the curviness of the scribble lines.
- *(Curviness) Variation*: Sets the range for variation in the Curviness value.
- *Spacing*: Set the space between scribble lines.
- *(Spacing) Variation*: Sets the range for variation in the Spacing value.

## Applying Effects

Effects can be applied to an object or to a layer. In this section, let's look at the difference between these two application methods. The commonly used Drop Shadow effect will be used in the examples that follow.

To apply an effect to an object, select the object in the work space using the Selection tool (⬛), then choose an effect. To apply an effect to a layer, click the target icon (⬛) of a layer in the Layers palette to select all the objects on the layer, then select the effect from the main menu.

◀Clicking on the target icon of the layer containing both objects and then applying the Drop Shadow effect will treat overlapping objects as one, applying the shadow only to the outer edges.

▲Applying the Drop Shadow effect to the cloud object and then the moon object creates an independent drop shadow for each object.

In the Layers palette, the target icon (◎) of a layer or sublayer changes to a shaded icon (◉) when an appearance attribute is applied. Appearance attributes include effects and transparency.

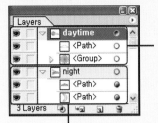

When an effect is applied to a layer, the target icon of the layer changes to a shaded icon to indicate that the layer has an appearance attribute. Notice that the target icons of the sublayers are not shaded.

When an effect is applied to an object, the target icon of the sublayer containing the object becomes shaded to indicate that the object has an appearance attribute. Notice that the target icon of the layer is not shaded.

When a new object is added to a layer containing an effect, the effect will be applied to the newly added object automatically.

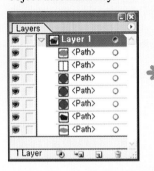

▲The Drop Shadow effect has been applied to the layer.

▲When a new object is added to the layer, the effect is automatically applied to the object.

## Deleting, Moving, and Copying Effects

To delete an effect from a layer or an object, click and drag the target icon (◎) of the layer or sublayer to the Delete Selection icon (🗑) in the Layers palette.

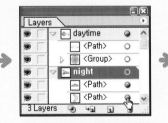

▲Note the drop shadow effect on the moon.

▲Dragging the target icon of the <Path> sublayer containing the moon object to the Delete Selection icon will remove the effect from the moon object.

▲The shadow around the moon is removed.

To move an effect from one layer or sublayer to another, drag the target icon (◎) from the source layer or sublayer to the target icon of the destination layer or sublayer.

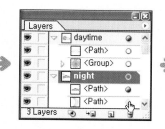

▲Note the drop shadow effect on the cloud.

▲Drag the target icon of the cloud sublayer to the target icon of the moon sublayer.

▲The shadow effect is moved from the cloud object to the moon object. The cloud's fill and stroke color will also be applied to the moon.

To copy an effect from one layer or sublayer to another, click on the target icon (⊙) of a layer or sublayer and–holding down the [Alt] key–drag the target icon to the target icon of the destination layer or sublayer.

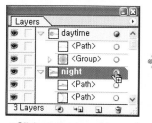

▲Click on the target icon of the daytime layer and, holding down the [Alt] key, drag to the target icon of the night layer.

▲The drop shadow effect of the daytime layer will be applied to the objects in the night layer.

## Transparency Palette

The Transparency palette is used to set the opacity of objects. You can use transparency in an image to create depth, simulate the effect of translucent textures, and create smooth color transitions. The Transparency palette is also used to create opacity masks that let you selectively change the opacity of an object. In addition, the Transparency palette is used to determine how overlapping objects blend visually.

## Opacity

To change the opacity of an object uniformly, select the object and enter a value in the Opacity field of the Transparency palette. Alternatively, click the triangle icon (⊙) to the right of the Opacity field and drag the pop-up slider.

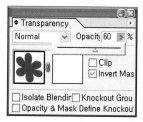

## Opacity Masks

To selectively change the opacity of an object, you need to create an opacity mask. Any object can be used as an opacity mask. The black areas on a mask make the underlying image transparent, while the white areas maintain the image's opacity. The gray areas alter the image's opacity to varying degrees, depending on shade. Let's learn to create an opacity mask:

1. In this example, the flower object will be masked using a gradient to gradually decrease the flower's opacity moving from left to right.

2. Create a mask object, such as a square, and make sure it is placed in front of the target object. Fill it with a black and white gradient. We'll use this to create a gradient opacity mask, by which the object will gradually transition from opaque (on the white side) to transparent (on the black side).

3. Select both the target object and the mask object and choose [Make Opacity Mask] from the pop-up menu ( ).

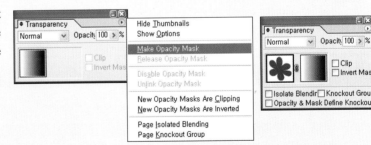

4. In the document window, the object will be masked according to the dark and light areas in the opacity mask. (The darker background area is included to better reveal the transparency on the right side of the flower.)

## Editing Opacity Masks and Masked Objects

To edit an opacity mask, click on the mask's thumbnail in the Transparency palette to select the mask. In the document window, edit the opacity and shape of the mask using any of the available tools. For example, you can paint the mask black to make it opaque or paint it black to make it transparent.

◄Clicking on the mask thumbnail selects the opacity mask in the document window.

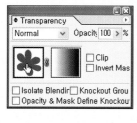

◄Click on the artwork thumbnail to select the masked object. In the document window, you can edit the masked object as you would any other object.

An opacity mask and the object that it masks are linked by default. When an object is linked to an opacity mask, you cannot move or edit the object independently of the mask. To unlink the object from the mask, click on the [Indicates opacity mask is linked to art] icon (⬛) between the artwork and mask thumbnails.

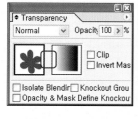

◄After the link is broken, the flower object can be moved independently of the mask.

To invert the tonal range of a mask, check the Invert Mask option in the Transparency palette. This will reverse the transparency effects of white and black.

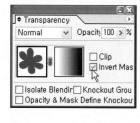

◄Checking the Invert Mask option reveals object areas that were previously hidden and hides areas that were previously shown.

# Blending Modes

Blending modes determine how overlapping objects will blend visually. The Transparency palette contains a number of preset blending modes you can choose from. In reading the following descriptions of the blending modes, note that "blend color" refers to the color of the selected object or layer, "base color" refers to the color in the underlying artwork, and "resulting color" refers to the color derived by blending the overlapping colors.

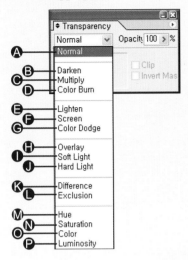

**Ⓐ Normal**: In this mode, the objects do not blend. This is the default blending mode.

**Ⓑ Darken**: Compares the blend and base colors, and displays whichever is darker.

**Ⓒ Multiply**: Multiplies the blend color by the base color. The resulting color is darker and the effect is similar to coloring with magic markers.

**Ⓓ Color Burn**: Darkens the base color when it uses the same color components as the blend color. For example, if both the blend and base colors contain yellow, the base object will appear darker and more yellowish. Since white contains no color components, a white blend color has no effect on the base color.

**Ⓔ Lighten**: Compares the blend and base colors, and displays whichever is lighter.

**Ⓕ Screen**: Multiplies the opposite of the blend and base colors to create lighter colors.

**G Color Dodge**: Lightens the base color when it uses the same color components as the blend color. For example, if both the blend and base colors contain yellow, the base object will appear brighter and less yellowish. Since black contains 100% of all the color components, a black blend color turns the base color white.

**H Overlay**: The blend and base colors are multiplied or screened. The resulting colors maintain the tonal range of the base color.

**I Soft Light**: The image is lightened if the blend color is less than 50% gray, and darkened if the blend color is more than 50% gray.

**J Hard Light**: The image is lightened if the blend color is less than 50% gray, and darkened if the blend color is more than 50% gray. The Hard Light blending mode is similar to the Soft Light blending mode, but has a stronger effect.

**K Difference**: Compares the brightness of the blend and base colors and subtracts the brighter color from the other.

**L Exclusion**: Compares the brightness of the blend and base colors and subtracts the brighter color from the other. The Exclusion blending mode is similar to the Difference blending mode, but it creates less contrast in the artwork.

**M Hue**: The resulting color takes on the hue of the blend color and the saturation and luminance of the base color.

**N Saturation**: The resulting color takes on the hue and luminance of the base color and the saturation of the blend color.

**O Color**: The resulting color takes on the hue and saturation of the blend color and the luminance of the base color.

**P Luminosity**: The resulting color takes on the hue and saturation of the base color and the luminance of the blend color.

## Isolate Blending Option

When you have an object that overlaps many objects underneath, the object will blend with all the underlying objects according to the blending mode you've specified. To make the object blend with only some of the underlying objects, you can check the Isolate Blending option in the Transparency palette to limit the blending to a layer or a group of objects. Let's have a look at the following example:

1. In this example, the blending mode of the orange polygon is set to Hue, while the blending mode of the yellow polygon beneath is set to Overlay. Notice that the polygons also blend with the underlying circle object. Select the yellow and orange polygons with the Selection tool and group them together using the [Object] - [Group] command.

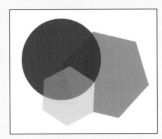

2. In the Transparency palette, select the Isolate Blending option so that the blending is limited to the yellow and orange polygons.

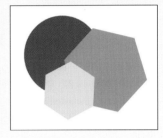

## Knockout Group Option

The Knockout Group option in the Transparency palette can be applied to an object to effectively erase any underlying object areas. This option works based on object groupings; when applied to a group of objects, the shape of the top-most object is used to knock out the areas of any other objects in the group that lie beneath it. In short, these areas are ignored by Illustrator and do not display in the document window. An example follows:

1. In this example, blending modes have been applied to the orange and yellow polygons. The polygons are selected and then grouped.

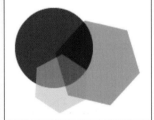

2. In the Transparency palette, the Knockout Group option is checked. The larger polygon, which is on top, now knocks out the smaller polygon where the two overlap (i.e., the red area in the first example graphic). One way to describe this is that the underlying circle object no longer "sees" this portion of the yellow polygon. Notice that the larger polygon does not knock out the circle object, which is not part of the knockout group.

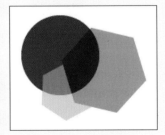

## Opacity & Mask Define Knockout Shape Option

While the Knockout Group option completely blocks out underlying objects in the same group, the Opacity & Mask Define Knockout Shape option in the Transparency palette creates a knockout effect proportional to the mask object's opacity. You can think of the Opacity & Mask Define Knockout Shape option as a combination of an opacity mask and the Knockout Group effect. Let's have a look at the following example:

1. The blending mode of the orange polygon at the top is set to Multiply, with Opacity set to 66%. No adjustments are made to the smaller polygon.

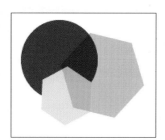

2. Group the two polygons together and select Knockout Group so that the the smaller polygon does not show through the larger polygon, which is on top. Note that the circle, which is not in the group, will still show through the larger polygon.

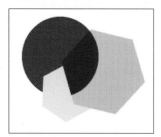

3. Use the Direct Selection tool ( ) to select the larger polygon, then check the Opacity & Mask Define Knockout Shape option. The larger polygon will now knock out the smaller polygon based on the Opacity value of 66%.

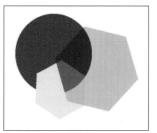

## Appearance Palette

When you select an object, you can view and edit details of the object's attributes–such as stroke color and transparency–in the Appearance palette. In addition, information on any effects that have been applied to the object can be view or edited. Note that appearance attributes are aesthetic properties that do not change an object's structure; they are reversable and easy to edit.

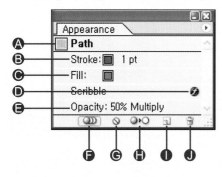

**Ⓐ Appearance Thumbnail**: Indicates the object or layer selected. When nothing is selected, the palette shows the attributes of the last selected item.

**Ⓑ Stroke Attributes**: Displays stroke attributes such as color, weight, brush type, opacity, and blending modes. Also indicates whether the stroke is dashed.

**Ⓒ Fill Attributes**: Displays fill attributes such as color, opacity, and blending modes. Effects applied to the fill area may be shown in the fill category or elsewhere in the palette.

**Ⓓ Effect Indicator**: Indicates that an effect has been applied. In this case, the Scribble effect has been applied to the object.

**Ⓔ Transparency Status**: Indicates the opacity and blending mode applied to the object.

**331**

**❻ New Art Has or Maintains Basic Appearance**: This icon toggles between [New Art Has Basic Appearance] and [New Art Maintains Basic Appearance]. Selecting New Art Has Basic Appearance applies a single stroke and fill, while New Art Maintains Basic Appearance applies the existing attributes to subsequent objects created in the artboard.

**❼ Clear Appearance**: Removes all of the appearance attributes.

**❽ Reduce to Basic Appearance**: Removes all appearance attributes except for a single fill and stroke.

**❾ Duplicate Selected Item**: Makes a copy of the selected appearance attribute in the Appearance palette. For example, if a scribble effect applied to the fill of an object is duplicated, a copy of the scribble effect will be created above the original scribble effect. This action is the same as applying the effect on the object again.

**❿ Delete Selected Item**: Removes the selected appearance attribute.

## Using the Appearance Palette

In the Appearance palette, effects are listed in the order they are applied. Strokes and fills, on the other hand, are always listed first, as these are considered the primary components of any object. The order they appear in has significance; strokes and fills applied to an object are "stacked" in the same way objects are stacked in the document window. In other words, a fill can be placed in front of a stroke, and vice versa.

You can move a stroke or fill to change its stacking order by dragging it in the palette. To move an effect from one item to another, simply drag the attribute from the palette to the destination object in the work space. To edit an attribute, double-click it in the Appearance palette to open the Color palette or the appropriate dialog box.

In the following example, let's learn to use the Duplicate Selected Item icon, then change the stacking order of some appearance attributes.

1. Selecting the star object in the artboard, choose the fill attribute in the Appearance palette, and click on the Duplicate Selected Item icon ( 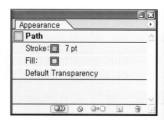 ) to make a copy.

2. Selecting the original fill attribute in the Appearance palette, select [Effect] - [Pixelate] - [Pointillize] from the main menu and set the blending mode to Multiply in the Transparency palette. Note that the green stroke is positioned right at the top of the object, and the yellow fill shows through the orange fill only because the orange fill has a Multiply blending mode.

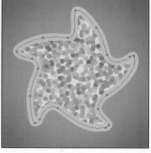

3. Clicking and dragging the stroke attribute to the bottom of the Appearance palette moves the stroke to a position behind the orange and yellow fills on the artboard.

 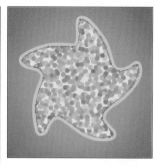

4. Dragging the orange fill item containing the Pointillize effect and Multiply blending mode below the yellow fill hides the orange fill completely.

## Saving Appearance Attributes in the Graphic Styles Palette

The appearance attributes of an object can be saved in the Graphic Styles palette. Doing so lets you apply an object's attributes to other objects easily. To save an object's appearance attributes as a graphic style, select the object and click the New Graphic Style icon ( ▣ ) in the Graphic Styles palette. You can then apply the saved style to another object by selecting the object and clicking the style.

▲Select the object containing the appearance attributes you want to save.

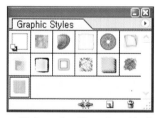

▲Click on the New Graphic Style icon ( ▣ ) in the Graphic Styles palette to save the object's appearance attributes.

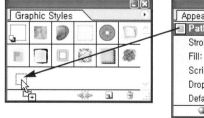 

◀Another way to save an object's appearance attributes as a graphic style is to drag and drop the Path appearance thumbnail from the Appearance palette into the Graphic Styles palette.

To change the attributes of a graphic style, whether it is a preset style that came with the program or one saved using the Appearance palette, select the style in the Graphic Styles palette and edit the style's attributes in the Appearance palette. When you are done, choose [Redefine Graphic Style] from the Appearance palette's pop-up menu (  ). Continuing with the previous example, let's change the fill color of the duck attribute to yellow:

1. With the duck's graphic style selected in the Graphic Styles palette, change the fill color to yellow in the Appearance palette.

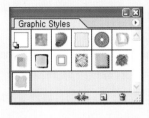
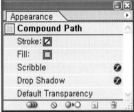

2. Choose [Redefine Graphic Style] from the pop-up menu ( ) in the Appearance palette. In the Graphic Styles palette, the graphic style will automatically be updated.

3. On the artboard, all objects created or edited with the graphic style will be updated.

<< tip

## Break Link to Style ( )

An object created or edited with a graphic style is linked to the graphic style in the Graphic Styles palette. As shown in the preceding example, when a graphic style is redefined, all the objects created or edited with the graphic style are automatically updated. To keep an object from being updated, you can select the object and click on the Break Link to Style icon in the Graphic Styles palette.

<< tip

## Rasterizing Objects

Rasterization converts a vector image into a bitmap. It is necessary to rasterize vector objects when you want to apply plug-in filters, use a file in a bitmap format for print or the Web, or convert non-native art into Illustrator objects. When you choose to export in a bitmap format, the file is automatically rasterized. To export an image, select [File] - [Export]. Select the desired bitmap format from the list of file formats in the dialog box.

<< tip

## Printing or Exporting Transparency

When printing or exporting an image with transparency to a file format that doesn't support Illustrator's transparency implementation, your artwork will automatically be flattened. The flattening process identifies overlapping transparent areas and divides them into separate objects. Illustrator then examines these components to see if they should be represented as vectors, rasters, or both. Because flattening an image is all about removing transparency information from the file, flattening does not apply to images without transparency.

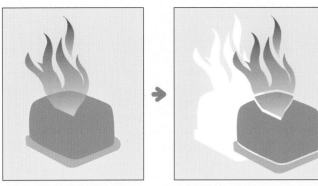

▲Image with Transparency

▲Flattening divides overlapping transparent objects into components, then decides whether these components should be represented using vectors or if they should be rasterized.

Illustrator's default flattening settings work well most of the time, but for images with complicated, overlapping transparent areas that you want to print at high resolution, you will need to adjust the flattening options. Basic flattening options can be found in the Transparency Flattener Presets dialog box, which can be accessed by clicking [Edit] - [Transparency Flattener Presets]. More advanced options are located in the Print dialog box and the Flattener Preview palette (see below). Select [File] - [Print] to open the Print dialog box. In the Print dialog box, choose the Advanced option and click on the Custom button to view all the flattening options.

## Flattener Preview Palette

If you do not see the Flattener Preview palette in your work space, select [Window] - [Flattener Preview]. The Flattener Preview palette is used for viewing any objects that will be affected by flattening the artwork. This information can then be used to adjust the flattening options to achieve your desired results. Click [Show Options] from the palette's pop-up menu to view all the options found in the Flattener Preview palette.

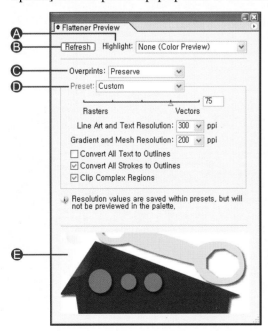

**Ⓐ Highlight Menu**: Isolate which objects are highlighted in the preview area. Use this option to isolate your preview based on specific criteria.

- *Rasterized Complex Regions*: Highlights areas that will be rasterized for performance reasons.
- *Transparent Objects*: Highlights any objects that contain transparency.
- *All Affected Objects*: Highlights transparent objects and objects overlapped by transparent objects.
- *Affected Linked EPS Files*: Highlights linked EPS files affected by transparency.
- *Expanded Patterns*: Highlights patterns that will be expanded because they are affected by transparency.
- *Outlined Strokes*: Highlights strokes that will be outlined (i.e., converted into filled paths) so that the stroke width remains consistent when flattened.
- *Outlined Text*: Highlights text that will be outlined (i.e., converted into filled paths) because they are affected by transparency and need to be outlined so that the text width remains consistent when flattened.

**Ⓑ Refresh**: Click this button to show or update the preview of the artwork at the bottom of the Flattener Preview palette.

**Ⓒ Overprint Menu**: Overprint means to print one color over another color. Choose Preserve to keep overprinting, Simulate to maintain the appearance of overprinting in a composite output, and Discard to ignore overprint settings.

**Ⓓ Transparency Flattening Settings**

- *Preset*: Choose Custom to create your own settings, or select High Resolution, Medium Resolution, or Low Resolution to load these presets.
- *Raster/Vector Balance*: Use this slider to adjust the degree of rasterization. Moving the slider towards the Vectors side will preserve more vector data.
- *Line Art and Text Resolution*: Determines the resolution for vector objects after flattening.
- *Gradient and Mesh Resolution*: Determines the resolution for gradients and mesh objects after flattening.
- *Convert All Text to Outlines*: Turns text into fill paths so that the text width remains consistent after flattening.
- *Convert All Strokes to Outlines*: Turns strokes into fill paths so that the stroke width remains consistent after flattening.
- *Clip Complex Regions*: Ensures that the edges of rasterized objects and vector objects fall on object paths so that the transitions are smooth.

**Ⓔ Preview Area**: Shows a preview of the artwork. The highlighted areas indicate the areas that will be affected by transparency. To zoom out of the preview area, hold down the [Alt] key and click in the preview area. To move the view of the preview area, press the [Spacebar] and then click and drag in the preview area.

# Using 3D Effects to Make a Flash Animation

This section shows the steps used to create a 3D Flash animation of a revolving globe. The 3D shape is created, then Release to Layers is used to export the shape as a Macromedia Flash file.

Original Image

**Start File**
\Sample\Chapter10\flash_ani.ai

**Final File**
\Sample\Chapter10\flash_ani_fin.ai

Final Animation

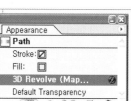

1  Open flash_ani.ai from the sample folder.

2  Create a copy of the object by holding down [Alt]-[Shift] keys and dragging the shape horizontally. Use the Group Selection tool ( ) to select the globe, then double-click 3D Revolve in the Appearance palette. Set the Position to Left.

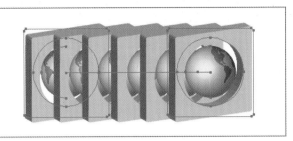

3 Select the grouped shapes and double-click the Blend tool (). Set Spacing to Specified Steps, enter 4, and click the vertex of the shapes to create the blend.

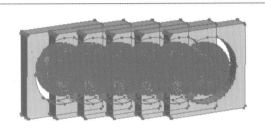

4 Choose [Object] - [Blend] - [Expand] and select all the objects. Choose [Object] - [Expand Appearance] to break apart the appearance attributes. Ungroup everything using [Edit] - [Ungroup]. Click the Vertical Center icon (⊞) in the Align palette to align all objects.

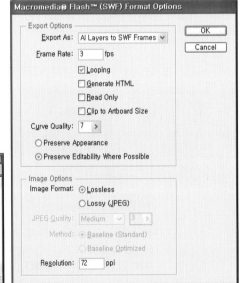

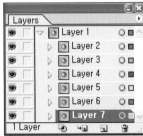

5 Select Layer 1 from the Layers palette and choose [Release to Layers (Sequence)] from the pop-up menu. This will release the grouped objects into layers. Choose [File] - [Export] and change the file format to SWF. Set Export As to [AI Layers to SWF Frames] and save. The animation of the revolving globe is now complete. This file can be viewed with your Web browser, or opened in Macromedia Flash for further editing.

# 2

# Effects and
# Blending Mode Basics

In this exercise, you will learn the basics of using effects and the Appearance palette by designing a CD jacket. Effects will be applied to the text, and the flowers will be edited using the Transparency palette.

Original Image

Final Image

**Start File**
- \Sample\Chapter10\decoration.ai

**Final File**
- \Sample\Chapter10\decoration_fin.ai

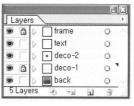

1 Open decoration.ai from the sample folder. This file contains text, flower images, and a background.

2 Use the Selection tool () to select the background.

3 Choose [Effect] - [Texture] - [Texturizer]. Set Texture to Sandstone, Scaling to 50%, Relief to 4, and Light Direction to Top Left. Click [OK] and lock the back layer.

**4** Use the Selection tool to select the white flower. Let's make changes to this flower shape.

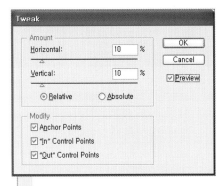

**5** Choose [Effect] - [Distort & Transform] - [Tweak]. Set Horizontal and Vertical to 10% and click [OK].

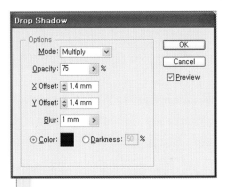

**6** Select [Effect] - [Stylize] - [Drop Shadow] and set X Offset to 1.4 mm, Y Offset to 1.4 mm, and Blur to 1 mm. Click [OK].

**7** In the Transparency palette, set the blending mode to Overlay and the Opacity to 45%.

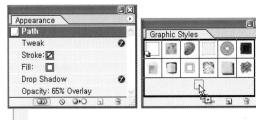

**8** Save the appearance settings by dragging Path from the Appearance palette to the Graphic Styles palette.

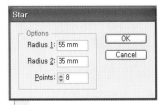

**9** Choose the Star tool ( ) and click the center of the flower. Set Radius 1 to 55 mm, Radius 2 to 35 mm, and Point to 8. Click [OK].

**10** Click on the style saved to the Graphic Styles palette. In the Color palette, adjust the color to R: 255%, G: 200%, B: 100%.

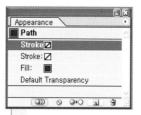

11 Choose [Object] - [Arrange] - [Send Backward].

12 Use the Selection tool ( ) to select the star object in the center of the flower. Click the Stroke item in the Appearance palette and click the Duplicate Item icon ( ).

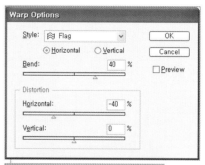

13 Apply a 1 pt white Stroke to the duplicated item. Choose [Effect] - [Distort & Transform] - [Tweak] and set Horizontal and Vertical to 10%. Click [OK] and lock the deco-2 layer.

14 Let's warp the text and add a border. Select the text and choose [Effect] - [Warp] - [Flag]. Set Bend to 40% and Distortion to Horizontal, -40%. Click [OK].

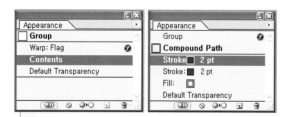

15 Double-click Contents in the Appearance palette to see the appearance items. Select the Stroke item and adjust the color to R: 25%, G: 0%, B: 190%. Set the Weight to 2 in the Stroke palette and then click the Duplicate Selected Item icon ( ).

16 Change the color of the new item to R: 120%, G: 165%, B: 255% and choose [Effect] - [Path] - [Offset Path] to offset the border 2 mm outward. You have completed this exercise.

# Using 3D Effects

*Exercise* **3**

In this example, 3D effects such as Revolve will be used to create a beer bottle, while the Map Art command will be used to map the beer labels onto the bottle.

**Start File**
- \Sample\Chapter10\lemonade.ai

**Final File**
- \Sample\Chapter10\lemonade_fin.ai

Original Image

Final Image

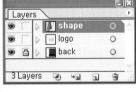

1 Open lemonade.ai from the sample folder.

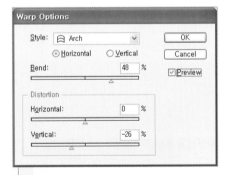

2 Choose [Effect] - [Warp] - [Arch] and set Bend to 48% and Distortion to Vertical, -26%.

3 Let's create a 3D look for the Lemonade text. Select the text with the Selection tool ( ).

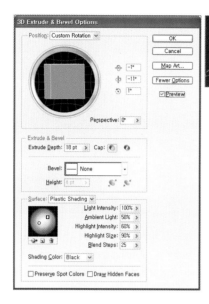

**4** Choose [Effect] - [3D] - [Extrude & Bevel]. Set the Position to X: -1, Y: -11, Z: 1 and Extrude Depth to 18. Set Surface to Plastic Shading and click the New Light icon (⬛). Arrange the light so that both lights create strong highlights. Click [OK].

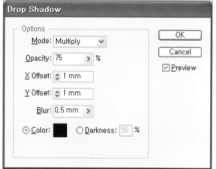

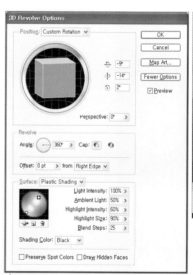

**5** Choose [Effect] - [Stylize] - [Drop Shadow] and add the following settings: X: 1, Y: 1, and Blur: 0.5.

**6** Save the finished effect to the Graphic Styles palette by clicking the New Graphic Style icon (⬛).

**7** Let's create the third bottle by extruding the path at the right. Then we'll use a mapping source to add the label. Use the Selection tool (▶) to select the bottle path and choose [Effect] - [3D] - [Revolve]. Set the Position to X: -9, Y: -14, Z: 2. In the Revolve section, set From to Right Edge. This will rotate the bottle towards the right. Click the New Light icon (⬛) and arrange the values as shown to create a shiny surface texture.

8 Click the [Map Art] button to create a wireframe object.

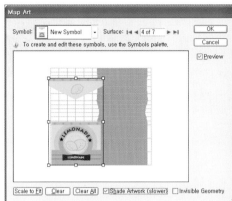

9 Keep clicking Next (▶) to select the bottle shape (4 of 7) and choose New Symbol. Use the anchors to make the symbol smaller, then position it on the lower-left side. Click Shade Artwork to add natural shadows and click [OK] twice.

10 We need to create the bottle reflections. Hold down the [Shift] key and select both the bottle on the left and the bottle on the right. Press [Ctrl]-[C] to copy the bottles and [Ctrl]-[F] to paste them in front. Choose [Object] - [Expand Appearance] to break apart the appearance attributes.

11 Double-click the Reflect tool (□) and select Horizontal. Click [OK]. Use the Selection tool (▶) to move the shape to the bottom, as shown. Arrange the duplicated bottles so that they line up with the originals.

<< tip

## Distorting Shapes

Use the Distort tool to distort shapes that have an effect applied.

12 In the Transparency palette set the Opacity to 55%. The completed image is shown above.

# Using the Scribble Effect

In this exercise, we'll learn how to add items to the Appearance palette. We'll then use the palette to apply multiple effects to the objects. We'll also work with the Scribble effect to make the original objects appear as if they were drawn by hand.

Original Image

Final Image

1 Open pimento.ai from the sample folder.

2 Select the yellow pimento with the Selection tool (⬆) and click the Fill item in the Appearance palette.

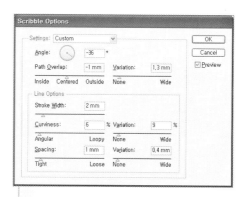

3 Choose [Effect] - [Stylize] - [Scribble]. Under Settings, enter Angle: -36, Path Overlap: -1, and Variation: 1.3. Under Line Options set Stroke Width: 2, Curviness: 6, Variation: 9, Spacing: 1, and Variation: 0.4. Click [OK]. The yellow pimento is filled with thick strokes.

4 Select the Fill item and click the Duplicate Selected Item icon (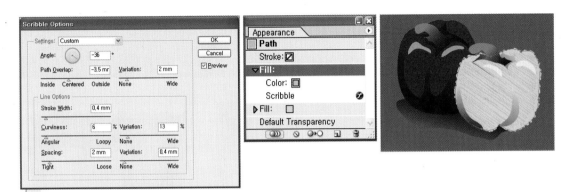). Click the duplicated surface and adjust the color to M: 20%, Y: 100%.

5 Double-click the Scribble item and change the Settings to Angle: -36, Path Overlap: -3.5, and Variation: 2. Set Line Options to Stroke Width: 0.4, Curviness: 6, Variation: 13, Spacing: 2, and Variation: 0.4. Click [OK] to see the thin, curved lines inside the path.

6 In the Appearance palette, select the second Fill item and click the Duplicate Selected Item icon (). Set the Color to Y: 100%.

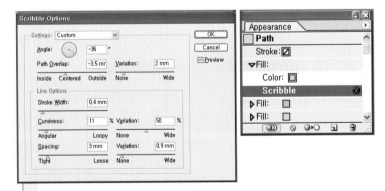

7 Double-click the Scribble item and change the Settings to Path Overlap: -35 and Variation: 2. Set the Line Options to Stroke Width: 0.4, Curviness: 11, Variation: 50, Spacing: 3, and Variation: 0.9. Click [OK]. This curves and spreads out the lines so they blend better with the orange lines.

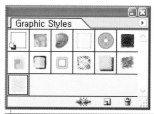

8 Click the New Graphic Style icon (⬜) in the Graphic Styles palette.

9 Let's apply a Scribble effect to the shadow. Hold down the [Shift] key and use the Selection tool (🔺) to select the shadow and the anchor points below the red and yellow pimentos as shown. Choose [Effect] - [Stylize] - [Scribble] and set the Settings to Angle: 144, Path Overlap: 0, and Variation: 1.7. Set the Line Options to Stroke Width: 0.5, Curviness: 10, Variation: 49, Spacing 0.5, and Variation: 0.2. Click [OK]. This creates a slightly curved line.

10 Select the red pimento and apply the graphic style saved from the yellow pimento.

11 In the Appearance palette, drag and drop the center Fill item onto the Delete Selected Item icon (⬜). Click on the Color item of each fill and adjust the color, from bottom to top, to M: 100%, Y: 100% and M: 30%, Y: 100%.

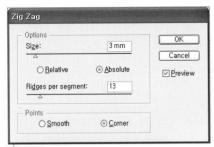

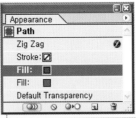

12  Select the background with the Selection tool () and choose [Effect] - [Distort & Transform] - [Zig Zag]. Set Size to 3 and Ridges per segment to 13. Click [OK].

13  Select the Fill item from the Appearance palette. Copy it with the Duplicate Selected Item icon () and set the Color to C: 80%, M: 30%, Y: 90%, K: 10%.

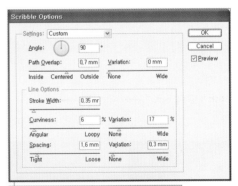

14  Click the Duplicate Selected Item icon () again and set the Color of the duplicated Fill item to C: 90%, M: 35%, Y: 100%, K: 26%.

15  Choose [Effect] - [Stylize] - [Scribble] and set the Settings to Angle: 90, Path Overlap: 0.7, and Variation: 0. Set the Line Options to Stroke Width: 0.35, Curviness: 6, Variation: 17, Spacing: 1.6, and Variation: 0.3. Click [OK]. This creates slightly thin and irregular lines.

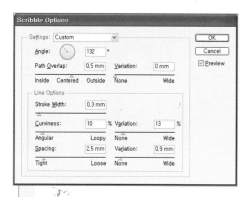

16 Select the third Fill item, click on the Duplicate Selected Item icon ( ) and set the Color to Y: 100%. Double-click Scribble and change the Settings to Angle: 132, Path Overlap: 0.5, and Variation: 0. Set the Line Options to Stroke Width: 0.3, Curviness: 10, Variation: 13, Spacing: 2.5, and Variation: 0.9.

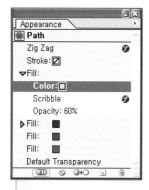

17 In the Transparency palette, set the Opacity to 60%.

18 Click the Fill item at the bottom of the Appearance palette and change the Color to C: 85%, M: 40%, Y: 100%, K: 40%.

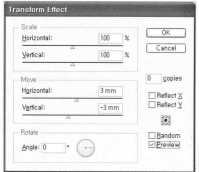

19 Choose [Effect] - [Distort & Transform] - [Transform] and set Horizontal to 3 and Vertical to -3.

20 Choose [Effect] - [Stylize] - [Scribble] and set the Settings to Angle: 132, Path Overlap: 0.5, and Variation: 0.8. Set the Line Options to Stroke Width: 1, Curviness: 6, Variation: 13, Spacing: 0.1, and Variation: 1. Click [OK]. This creates strong and slightly irregular lines at the edges. The image is now complete.

# Index › › ›